UNDERSTANDING & USING
EDUCATIONAL
THEORIES

Sara Miller McCune founded SAGE Publishing in 1965 to support the dissemination of usable knowledge and educate a global community. SAGE publishes more than 1000 journals and over 800 new books each year, spanning a wide range of subject areas. Our growing selection of library products includes archives, data, case studies and video. SAGE remains majority owned by our founder and after her lifetime will become owned by a charitable trust that secures the company's continued independence.

Los Angeles | London | New Delhi | Singapore | Washington DC | Melbourne

2ND EDITION

UNDERSTANDING & USING
EDUCATIONAL
THEORIES

KARL AUBREY AND
ALISON RILEY

Los Angeles | London | New Delhi
Singapore | Washington DC | Melbourne

Los Angeles | London | New Delhi
Singapore | Washington DC | Melbourne

SAGE Publications Ltd
1 Oliver's Yard
55 City Road
London EC1Y 1SP

SAGE Publications Inc.
2455 Teller Road
Thousand Oaks, California 91320

SAGE Publications India Pvt Ltd
B 1/I 1 Mohan Cooperative Industrial Area
Mathura Road
New Delhi 110 044

SAGE Publications Asia-Pacific Pte Ltd
3 Church Street
#10-04 Samsung Hub
Singapore 049483

Editor: James Clark
Editorial assistant: Diana Alves
Production editor: Nicola Carrier
Copyeditor: Audrey Scriven
Proofreader: Lynda Watson
Indexer: Gary Kirby
Marketing manager: Dilhara Attygalle
Cover design: Sheila Tong
Typeset by: C&M Digitals (P) Ltd, Chennai, India
Printed in the UK

© Karl Aubrey and Alison Riley 2019

First edition published 2015

Reprinted 2015, 2016 (twice), 2017 (twice) & 2018

This second edition published 2019

Library of Congress Control Number: 018930989

British Library Cataloguing in Publication data

A catalogue record for this book is available from
the British Library

ISBN 978-1-5264-3660-3
ISBN 978-1-5264-3661-0 (pbk)

PRAISE FOR THE FIRST EDITION

The chapters are accessibly written and accurate, serving to set the selected thinkers in context and draw the student's attention to key themes. I expect that this book will equip and inspire students to engage first-hand with the texts of these creative and influential educational writers.

David Aldridge, Brunel University London

Aubrey and Riley have gathered the backgrounds, theories and criticisms of educational theorists into one easy to read book. I would recommend this book to anyone studying to become a teacher.

Sam Emmett, Glyndwr University

The book gives a concise guide to some of the most relevant educational theories, providing background to the theorist and notes on critiquing and using the theory in practice. This book allows the student to explore further the educational theories that are relevant to their teaching practice and to enable them to begin to embed educational theory into their own teaching practice. The book also provides an excellent reference for their continued professional development as teachers.

Vikki Foley, Keele University

This book is a brilliant introduction to educational theories. There are short biographies of all the important theorists and the links between them are highlighted. A must for all teachers.

Malgorzata Hirst, University of Hertfordshire

This book is an invaluable resource to complement initial studies in all aspects of child development and educational theories. It offers a simple and understandable approach to key individuals and their research.

Elspeth Nelson, University of Hull

CONTENTS

ABOUT THE AUTHORS

Karl Aubrey is a Visiting Tutor on the Professional Studies in Education programmes at Bishop Grosseteste University. Prior to this Karl was the Programme Leader for a range of initial teacher education and professional development programmes at a large city further education college. Between 2003 and 2005 he was seconded to the DfES Standards Unit as a learning and teaching practitioner in the East Midlands. Karl has contributed to the *Oxford Dictionary of Education*. His doctoral thesis explored the reforms in further education teacher education from 2000 to 2010, from the viewpoint of teacher educators. Karl's research interests include inclusion, education policy, pedagogy and work-based learning.

Alison Riley is the Programme Leader for the BA (Hons) Early Childhood Studies degree at Bishop Grosseteste University, and she has also worked on a number of educational-related programmes at the university including initial teaching training courses. Prior to joining Bishop Grosseteste University Alison spent sixteen years working in primary education, as a classroom teacher, deputy head teacher and finally head teacher of a large junior school. She has been involved in a number of collaborative projects, and has recently been involved in an EU-funded project researching 'Creativity in Early Science and Mathematics Education'. Alison has recently commenced doctoral studies in which she is researching what influences the choices of pupils entering higher education.

ACKNOWLEDGEMENTS

SAGE would like to thank the following people whose comments helped to shape the first and second editions of this book:

David Aldridge, Brunel University London

Jane Andrews, University of the West of England

Ruth Barrington, Bath Spa University

Samantha Eason, Darlington College

Angela Fenton, Charles Sturt University

Wendy Garner, University of Chester

Glenn Stone, University of Chichester

Ian Summerscale, Oxford Brookes

James Williams, University of Sussex

NEW TO THIS EDITION

Welcome to the fully revised and expanded second edition of *Understanding and Using Educational Theories*. The scope and content of the changes made are a result of our reflections following constructive feedback from the reviewers, colleagues and students from the first edition. These changes, we feel, give the book an even wider-ranging and analytical perspective of the ideas of the educational theorists. The major revisions for this second edition are:

- Three new chapters, which follow the same format as the first edition, on the works of the following key educational thinkers: Albert Bandura, Dylan Wiliam, and Carol Dweck.
- An expanded introduction which offers an overview of the key schools of thought which have influenced educational theory.
- Each chapter has a glossary of the key words which are pertinent to that theorist's work.
- All chapters from the first edition have been reviewed and revised. Where appropriate updates include new references, links to current educational socio-political developments, and expansions to existing sections taking discussions and critical commentary further.

INTRODUCTION

WHY A BOOK ABOUT EDUCATIONAL THEORISTS AND THEIR IDEAS?

Although there are a number of texts which explore the work of education theorists, we have often found that undergraduates and students studying at Master's level have difficulty linking theory with practice. Therefore, the aim of this book is to offer a range of selected educational theorists and examine and critique their ideas, highlight links with other key thinkers and consider how these theories can be applied in practice. It was our intention therefore to produce a book which would serve as an accessible resource in which to give you the confidence to use theory in order to demonstrate your level of knowledge and understanding, and also enable you to apply theory in practice.

We would argue that currently education is being ideologically driven and promotes a traditional view of teaching and learning which is focused on the acquisition of knowledge and skills needed to compete in the global market, rather than for personal fulfilment and development. With this in mind, this book seeks to give a less competence-based view of education and proposes a more critically analytical approach based upon the research and ideas of the theorists discussed. Furthermore, we anticipate that the book will encourage you to reflect on your own learning development as adult learners as well as considering the learning development of the children and young people you may work with.

We should explain that this is not intended to be a comprehensive review of the work of each of the theorists included, but more an introduction to their works and applications of their ideas. It does however act as a valuable starting point for those who are interested in, and wish to delve deeper into, the thinking and background of the chosen theorists. Choosing which theorists to include in this book was a tricky proposition, especially with the vast array of thinkers who have made a significant impact on education. Having discussed the options between ourselves, colleagues and students, and amidst much disagreement on who to include and who to exclude, we were able to develop a set of criteria from which to work. We finally decided to include those theorists whose ideas covered a range of educational sectors: early years, primary, secondary, tertiary and adult. From dialogue with colleagues we have included those from approximately the last one hundred years, and reluctantly discounted older classical thinkers. We have also tried to use a range of international educational thinkers.

A major justification for this book is that we feel there is a definite place for theory in education. We ignore theory at our peril because of the potential effect this omission could have on the children and young people of the future. There is a danger, with the recent government discourse, that classroom practice is becoming a competence-based activity, and the rhetoric seems to suggest a return to the more traditional, didactic and examination-focused approaches which the likes of Dewey and Freire cautioned against. Much of this goes against what many of the influential theorists believe. These beliefs have emanated from the theorists' findings and evaluations following empirical research and from substantial observations of practice. If theory is discounted in education we risk formulaic and step-by-step approaches to teaching and learning, where there is a set of strict rules for those who work with children and young adults to follow. However, education in practice is a much more complex and messy phenomenon, with a multitude of contrasting facets to take into account which need a reflective and professional approach, involving 'not just knowing about what you do and how to do it. It is also about why you do it' (Williams, 2004: 5). It is our contention that theory enables practitioners to make informed judgements about their learners and their own actions. Perhaps the difficulty of knowing about, and using, theory is that there are so many contrasting educational theoretical opinions to consider and wrestle with. However, these competing schools of thought also offer a greater depth of understanding for us to reflect on and make judgements in differing situations.

EDUCATIONAL THEORIES: SCHOOLS OF THOUGHT

There are a number of educational theories, mostly emanating from differing educational psychological schools of thought. These theories have undergone an evolution; different ideas have been disputed, modified, and in some cases disregarded. This process of change, dispute and advancement of educational theory is similar to other fields of study (Williams, 2004). There are three main psychological schools of thought which are of relevance to education and learning theory: behaviourism, constructivism, and humanism. It should be acknowledged that although each of these have differing perspectives, they can at times complement each other and add to a body of knowledge about education. Indeed, in practice, the ideas of each of the schools of thought sometimes overlap (Petty, 1998).

Behaviourism is a school of thought which contests that 'behaviour can be predicted, measured and controlled, and that learning is simply a matter of stimulus and response' (Wallace, 2008: 32). Early behaviourists such as the Russian psychologist Ivan Pavlov researched the behaviour and reflexes of animals, in particular dogs. He found that the dogs he worked with could be conditioned to respond to environmental factors, and this he termed classical conditioning. Pavlov's research discovered that the dogs salivated when a bell sounded at the same time as their food was provided. In due course food was not required as a stimulus to start the dogs salivating, as the sound of the bell was sufficient to start this response. In classical conditioning, the recipient has no control over their behaviour. John Watson also used the general concept of classical conditioning in an attempt to illustrate human, rather than animal, behaviour. However, the idea was considered to be rather uncaring, simplistic and insensitive to be applied in any learning setting. A further development in behaviourist thinking was advanced by the American psychologist B.F. Skinner who further developed the work of Pavlov and Watson. Skinner's concept was termed operant conditioning; a more relevant and applicable concept for learning. Operant conditioning refers to the learner being conditioned to respond gainfully to a stimulus. Reinforcement is a crucial element for operant conditioning, such reinforcement can either be positive or negative as long as it produces the preferred responses. Disapproving stimuli or the threat of censure could bring about reduced responses from the learner (Williams, 2004).

The constructivist school of thought argues that learning is not something that can be delivered to students by them passively listening to a teacher dispensing knowledge. The constructivists believe that meaningful knowledge and understanding 'are actively constructed by learners ... which builds on what they already know causing them to change and adapt and invent ideas' (Wallace, 2008: 61). It is proposed that there are two main forms of constructivism: cognitive constructivism and social constructivism. Cognitive constructivism refers to the notion that for successful learning to take place any new knowledge encountered needs to be analysed in relation to what the learners already know. Theorists who were advocates of cognitive constructivism are Dewey, Piaget and Bruner. Social constructivism contends that the crucial aspect of effective learning is social interaction, which emphasises language and discourse, also taking into account the importance of the use of the cultural and social backgrounds of the learners in the construction of that learning. The main exponent of social constructivism was Vygotsky (Wallace, 2008).

The humanism school of thought argues that education should focus on the needs of the individual learner, and that what is important are the aspects of personal and emotional growth. These values they feel are being disregarded by society at large, and particularly in schools which promote academic achievement and give what they consider undue credence to test results. Humanists contend that the purpose of schools is to 'meet the needs of the individual learner not the other way round' (Petty, 1998: 8). They also feel that learners should be allowed to follow their own interests so that they can grow as a whole person in the way in which appeals to them as individuals. Humanists believe that students are thwarted in their learning because of oppressive classroom environments. Williams proposes that learning is hindered when students 'feel uncomfortable making mistakes or are afraid that their failure to grasp a new idea will result in ridicule or humiliation' (2004: 17). Instead teaching and learning should be learner-centred, and teachers should act as facilitators of non-threatening learning. There are a number of educational thinkers whose work can be aligned with humanism. Carl Rogers argued that facilitation, rather than didactic teaching, and the creation of positive and supportive classroom environments were key to meaningful learning. Rogers and Abraham Maslow also contended that learning should not be considered a finite objective but a process to advance the full potential of each individual learner. A.S. Neill's Summerhill School which encouraged learner choice and an environment of equality between students and staff offers an illustration of humanism in practice (Wallace, 2008).

Before we leave the overview of these schools of educational thought, and before readers delve into the contents of this edition, it is fitting that we offer a few words of caution about being too stringent in classifying the thinkers themselves. Some of the thinkers will come naturally within one of these three schools of thought and this will become apparent, while the concepts of others may overlap or indeed appear not to fit into any of the three. Others will transcend both educational psychological schools with wider issues of philosophy, including socio-economic and political aspects, most notably John Dewey and Paulo Freire.

WHO WOULD FIND THIS BOOK RELEVANT?

Firstly, we hope that many readers will find this book to be of interest, beneficial in their professional development and helpful in the synthesis of theory and practice. Perhaps you will be introduced to theorists you have never encountered before or have an opportunity to refresh your understanding of those you already know; this book will additionally allow you to make associations between theorists. Our aspiration is that it will be useful for both undergraduate and postgraduate students, and practitioners who are involved with learners in all sectors of education from early years through to adult education. We appreciate this is a wide remit; however, we are committed to reaching a broad range of readers whose practice does, or will, involve work with learners in formal education, such as in schools, further education (FE) colleges and universities, as well as informal education, such as early years, youth work and offender education. This breadth of readership will encompass those on work-based programmes, such as foundation degrees and their progression routes, as well as those traditional undergraduates undergoing initial teacher education for teaching in schools and FE colleges, education studies, and youth work undergraduates.

ORGANISATION AND STRUCTURE OF CHAPTERS

Chapters in this book are sequenced in an approximately chronological order, starting with John Dewey and finishing with Carol Dweck. We have adopted this arrangement so that readers can follow how educational thinking has evolved over time. Furthermore, the sequence makes it possible for the reader to make links not only between the theorists included here but also other significant thinkers they may wish to explore further. We have, again in this second edition, avoided organising this book into various schools of thought such as behaviourism, constructivism and humanism. This is because, as previously argued, we feel this is too simplistic and does not reflect the complexity and the multidirectional nature of many of their ideas.

Each chapter considers a particular theorist and follows a common arrangement of sections. Firstly, the learning outcomes indicate what readers should be able to do having read the chapter; this is followed by a list of key words which are pertinent to the theorist's work. The introduction aims to set the scene, by outlining the significance and impact of the theorist's work, before briefly considering their biography. The next section explores the theories in greater detail, then links these theories with other educational thinkers. This is followed by a critical examination of their ideas, based upon evidence from other theorists and other academic sources. The subsequent section offers suggestions of ways that a particular theorist's ideas could be applied in the reader's practice. Then, ahead of the summary, readers are invited to reflect upon the chapter and complete a task which ventures to consolidate theory with their current or future practice. Following the summary a glossary of the chapter's key words is included. Each chapter ends with a suggestion of further reading, which readers can follow for further in-depth study, as well as a list of references that have been cited in the chapter.

As we have noted, the opening chapter is about John Dewey. It is, we feel, a good place to start as many of those included in the following chapters have been influenced by his emphasis on reflection, learner-centred pedagogy and social learning. Chapter 2 then goes on to examine Montessori's impact on education, particularly in the early years, focusing on her child-centred approach to early years provision, which underlines the importance of the learning environment. Chapter 3 focuses on Piaget's notion of a staged cognitive development and the significant impact his prolific theoretical ideas and observations have had on how we perceive children's learning. This is then followed in Chapter 4 by an exploration of Vygotsky's concepts of cultural–historical activity, social constructivism and the zone of proximal development (ZPD), as well as the embryo model of scaffolding (which is later developed by Bruner, as discussed in Chapter 8, along with Bruner's concept of the spiral curriculum).

In contrast, Chapter 5 considers Skinner's behaviourist concepts of operant conditioning and positive and negative reinforcement. This is followed by Bloom's taxonomies and domains of learning in Chapter 6. Chapter 7 takes us to the domain of adult education exploring Malcolm Knowles' standpoint on adult education that offers the thought-provoking concepts of andragogy and social pedagogy. Chapter 9 explores the work of Albert Bandura, and the concept of learning through observation. In Chapter 10 we examine Urie Bronfenbrenner's bio-ecological theory, which argued that an individual's learning is heavily influenced by their social, historical and cultural background and circumstances. Chapters 11 to 14 return to more adult-based theories, starting with an exploration of Freire's progressive notions of problem-posing and liberating education. After this, Chapter 12 considers Schön's theory and his emphasis on the value of reflection 'in action' and 'on action' for educators, followed by Chapters 13 and 14 which examine the work of Kolb, then Lave and Wenger and their theories on experiential learning, situated learning and communities of practice, respectively. Chapter 15 evaluates Claxton's concept of learning power. Wiliam's ideas relating to assessment for learning are reviewed in Chapter 16. Finally, Chapter 17 appraises Carol Dweck's concepts of motivation and mindsets.

USING THE BOOK

There are a few ways in which this book can be used. It could be read as a whole text from start to finish and the chronological manner in which it has been written would certainly allow for this. Alternatively, you could dip into the chapters and use it as a source for each of the theorists to better understand their individual ideas, find out possible flaws in their concepts and consider ways to apply the theories. Another complementary option would be to follow the threads and links between theorists; and the further readings and references are presented as sources for those who want to get a deeper insight. We also suggest readers engage in the reflective tasks given towards the end of each chapter, which offer the opportunity to think not only about the theories but also about how they do, or could, complement professional practice. Whichever way, or combination of ways, this book is used we hope it will enhance your knowledge and understanding of the characters and their theories. It is also our wish that it will give food for thought, not only to help with building powers of critical analysis and synthesis in assignments but also to allow readers to critically reflect on the implications that these theories have on practice.

REFERENCES

Petty, G. (1998) *Teaching Today* (Second Edition). Cheltenham: Nelson Thornes.
Wallace, S. (2008) *Oxford Dictionary of Education*. Oxford: Oxford University Press.
Williams, J. (2004) *Great Minds: Education's Most Influential Philosophers* (A Times Education Supplement Essential Guide).

1
JOHN DEWEY

A DEMOCRATIC NOTION OF LEARNING

LEARNING OUTCOMES

Having read this chapter you should be able to:

- understand Dewey's major philosophical ideas
- be aware of his background as a person and as an educator
- consider his influence on later theorists and education today
- critically analyse his theoretical perspective
- create links between theory and practice.

KEY WORDS

experimentation; reflection; learner-centred pedagogy; democracy; active experience

INTRODUCTION

It seems fitting that John Dewey is the first theorist to be considered in this book, since he has influenced many of the educational thinkers who follow. Although a prolific writer on topics such as philosophy and politics, Dewey's impact on education was at the time, and arguably still is, profound, given the way in which he challenged more traditional notions of education and learning. He contended that learning should focus on practical life experiences and social interaction rather than the more traditional and staid manner of instruction and rote learning evident in late nineteenth- and early twentieth-century schools. For Dewey, the individual was at the centre of the learning process. He reasoned that for genuine learning to take place learners needed to make independent evaluations based on their interests and that school should be a place where challenges and difficulties are met and resolved. In summary he promoted the idea of learning by doing and experimenting rather than it being a passive experience: **experimentation** based on a scientific and reflective approach rather than an indiscriminate process. These ideas, outlined in *The School and Society* (1899) and *Democracy and Education* (1916), are closely aligned with the 'progressive education' movement which caused considerable interest and controversy at the time, but despite this interest his ideas were not adopted by American schools, his intended audience. However, the 'progressive education' movement enlightened UK educational philosophy in the 1960s which was substantiated by the 1967 Plowden Report regarding the future of primary schooling. It is somewhat ironic that in the following decade teaching staff from English schools travelled to the USA to coach 'US teachers on the implementation of practices that had their source in the American philosopher's own educational writing' (Bridges, 2007: xi).

In applying Dewey's ideas to both the study of education and those working with learners, there are two important and interlinked issues to be considered. Firstly, the role of the teacher within this learner-centred philosophy and, secondly, the importance he placed on **reflection** for both learners and teachers. It could be suggested that advocating a learner-centred approach might devalue the role of the teacher; however, this was not Dewey's viewpoint. He proposed that learners needed direction and that teachers have an important responsibility in facilitating learning by encouraging and channelling individuals' curiosity and motivation so they can develop intellectually. In other words teachers should develop a **learner-centred pedagogy** in which learners are encouraged to experiment based on their own interests rather than adopting a didactic model of teaching in which the learner has only a passive role. In doing this Dewey felt that a learning-centred pedagogy would enable learners to engage with learning while at the same time preparing them to be active members of their communities and society as a whole: 'To this end, Dewey viewed education and **democracy** as being intrinsically linked' (MacBlain, 2014: 210). Such democracy came from reflecting on experience rather than relying on the repetitious and passive pedagogic models employed in schools, which were disconnected from the realities of the social world.

Dewey also argued that teachers should look at learning as a cycle of experience where lessons are planned and executed based on observation and reflection from their own and their learners' previous experiences and interests (Woods, 2008).

JOHN DEWEY, THE PERSON

Born in Vermont in the United States in 1859, Dewey was brought up during a time of massive transformation in society, which lurched from rural subsistence to a more intricate system of commerce and industrialisation. The notion of society being democratic and just during this dramatic change in culture, brought about by the surge of industrialisation, was the focus of his philosophy throughout his life. Following graduation he taught both in high school and as the only teacher in a small rural setting. He completed his doctoral thesis on the psychology of Immanuel Kant prior to embarking on academic posts at the universities of Michigan and Minnesota before arriving at the University of Chicago as the chair of philosophy, psychology and pedagogy. While at the University of Chicago he established, along with his wife, an elementary-level Laboratory School to explore educational psychological ideas; the school was fundamental in helping trainee teachers get ready for their future practice. His major writings whilst at the University of Chicago were *School and Society* (1899), *The Child and the Curriculum* (1902), and *How We Think* (1910) (published after he left Chicago). Dewey's last and longest academic post was at Columbia University, from 1904 until he finally retired in 1939 at the age of eighty (Apple and Teitelbaum, 2001). During his time at Columbia University his published works included *Democracy and Education* (1916), and *Experience and Education* (1938) (Apple and Teitelbaum, 2001; Pring, 2007). Dewey passed away in 1952.

DEWEY AND THE NOTION OF PROGRESSIVE EDUCATION

Dewey's influence on education is multifaceted and still retains an air of controversy. His works encompass humanism, values education, learner-centred pedagogy and reflection; each of which will be addressed in this section. Dewey was an avid campaigner for an alternative and, for the era, radical approach to education. This is exemplified in the opening chapter of his seminal 1938 text *Experience and Education*, which called for a shift from traditional to progressive education. His philosophy argued for a move away from the rigid approach of passive learning towards a more participatory and democratic model. Doubtless influenced by his own breadth of social networking, Dewey argued that by accepting pupils from different classes, cultures and abilities, schools would thereby lay the foundations for building notions of democracy for children. For Dewey, school was not merely a physical establishment but rather a democratic community of learning. This progressive notion was exemplified by his idea that school should not only be a good grounding for life but also 'a representation of life itself … a purpose of improving and ameliorating the existing external world' (Howlett, 2013: 187). He called for a 'common school' which embraced and reproduced the similarities and differences found in the community. For Dewey the common school was a place where children from different religious faiths and social backgrounds could learn from each other in an environment of tolerance and understanding. The rise in the number of faith schools in England, along with the continued recourse to private education, seem to diminish Dewey's concept of the common school (Pring, 2007). Darling-Hammond contends that separate schools weaken Dewey's idea of democracy in keeping apart students because of religious and social backgrounds, 'by encouraging silence and separation where communication and connections are needed' (Darling-Hammond, 2010: 62).

At this time traditional education was exemplified by closely monitored and didactic pedagogy with the teacher very much the active, front-of-class participant and the pupil the passive recipient of knowledge. What was taught was controlled by a rigid curriculum. According to Dewey:

> The traditional scheme is, in essence, one of imposition from above and from outside. It imposes adult standards, subject-matter, and methods upon those who are only growing slowly toward maturity. The gap is so great that the required subject-matter, the methods of learning and of behaving are foreign to the existing capacities of the young. They are beyond the reach of the experience the young learners already possess. (1938: 18–19)

Progressive education, on the other hand, was much more of a liberal experience, with the child at the centre of the process. Learning was very much an **active experience**, typified by group discussions and activities, while the design of the curriculum should accommodate the needs of the individual learners rather than purely being shaped by subject-specific areas. These progressive ideas were paramount to Dewey's principles of children being ready to take an active and confident part in society as a whole in order to be fulfilled. In his view, learning involves active discovery and the gaining of procedural skills rather than the passive remembering of facts and figures. As such, he advocated the need for a flexible curriculum which was focused on resolving problems with subjects interwoven within it. He contested the position of the child being a submissive character to the curriculum; his pragmatist and social constructivist philosophy called for individual pupils to be 'actors' and not 'spectators'.

However, Dewey was critical about the notion that all experiences were equally beneficial to authentic learning. His stance that true learning is socially constructed permeates most of his educational philosophy. The significance of learning from and with others for the individual in the greater scheme of things is set out as follows:

> In a word, we live from birth to death in a world of persons and things which in large measure is what it is because of what has been done and transmitted from previous human activities. (Dewey, 1938: 39)

Dewey expressed that the interests of the individual child should be at the heart of active experience and this should be integral to the design of a flexible and integrated curriculum, together with teachers adopting learner-centred pedagogies. Active experience should be seen by the learner as a meaningful process of personal development rather than disjointed and separate silos of information, facts and activities. Active experience is nurtured by 'habits of criticism and free inquiry' as well as creating a trusting social environment for discussion and discovery without the shackles of traditional hierarchical boundaries between teachers and pupils (Carr, 2003: 223).

Although as a learner-centred educational thinker, who did not believe in the power of teachers imposing discipline and employing passive learning methods, Dewey did not accept that pupils could learn without the aid of the teacher. He believed their role was to create opportunities for active experience in the form of activities and resources which allowed pupils to construct connections between experiences. The role of the teacher, then, rather than being diminished becomes more multifaceted, intricate and learner-centred (Irwin, 2012). By adopting the socially constructed active experience, teachers needed to establish an environment that stimulated activities and opened debate within the 'principle of making things interesting' (Dewey, 1913: 24). From Dewey's viewpoint, teachers were to become facilitators, helping pupils to develop skills and processes to solve problems at times of possible uncertainty – skills which could be transferable to other subjects – and for them to thrive and contribute to a democratic society. For example, instead of the passive rote learning of times tables teachers should help pupils to develop skills of practical measurement, which in turn could be employed for other subjects such as geography and science (Carr, 2003).

Teachers, then, become the medium through which such 'skills are communicated' (Dewey, 1938: 18). Dewey spoke out about the need for teachers to have greater freedom in their interpretation of the curriculum. This freedom, he contended, was necessary not only to attract suitable candidates into teaching but also to help create learner-centred and socially constructed approaches. Additionally, he argued for a scholarly approach to teacher education. This scholarship included Dewey's idea of education as a science, not just focusing on the curriculum and how to teach it but also developing a greater understanding of how education as a whole is perceived by society (Lagemann, 2002). Dewey despaired at the way schools in the USA tried to function as businesses, and in the hierarchical manner in which they tried to resolve problems and create standard curricula. He contested the divisive way in which academic and vocational education were seen as separate entities, as well as the selection and separation of learners into different and streamed groups. He felt that learners should be listened to regarding the organisation of their learning, including curriculum content, methods of assessment, and resources to ensure they can make sense of their learning experience. Dewey would be despondent at the recent trend of reducing project and coursework in favour of submitting to more standard assessments of learning. As Pring states:

> The 'high-stakes testing' that has enthralled the USA and England not only fails to reflect that struggle to understand, that engagement in inquiry and that making sense of experience, but also makes these impossible. It has become an end in itself, an instrument in accountability based on an impoverished idea of learning. (2007: 168)

Rather, the voices of the learners should be central to the choice of assessment methods and in creating curricula which reflects their experiences, interests and anxieties.

Over the last thirty years reflective practice has been adopted as a tool for learning in a number of professional areas such as education, social and health care and the law. Dewey stressed the importance that, for reflective practice to be effective, each experience should be connected and reflected on holistically rather than being viewed in isolation. This in turn would build up a body of knowledge for the individual's future development. Dewey appreciated the intricacies and complications of cases in which decisions were required but often in a challenging and complex environment, such as a classroom, where decisions and answers were not easily remedied. It was only, he offered, through careful reflection that problems encountered could be resolved. This standpoint is exemplified by Dewey's philosophical pragmatism; a philosophy that through reflection knowledge is 'produced by an adaptive process in which the human organism succeeds in understanding and manipulating its environment' (Reynolds and Suter, 2010: 188). Thus, knowledge, through active experience and reflection, is created which will enable our practice to surmount problems encountered in the future within similar contexts.

What is important to note here in relation to Dewey's pragmatist approach to reflection is that, for some, it could be construed as a very simplistic process of 'learning by doing'. However, this disconnects the active experience of doing from thought and, as such, inhibits learning in a knowledgeable and forward-looking way. Furthermore, reflection requires the individual to respond creatively and imaginatively in times of doubt. Devout followers of Dewey's pragmatic philosophy would maintain learners need to be receptive and reactive to cope with the fast pace of change of modern society. However, from a teacher's point of view, responding to learner experiences and incidents through Dewey's idea of reflective practice in the 'messiness' and diversity of the classroom environment would be a challenging task (Elkjaer, 2009).

LINKS WITH OTHER THEORISTS

Connections with other thinkers are many: mostly those who have been influenced by his progressive views on education and for the most part would come under the humanist and social constructivist umbrella. The scope of this section is not broad enough to consider the influence Dewey has had on all educational thinkers. From an early stage he was interested in Darwin's evolutionary theory, he felt that humans were a higher form of living beings who could grow and develop in environments which nurtured social collaboration and culture (Pring, 2007). His philosophy was further influenced by Marx and Hegel. The link with Hegel, who championed the progressive concept of learners developing through creative and active experiences, is evident throughout much of Dewey's writing (Lawton and Gordon, 2002; Kegan, 2009). Dewey emphasised that reflective practice was a cyclical process which looked to the future. This concept was later, in the 1970s, developed by Kolb in his Experiential Learning Theory (ELT). Although Kolb was undoubtedly influenced by Dewey, especially in his adaption of the ELT learning cycle, there are differences. Whereas Dewey makes direct connections between active experience and thinking, Kolb contests that, in his learning cycle, the individual's learning styles are required for true active experience and thinking. Also, Kolb argued that active experience was not knowledge itself but only the groundwork for starting the knowledge-building process (Elkjaer, 2009).

Thinkers such as Froebel, Montessori, Vygotsky, and Piaget certainly related to Dewey, all maintaining that learners learn best when taking part in practical actions and by interacting with the environment. Piaget in particular is aligned with Dewey through his view of the teacher as a learning-centred facilitator. Dewey's philosophy can also be associated with Malcolm Knowles and his concept of andragogy in adult education. This concept stresses both the importance of the learner-centred approach and the significance of the experience that individuals bring to education. Perhaps the links between the two are not altogether surprising as Dewey was Knowles' first mentor in academia (Jarvis et al., 2003). Also undeniably inspired by Dewey's progressive views on learning was Howard Gardner's theory of multiple intelligences, which develops the notion that each learner is distinct and espouses the idea that learning, and hence intelligence, include a number of characteristics which are inherent in each of us and enhanced by experience.

The works of Carl Rogers and A.S. Neill, both humanists, were very much influenced by Dewey's progressive and liberal approach to education. Rogers replaced the term 'teacher' with 'facilitator'. This idea of mutual esteem between learner and facilitator was also very evident in the learner-centred and democratic 'free' school concept of A.S. Neill, the inaugural and long-term head teacher of Summerhill School, a famously democratic independent boarding school in England. However, Neill's philosophy of learner freedom and resulting practice at Summerhill were perhaps even too radical for Dewey's notion of progressive education, especially where the role and responsibilities of the teacher are concerned. Nevertheless, the work of both Dewey and Neill strived to develop 'confident, self-assured and responsible young people capable of critical reflection' (Carr, 2003: 226).

The ongoing importance of the influence of Dewey is also evident in the work of more contemporary thinkers. In his seminal text *Pedagogy of the Oppressed*, Paulo Freire warns against an information-giving or 'banking' approach and calls for a learner-centred education based on the needs and wants of individuals (Freire, 1996). Furthermore, the French sociologist and philosopher Pierre Bourdieu's concept of 'habitus' links with Dewey's term of 'habits', which explores the idea of learners being inducted and 'forming habits of action in conformity with … rules and standards' (Dewey, 1938: 18).

CRITIQUING THE THEORY

Although Dewey's influence is still very much evident in educational thinking and practice, his ideas raise some very pertinent and questionable issues which need consideration. Firstly, it may be interesting to reflect on the reason why his notions of progressive and learner-centred approaches to education were not readily acted upon in the United States. This could be because his left-leaning ideas were at odds with the majority of the American public, especially the policy makers, who traditionally shunned any suggestion of radical politics. This was certainly the case during and after the Cold War where a 'no-nonsense' approach to education in which the acquisition of skills to compete globally meant there was little room for Dewey's ideas to make progress (Howlett, 2013). The pursuit of a skill-based and economically-driven education system in many countries is even more appealing for government policy makers during the recent years of global recession. Many governments are now turning to more traditional approaches to the curriculum and assessment, with performance and attainment at the fore. It is doubtful whether Dewey's idea of learners taking part in the common good of society is truly possible in an increasingly commercial, market-driven and unfair world (Apple and Teitelbaum, 2001). However, despite the impact of market-focused education policy, models of progressive pedagogy continue to thrive in a number of schools (Bates and Lewis, 2009). This is surprising, as policy is increasingly resulting in content-heavy and subject-specific curricula with teachers constrained to a standardised and performance-driven culture.

There are some convincing arguments opposing Dewey's concept of devaluing the use of theories and facts. For some this is a misconception, because learners need to have an understanding of the point of their active experience to make sense of their subsequent investigations. Hence subject-specific facts and the basis of theory are necessary for learning to be created and built; it cannot take place just by active experience. Dewey's pragmatism therefore could be seen as somewhat naïve. There is then an argument that suggests knowledge and understanding are both detached from individual beliefs and preferences (Carr, 2003). Pragmatism focused on active experience, learner-centred, learning by doing and catering for individual interests, have been transformed by some critics into playing rather than learning, lacking focus, poor levels of literacy and numeracy and overall 'exaggerated subjectivizing' (Geiger, 1958: 8). Reflective practice is still very much a part of teacher education today. However, from an educator's point of view, responding to individual learner experiences and incidents through reflective practice in the 'messiness' and diversity of the classroom environment would be a challenging task (Elkjaer, 2009). This is particularly so in the current climate of an increasingly standardised curriculum and teacher performativity. In short, the overarching criticism which possibly fits Dewey best is that he had 'modernist (and romantic) faith in human reason and democratic community' (Irwin, 2012).

APPLYING DEWEY IN THE CLASSROOM

When considering the application of Dewey's theory to practice one of the biggest challenges perhaps lies in the lack of any specific acknowledgement of his work in classroom practices. In contrast to the work of his contemporaries, such as Steiner and Montessori, where an explicit approach to classroom procedure has been developed in their names, the same cannot be said for Dewey, and there is no 'Dewey system of education' which can be adopted or replicated in schools today. That said, in probing education systems, past and present, it is not difficult to identify where Dewey's theory and philosophy might have influenced practices, which perhaps explains why Carr and Hartnett (1996) refer to him as the philosopher who has had the greatest influence on education in the last century, and why Seigfried states 'Dewey has been called the last of the great public intellectuals because his own practice informed his theory and his theory was carried out in practice' (2002: 2).

Dewey's application of theory is manifest throughout his writing and it is quite impossible to doubt his convictions and sincerity in developing democratically minded and inquisitive young learners for the future. Although he championed the cause of teachers' freedom so that they could facilitate his progressive style of education, his main focus was on learners and promoting the significance of their experience. Consequently, when considering applying theory to practice here it can really only be viewed from Dewey's learner-centred perspective.

An examination of curriculum developments in England in recent years reflects the influence of Dewey's philosophy, particularly in primary education, where a shift from a more traditional knowledge-based system to a more learner-centred one has been a key focus of education policy. Perhaps the most significant period, in which a move to a more progressive education system can be seen, is during the 1960s when British education was influenced by the government-endorsed Plowden Report (1967). The Plowden philosophy reflected Dewey's work, showing progressivism through advocating that 'activity and experience, both physical and mental, are often the best means of gaining knowledge and acquiring facts' (Plowden Report, 1967: 195), and emphasising the importance of teaching the skills of reading and writing in the context in which they might be used by the children. Indeed, the most significant similarity between Plowden's findings and Dewey's philosophy is the learner-centred approach advocated by both. While Dewey explains this in metaphorical terms:

> … the change which is coming into our education is the shifting of the centre of gravity. It is a change, a revolution, not unlike that introduced by Copernicus when the astronomical centre shifted from the earth to the sun. In this case the child becomes the sun about which the appliances of education revolve; he is the centre about which they are organised. (1899: 151)

Plowden applies a more practical approach, stating that 'at the heart of the educational process lies the child' (Plowden Report, 1967: 7) and reinforcing that any change in policy and acquisition of resources must be in harmony with and acceptable to the child. While a more progressive approach to education was perhaps inevitable at the time – a period in which people were looking towards a more optimistic future following the post-war years – this was very much a honeymoon period lasting just a decade till the advent of the right-wing Conservative Thatcher government in 1979, which quickly reaffirmed the more traditional subject-based curriculum in the education system. Nevertheless, the appeal of a learner-centred approach to learning did not completely disappear and in subsequent revisions of curriculum policy a learner-centred approach to learning continued to make a significant contribution to the pedagogical framework. In the early 2000s, for example, a drive towards a creative curriculum which applied a thematic approach to teaching subjects began to gather pace following the Rose Review of the Primary Curriculum (Department for Children, Schools and Families, 2008); however, this was not embraced by the 2010 coalition government whose most recent iteration of a National Curriculum, the 2014 National Curriculum in England, was a return to a subject-based approach. Interestingly, the most recent revision of the Early Years Foundation Stage curriculum (2012) does however embrace the unique child and the importance of teachers' planning experiences, which start from the child and their own unique experiences. This is reflective of Dewey's theory in which he proposes a curriculum in which 'the child and the curriculum must interact' (Noddings, 2010: 269).

It could be assumed, then, that the application of Dewey's theory in practice is very much dependent upon the political position of the country at the time, since this undoubtedly will influence educational policy and its intentions. Dewey's assertion that learners become collaborators with other learners and teachers to create their own understanding by solving problems they encounter in a variety of situations is perhaps seen as a risky approach to pedagogy in the results-driven environment which currently typifies the English education system; and the view of teacher as facilitator and co-collaborator calls into question the role of the teacher and their responsibility in terms of achievement and attainment of the learner. This may also explain why this aspect of Dewey's philosophy was only fully embraced in early years education, where the stakes were deemed lower than in secondary education when education 'began to count'.

In reality, then, subject-based facts and theories are fundamental to learning, especially in secondary and tertiary education, and in the content-driven curriculum we see today. However, this is not to say that educators cannot consider ways of developing learners' reasoning proficiencies, which individual subjects look to cultivate, and encourage activities which are pragmatic and true to real life. Petty offers pertinent practical examples of this, although he also states that planning and managing such activities is not an uncomplicated undertaking:

Your subject is a way of thinking, not just a body of facts … So set tasks which require your students to reason. Get them thinking like real scientists, historians or social scientists. It is important to recognise that delivering the content and ideas on your topic is not enough. You are not a petrol pump attendant filling the students' empty tanks! A closer analogy is that you are an athletics coach, developing your students' abilities through the students' *own* exercise and practice. You may be structuring the exercise programme, but like athletes, it is the students who must do the practice, provide the effort, and create the gains. (1998: 358–9)

Therefore, even within a subject-driven curriculum it is conceivable that the skilful teacher can deliver subjects in a manner which still reflects the learner-centred approach which so impassioned Dewey. Indeed, despite a curriculum which is firmly rooted in a subject-led approach, the most recent National Curriculum for England still states that:

… teachers [should] develop exciting and stimulating lessons to promote the development of pupils' knowledge, understanding and skills as part of the wider school curriculum. (Department for Education, 2013: 5)

At this juncture it would be erroneous not to acknowledge the influence of Dewey's democratic ethos on education, and here we can see his theories influencing many aspects of education, but perhaps most significantly in aspects of higher and further education. His view of democracy was not one that reflected a political perspective, but rather was associated with 'a mode of associated living, of conjoint communicated experience' (1916: 93). He believed that education should be embedded within society and it should encourage students to become good and active citizens. This too links with his approach to learning, since he suggested that students who were active and engaged within society could more readily bring their experiences to their learning. This mode of learning is embodied in 'Citizenship Education', which can be seen in Key Stages 3 and 4 of the National Curriculum in England and aims to 'provide pupils with the knowledge, skills and understanding to prepare them to play a full and active part in society' (Department for Education, 2013: 201). A lighter touch, but no less important, approach to democracy in education is the rise of student councils in education settings, which present pupils with the opportunity to have their say in how their school is run.

However, perhaps the most significant area in which Dewey's democracy in action can be seen is in higher education, where universities are becoming increasingly influenced by student feedback and input. It is common for universities to have staff–student committees, which work at both departmental and institutional level, and there is an increasing focus on the results of the National Student Survey to inform and develop practice, all of which suggests that the democratic ethos of Dewey's work is a way of life in terms of higher education structure and procedures.

This section has touched upon a number of areas where Dewey's philosophies could be transferred into practice in the classroom, workshop or other learning environments. All these areas for practice aim to achieve the learner-centred and active experience espoused by progressive education. There is one further, central, aspect to Dewey's thinking to be considered by educators and that is inclusivity, which comes from his overarching principle of democracy. His standpoint on inclusivity came from him witnessing the damage done by privilege and elitism. He argued for all learners contributing what they could and building knowledge for the shared benefit of all, despite perceived levels of abilities, in an environment which celebrated difference. This is achieved by setting differentiated tasks and objectives for all learners and is enabled through open-plan classrooms and workshops which encourage participation and dialogue by all. All of these areas covered here require reflection, effort and in some cases courage to put into practice – skills and qualities Dewey was trying to nurture in his philosophy of progressive education. As a summary to this section, Pring outlines four skills and qualities that teachers require to facilitate Dewey's philosophy:

> First, the teacher has to know the child very well, the interests that engage his or her attention ... Second, the teacher must be knowledgeable of the cultural inheritance (embodied formally in various subject matters) that illuminates and enriches those interests. Third, the teacher is able to link the two through the process of inquiry, helping to identify the problem, to formulate hypotheses, to suggest possible solutions and to test these out in experience. Fourth, the teacher is to coordinate such inquiry among those belonging to the community of young people, respecting the different ways in which the various interests interact and the subject matter is interpreted by these individuals. (2007: 124–5)

REFLECTIVE TASK

You will not find a 'Dewey Curriculum' or 'Dewey Approach' to learning; however, look into any educational system or curriculum and you won't have to look too hard to find where the work of John Dewey has influenced both theory and practice.

Look for policies and curriculum frameworks in your own setting. Can you find any influences of Dewey's philosophies?

Are there any aspects of the curriculum and policy which reflect Dewey's progressive notion of education or do they follow a more traditional route? Why do you think this?

SUMMARY

It could be argued that John Dewey was a philosopher who was ahead of his time. A philosopher and educator, his humanistic views of individual self-worth and self-determinism, set in his democratic notion of education, challenged the traditional view of education and encouraged a more radical way of thinking in terms of putting the learner at the heart of the educational system.

Dewey questioned the traditional model of the educational system, in which pupils were the passive recipients of knowledge, instead championing a more participatory and democratic model, yet despite presenting a strong case for an educational setting that was a democratic community of learning in which the curriculum began with the learner, his ideas were not immediately endorsed. In fact, it could be argued that his vision for education is reflected on much more now than when he first presented his ideas, over a century ago.

Dewey's work is far-reaching, not just in terms of the development and organisation of school settings, but also in relation to the role of the teacher as a reflective practitioner, which was seen as a cyclical process designed to enable practitioners to develop and improve their practice – theories which were later developed by Schön and Kolb respectively.

Dewey also acknowledged the importance of experiential learning, which in itself was influential in curriculum development, particularly in the arena of the lifelong learning sector and vocational education. Dewey did not view these as separate entities, but viewed every experience as fundamental to what follows in an individual's learning journey, emphasising the importance of a vocational and academic curriculum to be delivered side by side in the best interests of the learner.

GLOSSARY OF TERMS

Active experience

Learning as an active process which involves the interests and experiences of the individual children rather than being restricted to single subject teaching sessions. In active experience teachers act as facilitators, enabling the learners to make connections between different experiences through socially interactive techniques such as discussions and debates which stimulate inquiry and discovery.

Democracy

For Dewey, democracy in society and democracy in education were naturally connected. Giving children choices in how and what they learned, which reflected their interests and experiences, helped prepare them to become inquisitive and critically active members of a democratic society.

Experimentation

A scientific, reflective and interactive approach where children learn by discovery and inquiry to make sense of their worlds rather than being docile receivers of information. The children then become active contributors in a social and cooperative learning environment.

Learner-centred pedagogy

Teachers empower children to explore their interests and experiences in depth as part of their learning process. In doing so, the teacher facilitates the learner to follow their curiosity and enthusiasm so that they can develop intellectually and as a whole person.

Reflection

Dewey felt the use of meaningful reflection was an important acquisition for both teachers and learners alike, that reflection was more than 'learning by doing', it was a deeper phenomenon based upon observation and deliberation from experience. As such reflection is closely aligned with the process of active experimentation as they both combine to make learning forward-looking that can be used to respond creatively to solve problems, as well as in times of uncertainty.

 ## FURTHER READING

Addams, J. (2002) A toast to John Dewey. In: Seigfried, C. (ed.) *Feminist Interpretations of John Dewey*. University Park, PA: Pennsylvania State University Press.

A celebration of Dewey's contribution to education from a feminist viewpoint.

Dewey, J. (1933) *How We Think* (Second Edition). New York: DC Heath.

A seminal text which explores and promotes a scientific approach to teaching which engages children's natural curiosity.

Osterman, K. and Kottkamp, R. (1993) *Reflective Practice for Educators: Improving schooling through professional development*. London: Sage.

Linking Dewey's ideas of reflective practice to the role of teaching.

Wenger, E. (1998) *Communities of Practice: Learning, meaning, and identity*. Cambridge: Cambridge University Press.

A contemporary notion of Dewey's ideas of theory.

REFERENCES

Apple, M. and Teitelbaum, K. (2001) John Dewey, 1859–1952. In: Palmer, J. (ed.) *Fifty Major Thinkers on Education: From Confucius to Dewey*. Abingdon: Routledge.

Bates, J. and Lewis, S. (2009) *The Study of Education: An introduction*. London: Continuum.

Bridges, D. (2007) Foreword. In: Pring, R. (ed.) *John Dewey*. London: Bloomsbury.
Carr, D. (2003) *Making Sense of Education*. London: RoutledgeFalmer.
Carr, W. and Hartnett, A. (1996) *Education and the Struggle for Democracy*. Buckingham: Open University Press.
Darling-Hammond, L. (2010) *Flat World and Education: Lessons from exemplary programs*. New York: Teachers College Press.
Department for Children, Schools and Families (2008) *Independent Review of the Primary Curriculum: Final report*. Nottingham: DCSF Publications.
Department for Education (2013) *The National Curriculum in England: Framework document*. London: Department for Education.
Dewey, J. (1899) *The School and Society*. Chicago, IL: University of Chicago Press.
Dewey, J. (1902) *The Child and the Curriculum*, reprinted in Garforth, F. (1966) *John Dewey: Selected writings*. London: Heinemann.
Dewey, J. (1910) *How We Think* (New Edition, 1997). Mineola, NY: Dover Publications.
Dewey, J. (1913) *Interest and Effort in Education*. Bath: Cedric Chivers.
Dewey, J. (1916) *Democracy and Education: An introduction to the philosophy of education*. New York: The Macmillan Company.
Dewey, J. (1938) *Experience and Education*. New York: Kappa Delta Pi.
Elkjaer, B. (2009) Pragmatism: A learning theory for the future. In: Illeris, K. (ed.) *Contemporary Theories of Learning: Learning theorists … in their own words*. Abingdon: Routledge.
Freire, P. (1996) *Pedagogy of the Oppressed* (Revised Edition). London: Penguin.
C … k: Oxford University Press.
H … *roduction*. London: Bloomsbury.
I … London: Continuum.
J … *nd Practice of Learning* (Second Edition).

K … ed.) *Contemporary Theories of Learning:* … Routledge.
L … hn Dewey and Ella Flagg Young at the … *minist Interpretations of John Dewey*. … ress.
L … *ducational Ideas*. London: Woburn Press.
M … .
N … A critique from the perspective of care … *anion to Dewey*. Cambridge: Cambridge … ublishingonline.org/cambridge/compan

P … tenham: Nelson Thornes.
P … *chools: A report of the central advisory*

P …

ethical element
encompasses
an established
set of ideas
about professional
expert approaches
morals + outlooks

Reynolds, B. and Suter, M. (2010) Reflective practice. In: Avis, J., Fisher, R. and Thompson, R. (eds) *Teaching in Lifelong Learning: A guide to theory and practice*. Maidenhead: Open University Press/McGraw-Hill Education.
Seigfried, C. (ed.) (2002) *Feminist Interpretations of John Dewey*. University Park, PA: Pennsylvania State University Press.
Woods, A. (2008) Dewey. In: Wallace, S. (ed.) *Oxford Dictionary of Education*. Oxford: Oxford University Press.

2
MARIA MONTESSORI

LIBERATING THE CHILD

LEARNING OUTCOMES

Having read this chapter you should be able to:

- recognise Montessori's background as a person and as an educator
- understand her major philosophical ideas
- critically analyse her theoretical perspective
- evaluate how her work has influenced other philosophers
- consider how her theories could be applied in practice.

KEY WORDS

spiritual embryo; absorbent mind; conscious mind; abstract thinking; sensitive periods; directress; prepared environment; child-centred

INTRODUCTION

Maria Montessori is one of the most well-known educationalists in the field of early education. It is a testament to her hard work and tenacity that, despite advocating a style of education which was in opposition to the ideas and philosophies of the time, Montessori schools are as prevalent now as they were a century ago and her philosophy continues to influence practice in mainstream settings today.

From her work as a clinical paediatrician, Montessori developed a unique approach to teaching which relied heavily on careful and clinical observation originating from her work with special needs children. She identified that by 'tapping into' the individual needs of these seemingly uneducable children she was able to teach them to attend to their personal needs and care for their environment, as well as in some cases learning the three Rs (writing, reading and arithmetic) using specially designed materials developed from her work with Jean-Marc-Gaspard Itard and his pupil Édouard Séguin.

Keen to try her ideas on 'normal' children, Montessori applied her ideas to her work with children in the *Casa dei Bambini*, the school she set up to meet the needs of the children in the slum areas of Rome.

Her work began with practice and from this her theories naturally developed and evolved. Relying on careful observations of the children in her care, she identified where learning potential lay and maximised this in terms of the materials and experiences she provided. She also drew from her first-hand experiences of education, identifying that children were learning in a largely didactic manner, working from a curriculum designed for societal interest rather than the needs of the child. She saw this educational experience as one which was largely demotivating and responsible for some of the problems inherent in education at the time.

Through allowing children a sense of freedom in their education and the opportunity to select their own learning experiences, within the boundaries of respect for the materials and one another, Montessori observed that they could sustain interest in an activity for significant periods of time and would frequently repeat experiences until mastery was achieved. At this point they would return the materials to the shelf from which they came before proceeding to the next learning experience.

It is from these early observations that the Montessori Method was born, which not only forms the basis of Montessori Education today but has also influenced some of the key features of early years education and beyond. Montessori left a legacy which has not only impacted on the way in which children are educated but also encourages reflection on the role of the teacher from educator to facilitator.

MARIA MONTESSORI, THE PERSON

Maria Montessori was born in Chiaravalle, Italy, in 1870, the same year in which the unification of Italy took place. She was born into a country which was undergoing significant political, social and economic change, in which there was considerable political and economic struggle between the classes and which was predominantly governed by a male-dominated electorate. It could, however, be said that she herself was to some extent protected from the class struggle going on around her, being brought up as part of Rome's growing middle class because of her father's work as a civil servant.

Montessori's upbringing was traditional, although her parents had somewhat contradictory views on life. On one hand, her father, Alessandro Montessori, was conservative and naturalistic, discouraging Maria from following an academic path and encouraging her into teaching, which at the time was perceived to be an appropriate role for a woman. On the other hand, Montessori's mother, Renilde Stoppani, had more liberal and progressive views and it was perhaps her influence which led Montessori to pursue a technical rather than classical education, which ultimately resulted in her studying medicine at the University of Rome in 1892. It is a testament to her determination and tenacity that she succeeded in a male-dominated environment, being the first woman to graduate from medical school in Italy. Despite the challenges which this presented, including her father's disapproval and ridicule from fellow students, Montessori went on to exceed all expectations, including being awarded the Roti prize and the scholarship that accompanied it.

On graduating in 1896, her early work was at San Spirito Hospital, working as a surgical assistant, which later led to her working at children's and women's hospitals and then establishing her own private practice. It was while working at the clinic that she became involved with a colleague with whom she had a son, Mario. The couple never married and, as a result of the stigma attached to unmarried mothers in Catholic Italy, Mario was sent to live with foster parents in the countryside. Montessori remained in contact with her son but presented as his aunt. Mario was later acknowledged by Montessori and grew very fond of his mother, continuing to promote her ideas after her death (Kramer, 1976; Gisolo, undated).

In her role as a physician Montessori was exposed to the hardships of the class society in Italy and here she showed a social responsibility which exceeded expectations. It was this work that resulted in her being invited to visit Rome's asylums where she first met the children who were to change the course of her life and the direction of her work from medicine to education, for which she is best known today. She became fascinated by the 'idiot children' in the asylums and began to apply some of her medical techniques to observing children with learning difficulties. Through astute observation she noticed that children who had previously been thought to be uneducable responded to her methods. This she attributed to her careful observations which meant that she was able to respond to their individual needs, and she began to deduce that the problem lay with the approaches of the teachers and the environment, not with the children as was the common misconception. Influenced by the work of the French physician Jean-Marc-Gaspard Itard and his pupil Édouard Séguin, she began to develop her own methods for teaching pupils with special needs.

In 1906 Montessori was invited to work with the children of migrant workers living in the tenements of the San Lorenzo district of Rome, viewed as one of the worst slum areas in Rome; the original intention was to prevent the children roaming the streets and 'getting up to mischief' while their parents were at work. Montessori's response was to create the first *Casa dei Bambini*, or Children's House, which was designed as a home environment in which the children could develop their own activities. With a limited budget at her disposal she furnished the environment simply, using miniature versions of equipment which would be found in their own environment, often making the resources herself. Once established, she applied her skills as a medical practitioner and observed the children at work with the equipment, evaluating closely which equipment the children responded to best and discarding any that they did not use.

Through her observations Montessori noted that the children could sustain concentration on an activity for considerable periods of time, and that through absorbing information from their environment they possessed the ability to educate themselves. As with her earlier observations in the asylums she ascertained that with the right motivation children were equipped to learn and, more importantly, were motivated to do so. By providing a structure in which children took personal responsibility, Montessori realised that they learned very easily and gained considerable self-worth from doing so.

It was these early observations at the first *Casa dei Bambini* that set the context for Montessori's subsequent work with children as she continued to develop methods and materials which are still associated with Montessori schools today. Her work bucked the educational trends of the day, in which children were not seen as individuals with specific needs and in which all children were given the same work which was delivered in the same way. Montessori started from the child, recognising that learning began with the senses and providing materials which allowed them to explore and investigate using all their senses, but perhaps of more significance was her work with the families of the children who lived in the slums. She saw school as an extension of the home environment and believed in the importance of building relationships with the parents and encouraging them to realise how special their children were (Daly et al., 2006).

Maria Montessori died in 1952 and left a legacy of theories and writings which have had a significant influence on practice today. The *Casa dei Bambini* became 'a tool for social change both for children and their mothers' (Isaacs, 2007: 8) in Italy and gathered worldwide acclaim, particularly between 1907 and 1914 when opportunities arose for Montessori to promote her unique view of children and their learning (Isaacs, 2007).

MONTESSORI'S THEORY

As discussed earlier in the chapter, Montessori's theory was grounded in her careful and clinical observations of the children with whom she worked, initially in the mental asylums of Rome and later in the *Casa dei Bambini*. Montessori applied the methods used with mentally deficient children to her work with 'normal' children, stating:

> After I had left the school for deficients I became convinced that similar methods applied to normal children would develop or set free their personality in a marvellous and surprising way. (1919: 33)

Montessori placed the child firmly at the centre of her work. She saw the child as unique and individual, a '**spiritual embryo**', with an inner potential which would develop naturally with the right guidance (Miller and Pound, 2011). She emphasised the importance of social liberty; rather than a curriculum designed to meet societal needs, she developed activities and classroom arrangements fashioned to meet the needs of the child based on her observations. She then formulated her method around three interrelated components: the child, the favourable environment and the teacher.

As a result of her observations of the child Montessori identified a series of stages or planes, each associated with physical changes in the body and which characterised a child's development, each with its own unique qualities and characteristics.

The stages as identified by Montessori are:

- birth to 6 years (subdivided into 0–3 years; 3–6 years) – **an absorbent mind**
- 6–12 years (subdivided into 6–9 years; 9–12 years) – **a conscious mind**
- 12–18 years (subdivided into 12–15 years; 15–18 years) – **abstract thinking**
- 18–24 years – adulthood

(1967: 19)

Montessori was one of the first theorists to acknowledge the importance of the first few years of a child's life, stating that the period from birth to three years was one in which, 'the fundamental features of development which characterise the human potential are established' (Montessori, 1948: 90). Until this time attention given to the newborn was in respect of the physical needs which had to be met rather than seeing the child as having any psychological needs; however, Montessori argued that this was when a child's personality began to develop and 'the first care of the new-born babe ... must be care of his mental life, and not just his bodily life' (Montessori, 1967: 61). Indeed, she saw the first few years of life as having remarkable potential in terms of developmental progress due to the child's *unconscious absorbent mind*, which allowed them to absorb and make sense of the environment around them, which helped to shape their personality.

In order for children to make sense of their environment Montessori accentuated the importance of the senses as a means of refining the learning experience. She observed that the child was a spontaneous learner with an inner drive or energy, termed 'the horme' by Montessori, and this was typified by **sensitive periods** in which the child was predisposed to acquire certain skills and attributes. The six key sensitive periods relate to movement, language, order, small detail, refinement of the senses, and the social aspects of everyday life, and these are present in all children around the world. She believed that sensitive periods were present with the child from birth and ran concurrently, although some sensitivities were more prevalent at certain times than others; for example, the prenatal child has a sensitivity to language, being predisposed to respond to the human language, and recognising its mother's voice whilst still in the womb.

Montessori's early work was very much built on her observations of the children in the *Casa dei Bambini* who she saw as progressing through the unconscious absorbent mind, where the child 'learns everything without even knowing he is learning it' (Montessori, 1975: 73), into the absorbent mind plane. During this period Montessori saw the child as translating the unconscious into the conscious through the physical exploration of the environment. She observed that 'he was always busy with his hands' and 'cannot think without his hands' (Montessori, 1973: 63, 67).

The child's need for order and structure is also prevalent at this stage, with children needing to feel secure in their environment. Here Montessori noted that the child developed a familiarity with their environment during the unconscious absorbent stage and as they moved into the absorbent mind stage would show anxiety and discomfort if the routines and structures changed. For example, a child who expects to find a certain toy in its usual place may become unduly stressed when it is not where it should be.

An underlying feature of the Montessori Method is the importance of freedom and individual choice, with Montessori strongly advocating the importance of allowing children choice if they were to become individual and creative learners who were to fully absorb the world around them. In harmony with this notion was the favourable environment, which allowed children this freedom of choice and gave them the confidence to become active agents of their own learning. She believed that the environment should be structured in such a way that children were able to choose their own activities using resources which scaffolded their learning. Through this, children developed a sense of self-control and self-respect, with freedom coming with responsibility rather than being seen as a laissez-faire approach to learning. She also believed that through this method children developed into independent and confident decision makers who were capable of taking responsibility for their own learning and that of others.

Perhaps the most controversial feature of the Montessori Method at its time was the role of the teacher, who Montessori referred to as 'the **directress**'. At a time when the role of the teacher was to present knowledge and facts in a largely didactic manner, Montessori instructed her teachers to step back and observe, reflecting her own methods in the *Casa dei Bambini*. The teacher was to regard the child respectfully, appreciating their unfolding development, and respond to their specific needs. While this may have appeared a somewhat passive role Montessori did not want the children's natural tendencies to be suppressed, but instead wanted the teacher to be able to act as a facilitator of the child's learning, creating and maintaining an environment which was conducive to learning, while also acting as scientist and researcher learning from her observations of the child and acting accordingly.

It is fair to say that Montessori's theories predominantly lay in her work with children in the early stages of development. However, this is not to say that other stages of development were neglected and in her later work she focused on the later stages of childhood (6–12 years), which she saw as a period of great transformation and metamorphosis (O'Donnell, 2013). In this period the child is no longer controlled by the absorbent mind, but begins to develop their own freedom of mind, showing a thirst for knowledge and a desire to learn. At the same time children develop a sense of moral responsibility and social justice, wanting to become part of the social hierarchy of the classroom. Montessori also observed that children at this stage show a natural desire to help others, which supported the parallel teaching that was seen in her classrooms with older children supporting the learning of their younger peers.

As a prolific writer and observer of children it is impossible to capture the full range of Montessori's theories in this chapter. However, it is important to note that she saw her work as being first and foremost with the children, the influence on practice by far superseding the theory behind it. Montessori's theories were developed alongside her work with the children and evolved from her observations that schools were not happy places for them.

LINKS WITH OTHER THEORISTS

Montessori was one of several philosophers who rejected the idea that children were empty vessels who were waiting to be filled and shaped through a curriculum in which children were not seen as individuals with specific needs, but in which all children were given the same work at the same time (Daly et al., 2006). The notion of children as individuals was first advanced by John Locke in the seventeenth century who suggested that, rather than empty vessels, newborn babies were 'like a blank slate' who could be shaped by the social and environmental experiences which would affect their character and mental abilities in later life (O'Donnell, 2013). However, Locke himself was not known to put his theories into practice and it was the work of subsequent philosophers, including Montessori, which was responsible for changing the views of educators towards how children were perceived through the practical application of their theories.

This 'progressive' view of education was first theorised by Jean Jacques Rousseau who saw children as individuals capable of exploring the world around them, acquiring knowledge through their explorations. In opposition to Locke, who firmly believed in nurture as the force behind development (O'Donnell, 2013), Rousseau advocated nature, viewing the child as 'a noble savage who would develop intellectually if left uninhibited' (Beatty, 1922: 76). Rousseau developed a stage theory, believing that children developed in stages and that at each stage they had their own specific needs.

A century later, as Montessori developed her own philosophies, echoes of both Locke and Rousseau's work can be seen, reflected through her own stage theory as well as her view of the child as an individual who was heavily influenced by the environment. However, Montessori incorporated both nature and nurture into her own theories believing both to have equal importance in the development of the child.

Comparisons can also be made with the work of Friedrich Froebel who believed that children were inherently creative and play should be used as a vehicle to facilitate a child's creative expression. Froebel also advocated the environment as essential to educating young children, creating the *Kindergarten*, meaning 'children's garden', as a place for children to learn. Like Montessori, Froebel developed his own set of learning materials which he called gifts, designed to maximise the senses to enhance learning. However, there are differences in the application of these materials since, while Froebel advocated creative expression and imagination as a means for learning, Montessori herself rejected the idea of creativity and imagination, believing children should be engaged in activities which mimicked 'real life', seeing play as the child's work.

Montessori was also influential in the work of key theorists in the field of education, including both Piaget and Erikson. Piaget's *La Maison de Petits* where his experimental work with children took place in the 1920s, was originally a modified Montessori institution and Piaget himself was president of the Swiss Montessori Institution in the 1930s (O'Donnell, 2013). Both Montessori and Piaget were constructivists, believing that children constructed their knowledge from the world around them. They both developed their own stage theory, although here their theories differed. Piaget's theory centred on a hierarchical structure, in which children passed through specific stages at a certain age; Montessori, however, disagreed with this, and while her 'sensitive periods' could be seen mirrored in Piaget's work she acknowledged that all children were different and sensitive periods could not be determined by a specific age. Indeed, despite the obvious influence of Montessori on Piaget she later came to disagree with much of his work, particularly regarding how his work was conducted.

CRITIQUING MONTESSORI

It cannot be denied that Montessori's work transformed attitudes towards early childhood education in the early twentieth century and many aspects of her work can still be seen reflected in early years practice today. Yet her work was not without its critics and it is important to consider whether all her philosophies and principles can be applied to education today. Indeed, while the Early Years Foundation Stage curriculum in England has echoes of her work, it could be argued that there are many elements which are not evident, suggesting that these may be outdated and not relevant or transferable to society today.

The Montessori system of education has been criticised for its rigidity, and the idea of all settings using replica materials delivered in an identical way could be seen as contradictory to a system which prides itself on seeing every child as unique and individual, particularly in a society which is becoming increasingly diverse. Montessori 'spoke [of a] vision for a better world in which education would be a catalyst and principal agent for global harmony, peace and happiness' (O'Donnell, 2013: 172), and even acknowledged the need to adapt to an increasingly technological society, reflecting again a philosophy which was ahead of its time, yet she could never have predicted the way in which changes would happen and, in view of this, the lack of perceived flexibility in the Montessori approach must call into question its relevance in the fast-moving society of today.

Even at its peak the Montessori Method was not without its critics, particularly in respect of Montessori's attitude towards play and imagination. John Dewey criticised Montessori for curbing children's creativity, believing that children should be allowed to explore materials in whatever way they wished rather than the strict approach adhered to by her. On visiting Montessori environments in America, Beth Stubbs noted an absence of materials for dramatic and imaginative play (O'Donnell, 2013) – not surprising given Montessori's view of fantasy play as having little or no importance in a child's education (Roopnarine and Johnson, 2005). This was elaborated on in a disparaging report by William Heard Kilpatrick (1914), who stated that the apparatus in the Montessori school offered a 'meagre diet for normally active children' (Kilpatrick, 1914: 28) and noted that playing with the didactic material was strictly prohibited, reflecting Dewey's view that strict adherence to the intended function of material stifled creativity.

A further criticism of the Montessori approach can be seen in respect of the lack of social interaction, with some critics claiming that Montessori made no emotional provision in her approach to education (O'Donnell, 2013). While she had indeed provided an environment designed to meet the social and emotional needs of the children, critics suggest that the discouragement of social interaction between children within this environment was in discord with their emotional needs. When seen in the context of a lack of opportunity for children to work out their emotions through the medium of play, it can be argued that the environment could indeed stifle a child's social and emotional well-being. This too was observed by Kilpatrick who saw the Montessori child as 'an isolated worker' (1914: 14) where even the teacher, or directress, was seen to stand to one side, rarely interposing.

APPLYING MONTESSORI IN THE CLASSROOM

The application of theory to practice is not difficult to see in terms of Montessori education, principally because Montessori's theories were centred on classroom practice and improving learning conditions for children. According to the North

American Montessori Teachers Association (NAMTA, n.d.) there are approximately 25,000 Montessori schools worldwide, with around 18% of these being in the United States. However, statistics are invariably difficult to pin down given that some schools are operating under the Montessori name without gaining the required certification needed to demonstrate they are complying with the specific criteria of a Montessori school.

Maria Montessori had a clear vision for the education of young children which was based around her view that an educational environment should attend to the holistic needs of each individual child. Each child should be allowed to proceed at their own pace, using imaginative teaching materials designed to be self-correcting in order that they could identify and correct their own mistakes. The role of the teacher was one of facilitator who was guided by the child. Montessori ensured that all teachers were trained in her methods and any setting which carried the Montessori name would have a consistent approach to design and use of the environment and the materials within it.

Montessori's legacy still remains in the Montessori schools of today, and while materials and environments may have evolved to reflect each decade, the principle remains the same. In every Montessori classroom learning resources are developed from high-quality materials and are designed to develop a child's senses individually. It is rare to see textbooks in a Montessori classroom – children learn from the environment and the materials within it with a sense of freedom to move around the classroom choosing where they wish to learn and with what. While this may appear a somewhat arbitrary approach to a child's education, learning is certainly not left to chance – 'the children were introduced to each piece of material individually by silent demonstration or a three-period lesson' (O'Donnell, 2013: 164) – and it is not unusual for children from the age of four years to show an interest in reading and writing using Montessori's specially designed metal insets, sandpaper letters and movable alphabet (O'Donnell, 2013).

Children in a Montessori classroom are encouraged to work independently but in parallel with others. Montessori firmly believed in the rights of the child and while she recognised the rights of each child to an individualised education, she also instilled into the children their responsibility towards others in their environment and the environment itself. Therefore, it is not unusual in a Montessori classroom to see older children teaching their younger peers, supported by parallel grouping, and all children regardless of their age know to return equipment to its rightful place once finished with. Indeed, a key principle of the Montessori approach sees children undertaking practical life skills alongside the more commonly recognised curriculum areas. Such skills require children to take first-hand responsibility for their environment, including care of plants and animals, cleaning equipment and undertaking household chores.

Montessori education advocates a stress-free environment in which children are protected from the tests and examinations which characterise mainstream education. Montessori teachers are skilful observers of their pupils, rendering summative assessments unnecessary since they already have a clear knowledge and understanding of their children's progress. Likewise, Montessori classrooms lack the competitive nature of mainstream classrooms, since Montessori advocated self-discipline, borne from children being interested and engaged with activities – there is no place for the rewards and sanctions which typify classrooms today. She believed that self-dignity was best developed through intrinsic rather than extrinsic motivation (Roopnarine and Johnson, 2005).

While Montessori schools remain faithful to the philosophies and theories of their founder, it should not go unobserved that Montessori's philosophy can also be seen as influencing practice in mainstream schools and, whilst not officially acknowledged, the parallels between her work and the current Early Years Foundation Stage philosophy cannot be refuted. As observed by O'Donnell:

> It is also worthy to note that during the last century many of Montessori's principles and materials have been integrated into mainstream early childhood education often without acknowledgement. (2013: 167)

There has been a keen interest in early years education over the past twenty years, with the most recent guidelines for practitioners being published in 2017. This revised Statutory Framework for the Early Years Foundation Stage (EYFS) (Department for Education, 2017) has been built on the previous 2012 document, which itself was a revision of the original 2008 document following the Tickell Review (Department for Education, 2011). The statutory document 'sets out the standards that all early years providers must meet to ensure that all children learn and develop well and are kept healthy and safe' (Department for Education, 2017: 5). The document emphasises the importance of the 'unique child', stating that 'every child is a unique child, who is constantly learning and can be resilient, capable, confident and self-assured' (Department for Education, 2017: 6). It would be difficult not to see the parallel here with Montessori's recognition and celebration of the unique individuality of each child, and this is reflected in the current drive towards starting from the child's own interests, which also reflects Montessori's theory that children are increasingly motivated if allowed to take control of their own learning. Equally, the holistic needs of the child are a central feature of early education today and, just as Montessori recognised the rights of the child, there is currently a drive towards attending to a child's personal, social and emotional needs, with personal, social and emotional development being one of the three prime areas of the curriculum.

A further parallel which cannot be ignored is the value placed on the environment as a key factor in a child's learning and development. Montessori stressed the importance of the '**prepared environment**' which she developed from her observations of the children in the *Casa dei Bambini* and which was designed to allow children to take control of their own learning through centrally resourced materials that were accessible to children at all times. The aforementioned EYFS documentation states that 'children learn and develop well in enabling environments', recommending that 'experiences should respond to their [children's] individual needs' (2017: 6) and advocating strong partnerships between parents and teachers. EYFS classrooms today are, then, designed to encourage child agency, and while they may not have the same calm atmosphere as Montessori originally intended (believing children should not be over-stimulated by busy classrooms), current practice does indeed encourage the importance of a well-planned and organised learning environment with appropriate resources which children can freely access.

Montessori had clear ideas on the role of the teacher as educator and moved away from the didactic form of teaching which was common at the time. This perhaps is an area of tension between Montessori's theory and current classroom practice, since while teachers might well define their role as a facilitator who makes formative obser-vations of the children in their care, the current education climate, which relies heavily on assessments and targets, creates a challenge for teachers simply standing back as mere observers. While the current drive is for well-qualified staff who are capable of providing the best possible conditions for children, the reality is perhaps more of a challenge in terms of meeting the expectations of all stakeholders, who may well have conflicting expectations of the role of the practitioner.

Although there has been little opportunity to focus on the subject of parents as partners it should not go unnoticed that Montessori was ahead of her time in terms of involving parents in the education, as well as the care, of their children. A main feature of Montessori education was 'the union of the family and school' (Montessori, 1964: 63), and this too is a key feature of current practice where parents as partners is fundamental to provision.

It can be seen, then, that features of Montessori's theory and philosophy are prev-alent throughout early years education today, most significantly in terms of how the child is perceived and the approach to ensuring that each child's needs are met. An integrated curriculum which is developmentally appropriate to the children for whom it is designed, and a focus on active learning, show clear parallels with the Montessori approach, and while some areas are less well represented, it cannot be denied that Montessori's legacy is alive and well in early years settings today.

REFLECTIVE TASK

'No prizes and no punishments'

Montessori believed that children were inherently good and as such did not require any behaviour management systems since they had an internal capacity to guide themselves.

Do you believe it is possible to encourage a system in your own setting which relies on intrinsic rather than extrinsic motivation?

SUMMARY

It cannot be denied that at the heart of Montessori's work was the child, and while critics may have questioned her methods, her belief in the child as an individual and a desire to move away from the teacher-centred approach of the time, were certainly a catalyst in encouraging people to question how they viewed children. Montessori's work must be seen as a key driver for the **child-centred** approach to education that we see today, as were her views of the teacher as observer, preparing and adapting materials to meet the specific needs of the child.

Montessori was one of the first people to acknowledge the child as a unique individual; she championed the rights of children and gave them a responsibility which others would have repudiated, allowing them to take control of their own learning in an environment designed to suit them. In return, the children demonstrated to Montessori that they could indeed take responsibility for themselves: their learning, their care and their environment. It was her conviction in their abilities that made her work the success it was and ensured that it has prevailed for over a century.

GLOSSARY OF TERMS

Absorbent mind

The period from birth to six years which Montessori believed to be the most important in terms of mind growth and development. She believed that children learned more in this period than any other, and advised that the adult was essential in ensuring that the child's natural impulse to learn was initiated during this phase.

Abstract thinking

Abstract thinking occurs when the individual no longer needs the physical presence of an object to think about it, instead inferences can be drawn, and concepts and generalisations formed, without the need for a concrete object to be present. The materials developed by Montessori allowed children to work through and internalise exercises through the use of concrete materials which were designed to ease the way to abstract thinking.

Child-centred

An approach to learning which allows the child to take control of their environment and develop their own learning, the role of the teacher is to facilitate this by creating a learning environment which promotes independence in the child. Montessori advocated this method of learning, in which adults were encouraged to follow the child's lead.

Conscious mind

Montessori suggested that this was when a child could make conscious decisions based on the information which they had gleaned from the environment.

Directress

This is the name which Montessori gave to teachers in her settings; she saw this role as a guide or facilitator, whose role was to support the child in their self-development. In Montessori schools today the directress has a teaching qualification, alongside a specific Montessori teacher educator diploma.

Prepared environment

For Montessori the prepared environment was calm and well ordered, in which everything the child encountered was designed to maximise their learning potential. Children had the right to choose activities which they worked on at their own pace. The prepared environment was designed to encourage freedom and self-discipline in the children.

Sensitive periods

Periods in a child's life when they have a propensity to learn a certain knowledge or skill, commonly referred to today as a developmental milestone. For Montessori, this was a window of opportunity for the directress to support the child in the mastery of that skill since the child will repeatedly work on the skill with passion and conviction, until mastery has occurred. Montessori also believed that the sensitivity only lasted for a certain period, after which it would not reoccur.

Spiritual embryo

The second, and most significant, stage in a child's development. Montessori believed that at this stage the child was most vulnerable to its environment, and it was during this period that personality, intelligence and emotional make up would be developed. Montessori reinforced the important role of the supportive adult at this stage of development.

FURTHER READING

Blundell, D. (2012) *Education and Constructions of Childhood*. London: Continuum.

An examination of the social constructs of childhood through the lens of key theorists, philosophers and contemporary issues which have shaped childhood today.

Cohen, S. (1974) The Montessori Movement in England 1911–1952. *History of Education*, 3(1), 51–67.

An overview of Montessori's work and where it sits in relation to education in England.

Kramer, R. (1976) *Maria Montessori: A biography.* Oxford: Basil Blackwell.

A biography of Montessori, examining her contributions to child development and social reform, alongside some of the controversies surrounding her work.

Polk Lillard, P. (1997) *Montessori in the Classroom*. New York: Schocken Books.

An overview of the Montessori Method which sets the work in the context of its relevance in society today.

Seldin, T. and Epstein, P. (2003) *The Montessori Way: An education for life*. Bradenton, FL: Montessori Foundation.

A guide to Montessori's work across the whole age range, offering practical guidance as to how the Montessori Method might be applied in the home and school environment.

REFERENCES

Beatty, H.M. (1922) *A Brief History of Education* (Reprint 2012). London: Forgotten Books.

Daly, M., Byers, E. and Taylor, W. (2006) *Understanding Early Years Theory in Practice*. Oxford: Heinemann.

Department for Education (2011) *The Early Years Foundation Stage (Tickell Review): Report on the evidence*. London: Department for Education.

Department for Education (2012) *Statutory Framework for the Early Years Foundation Stage*. London: Department for Education.

Department for Education (2017) *Statutory Framework for the Early Years Foundation Stage: Setting the standards for learning, development and care for children from birth to five*. London: Department for Education

Gisolo, G. (undated) *Montessori, Maria*. Available from: www.learningtogive.org/resources/montessori-maria [accessed 5 March 2018].

Isaacs, B. (2007) *Bringing the Montessori Approach to Your Early Years Practice*. Abingdon: Routledge.

Kilpatrick, W.H. (1914) *The Montessori System Examined*. New York: Houghton Mifflin. Available from: https://archive.org/details/montessorisystem00kilprich [accessed 5 March 2018].

Kramer, R. (1976) *Maria Montessori: A biography*. Chicago: University of Chicago Press.

Miller, L. and Pound, L. (2011) *Theories and Approaches to Learning in the Early Years*. London: Sage.

Montessori, M. (1919) *The Montessori Method: Scientific pedagogy as applied to child education in 'The Children's House'*. London: Heinemann.

Montessori, M. (1948) *What You Should Know About Your Child*. Madras, India: Kalakshetra.

Montessori, M. (1964) *The Montessori Method* (Reprint 2008). Blacksburg, VA: Earth Angel Books.

Montessori, M. (1967) *The Absorbent Mind* (Reprint). New York: BN Publishing.

Montessori, M. (1973) *From Childhood to Adolescence* (Reprint). Santa Barbara, CA: ABC-CLIO Inc.

Montessori, M. (1975) *The Formation of Man* (Reprint). Santa Barbara, CA: ABC-CLIO Inc.

NAMTA (North American Montessori Teachers Association) (n.d.) Available from: www.montessori-namta.org/ [accessed 5 March 2018].

O'Donnell, M. (2013) *Maria Montessori: A critical introduction to key themes and debates*. London: Bloomsbury.

Roopnarine, J.L. and Johnson, J.E. (2005) *Approaches to Early Childhood Education*. Upper Saddle River, NJ: Prentice Hall.

3
JEAN PIAGET

UNDERSTANDING THE MIND OF THE CHILD

LEARNING OUTCOMES

Having read this chapter you should be able to:

- recognise stages of child development according to Piaget
- understand how his work has influenced past and present education practice
- recognise how his work changed the way in which the child was viewed
- critically evaluate his work.

KEY WORDS

cognitive development; adaptation; schemas; equilibrium; disequilibrium; assimilation; accommodation; preoperational; sensorimotor; egocentric; conservation; concrete operational; formal operational

INTRODUCTION

Jean Piaget was just eleven years of age when he wrote his first scientific article on the subject of albino sparrows; this work marked the beginning of a brilliant scientific career in which he wrote several hundreds of articles and papers and over 60 books (Halpenny and Pettersen, 2014). Despite having no official qualification in psychology, sociology or epistemology he was arguably the most dominant voice in child psychology for a large part of the twentieth century (Schaffer, 2004; Kohler, 2008), and while he never intended his work to directly influence educational pedagogy, we will see in the latter part of this chapter that curricula past and present have been guided by Piagetian principles.

Piaget was one of the first theorists to study how children think and learn, and while his contemporaries saw learning as either intrinsic, from the child, or extrinsic, from the environment, he believed that neither fully expressed learning and that it was the child's interactions with the environment that generated learning (Mooney, 2000). He saw children as constructors of their own knowledge, taking information from the people and objects in their environment and making meaning from them.

Piaget used his observations of children as a basis for his work and established from this that children's own curiosity would drive their learning, and that the most effective way of enabling learning was to provide an environment which promoted curiosity and challenge and allowed children to control their own learning. This required those working with young children to facilitate the appropriate learning experience, nurturing enquiry and supporting children in finding their own solutions to problems.

Piaget is perhaps most well known for his stages of development and these have been the subject of the most significant critiquing of his work. Through both his observations of children and his experimental work, he established that children pass through a series of stages when developing their thinking skills, and while an approximation of the age in which stages were passed through was given, he believed that this was sequential and each stage must be fully achieved before the next could commence. In view of this he did not believe that a concept could be 'taught' directly to children; rather, children must build their own knowledge of a concept based on their previous experiences.

While many would argue that this is an outmoded way of thinking and that children develop much sooner than Piaget's theories would suggest, we will see throughout the course of this chapter that his influence in the field of psychology is unquestionable and the impact of his work in the field of education is vast. As Schaffer states:

> ... his enormous output of theoretical propositions and empirical observations during a long life time transformed our way of thinking about children and their intellectual development. (2004: 160)

JEAN PIAGET, THE PERSON

Born in Neuchâtel, Switzerland, in 1896, Piaget was the eldest child of Arthur Piaget, a professor of medieval literature at the University of Lausanne, and Rebecca Jackson. He was brought up in a household with conflicting religious views, since while his mother was a devout Christian, his father was a staunch atheist and, as described by Halpenny and Pettersen, 'it appears that these conflicting religious views and beliefs were the origin of many a conflict in the Piaget household'; they also go on to suggest that this may in part be the reason why Piaget began to 'develop an interest in intellectual discussion and hypothesis' (2014: vii).

Although Piaget is best known for his work on the **cognitive development** of children his early interest was in fact in biology, and having written his first article on the subject of albino sparrows, he then went on to write and publish a number of papers on molluscs. Despite his young age (he was still in his teens when the papers were published), many people considered the young Piaget to be an expert in the field of malacology (the study of molluscs). This interest in biology resulted in his studying zoology at Neustadt University where he was awarded a PhD in the natural sciences in 1918.

Piaget's interest in psychology, and psychoanalysis, began following a period studying under Carl Jung and Paul Eugen Bleuler at the University of Zürich, and following this he spent a year in France working at an institute for boys created by Alfred Binet, *l'Ecole de la rue de la Grange-aux-Belles*. Binet was responsible for devising a series of tests designed to measure intelligence and Piaget, working under the directorship of Binet's colleague Theodore Simon, was tasked with standardising Binet's test of intelligence. However, Piaget became less concerned with the results of the tests, focusing instead on how the students had come by their answers rather than the answers themselves, hence the development of his first experimental studies of the mind.

Like many of his contemporaries Piaget held numerous positions, successively and simultaneously, in the fields of psychology, sociology and science, in a range of institutions, including the University of Neuchâtel (1925–9), the International Bureau of Education (1929–67) and Lausanne University (1938–51). Throughout his tenure in these positions Piaget built on his observations at *l'Ecole de la rue de la Grange-aux-Belles* and sought to find out how knowledge grew.

As a genetic epistemologist Piaget was interested in human knowledge, most specifically the nature of thought and how it develops: 'while others asked what children know or when they know it, Piaget asked how children arrive at what they know' (Mooney, 2000: 59). Building on this concept he researched and wrote prolifically on the subject of child development for over sixty years. In his early studies he observed children at play and noted that those of the same age tended to make similar mistakes. From this he ascertained that children 'do not just know less but think differently from adults' (Jarvis and Chandler, 2001: 131). He then went on to conduct a number of experimental studies on children, initially using his own children, whom he studied from their infancy, and later studying larger numbers of children in a psychology laboratory.

From his experimental work Piaget postulated that children pass through stages as they develop towards adulthood and that it is necessary for each stage to be success-fully accomplished before moving on to the next. He did not believe that cognitive development was a continuous process, but rather a cognitive revolution (Mitchell and Ziegler, 2007), in which the child sheds early cognitive limitations as they shift to a 'new and more sophisticated plane of intelligence' (Mitchell and Ziegler, 2007: 10). Indeed, he was particularly interested in the development of intelligence and believed that this was an important factor in explaining how children adapted to their environ-ment. He categorised the environment into two distinct areas: the human, social or psychological environment and the physical environment, in which adjustments to both were of equal importance. Many of his early theories centred on the idea of **adaptation**, in which in order to move through the stages of development, adaptation to existing **schemas** was required in order to develop schemas to fit a new situation. This will be explored further in the next section of the chapter.

Piaget's work has directly influenced American pre-school programmes and many elements of his theory can be seen within the English Early Years Foundations Stage curriculum, which will be discussed later in the chapter. While his work has often been described as being difficult to read and intimidating to the classroom teacher (Mooney, 2000) and despite criticisms of the processes of that work, it cannot be denied that it has helped practitioners in early education to consider more closely how children think. Piaget was an active researcher for over sixty years, publishing 40 books and over 100 articles on the subject of cognitive development. On his eightieth birthday he decided to rectify his missing psychology qualification by taking an examination, subjecting himself to a colloquium for PhD candidates (Kohler, 2008). However, Kohler (2008) explains that since the examination could not be held under the official university authority he never achieved this formal qualification, citing Piaget (1976) who observed 'I shall die without an actual degree and shall take the secret of my educational shortcomings to my grave' (cited in Kohler, 2008, p. 238). He remained active in the field of cognitive psychology up until his death in 1980.

 ## PIAGET'S THEORY OF COGNITIVE DEVELOPMENT

Piaget's theories centred on his fascination with how children think and learn, and from this he focused his work on three specific areas: how children acquire knowl-edge, how their thinking differs from that of adults, and how cognitive development can be classified into stages (Jarvis and Chandler, 2001). Through his observations of children he identified that even very young children are intrigued by their environ-ment and their own abilities to interact with it. He theorised that it is through their interactions with the environment that learning proceeds; however, in order for learning to take place it is necessary for children to construct their knowledge by making meaning of their experiences. He proposed that the human mind contains structures which allow it to make sense of the world, namely schemas and operations (Jarvis and Chandler, 2001).

A *schema* refers to the mental structures in the mind in which the individual stores all the information gathered from the world around them. Piaget believed that babies are born with innate schemas which enable them to interact with others; however, as their experiences increase they begin to form a plan or representation in their brains which aids them in developing new schemas. The more experiences an infant has, then the more schemas they construct. Once the infant can comprehend everything around them they are said to be in a state of **equilibrium** – this being a state whereby the world can be understood through the existing schemas. Of course, given the vast number of experiences the infant is likely to be exposed to, it is frequently the case that existing schema cannot explain a new situation, in which case the infant finds themself in a state of **disequilibrium**.

According to Piaget, human beings are programmed to try and make sense of the world, and therefore a state of disequilibrium is an uncomfortable place to be. He identified two processes by which equilibration (attaining equilibrium or balance) could take place: **assimilation** and **accommodation**. Through the process of assimilation the infant is able to adapt an existing schema in order to make sense of a new experience. For example, an infant may have already developed a 'bird' schema constructed through experience with the family canary, which will then be assimilated to accommodate a first encounter with sparrows in the garden since these too will fit into the 'bird' schema (Jarvis and Chandler, 2001). However, in the case of accommodation an experience may not readily fit into the existing schema and a new schema will be required. So in the case of the 'bird' schema, on their first encounter with an aeroplane the infant will find the object too distinctive to fit into the existing 'bird' schema, in which case an 'aeroplane' schema will need to be formed. Once the processes of assimilation and accommodation have been achieved then the infant is in a state of adaptation.

Piaget also recognised that as well as making sense of the world around them, children need to understand the rules by which that world functions, referring to these rules as operations. He believed that these operations develop as the brain matures rather than through experience; as such, whether or not the child has any operations will be dependent upon their age. He referred to the very young child as **preoperational** since they have not yet developed the brain capacity to form operations. As the brain develops then so does the child's ability to form and understand operations, and it is on this basis that he formed his stage theory of development.

Piaget identified four stages of development and while he suggested an age for each stage, these were only intended as a rough guide (Mitchell and Ziegler, 2007). More importantly, he theorised that stages were fixed and invariant, that each stage served as a foundation for the next, and that no stage could be missed or rendered incomplete. He believed that each stage was reached as the brain matured, permitting 'the use of new types of logic or operations' (Jarvis and Chandler, 2001: 138).

Looking at each stage independently the first stage identified by Piaget was the **sensorimotor** stage, occurring approximately between the age of zero and two years. At this stage he suggested that the main focus is on the development of senses and movement, by which the infant makes sense of the world directly from information gathered through sensory experiences. Infants at this stage are fascinated by their own bodies and what they can do with them and will quickly transfer their experimentations with their own bodies to the objects around them. Towards the end of this stage infants experience increased mobility and they will actively explore their environment and their innate curiosity will lead them to further experimentation within their wider environment.

It is during this stage that Piaget suggested infants develop their understanding of object permanence – that is, knowing objects have a permanence in the world, and that 'out of sight' is not 'out of mind' (Brain and Mukherji, 2003). Once object permanence has been developed the infant will await the return of an object because they know it exists even when they can't see it. It is also at this stage that the infant develops an awareness of themselves as separate from the world.

Piaget referred to the second stage of development as the **preoperational** stage, occurring between two and seven years of age. His assertions at this stage focused on what the child was unable to do, and he believed that during this stage the child needed constant stimulation in order that new schemas could be formed through the joint processes of assimilation and adaptation. He did, however, recognise that at this stage the child had developed sufficient language for thinking to be based around symbolic thought rather than through physical sensation (Jarvis and Chandler, 2001), although as the stage name suggests they are not yet able to grasp logical rules or operations. At this stage Piaget saw the child as being highly **egocentric** – that is, they can only view the world from their own point of view.

He also suggested that the preoperational child has difficulty in understanding the concept of **conservation** and many of his early experiments focused on conservation tests. He established that children in the preoperational stage lacked the ability to understand that a concept such as volume, mass or number stays the same even if the situation has changed. So, for example, one of his most well-known experiments required pouring the same amount of water into two identical beakers. Once the child had agreed that the volume was the same Piaget would transfer the contents of one beaker into a wider beaker. A child at the preoperational stage would automatically assume that there was less water in the shorter beaker because the water level was lower, even though they had seen the water being transferred. Hence he deduced that the child was unable to understand the concept of conservation.

Piaget theorised that cognition develops over time and a certain level of maturity is required before stages can be reached. Children who cannot conserve are said to be unable to decentre – that is, they are only able to focus on one thing at a time. For example, if given sets of pencils, red and blue, and long and short, the preoperational child would only be able to sort these into two groups, either red or blue or long or short, not a combination of each.

Piaget's third stage of development occurred between the ages of seven and twelve years and he referred to this stage as **_concrete operational_**. At this stage the child is able to perform more complex mental operations and, significantly, is now able to decentre. They can conserve volume and number and are able to take in the viewpoints of others. While Piaget recognised that children at this stage had the capacity to solve problems, the problems had to be real or concrete and they were not yet able to solve imagined or hypothetical problems (Mitchell and Ziegler, 2007).

It is not until the final stage, **_formal operational_**, that children are able to solve hypothetical problems and this, according to Piaget, occurs between the ages of twelve and nineteen years. At this stage children no longer require actual concrete objects to solve problems and are able to carry out mental problems in their heads using abstract terms. He 'suggested that not everybody achieves formal operational thinking' (Mitchell and Ziegler, 2007: 25) and in order to reach this stage a wide range of experiences is required.

It would be impossible to cover the depth and breadth of Piaget's work in a chapter of this length; however, that work can be found documented in a vast number of texts related to child psychology and development and further engagement with such texts is highly recommended.

LINKS WITH OTHER THEORISTS

Piaget was influenced by the work of Maria Montessori, particularly the importance of facilitating first-hand experiences for the child in order to support their cognitive development. Like Montessori, he recognised and valued the importance of play as a vehicle by which children could construct knowledge and he linked this to his stages of development, suggesting that at each stage a different type of play could be observed based on what the child was capable of. Montessori, too, subscribed to the idea that children have a readiness to learn at certain developmental stages and, as such, she suggested that the learning environment should be a supportive one allowing cognitive development to proceed through free exploration. While Piaget recognised the importance of such free exploration, he was also critical of Montessori's work, suggesting that it was not open-ended enough and lacked the opportunity for creativity and exploration to take place (Halpenny and Pettersen, 2014).

Dewey's work can also be seen reflected in Piaget's theories since, like Dewey, he recognised the importance of satisfying a child's curiosity in order for learning to take place. Indeed, he believed that a child's curiosity is responsible for driving their learning (Mooney, 2000). As seen in Dewey's work, Piaget reinforced the idea that the teacher should facilitate rather than teach, presenting children with problem-solving challenges rather than merely imparting knowledge and, as Mooney suggests, this 'requires changing the image of a teacher into someone who nurtures inquiry and supports the child's own search for answers' (2000: 62).

While Piaget's work is undoubtedly the most well known when examining cognitive development (Jarvis and Chandler, 2001), when considering links to other theorists it is pertinent to consider the work of other cognitive theorists, namely Vygotsky and Bruner, whose work is examined in Chapters 4 and 8 of this book.

Vygotsky, a contemporary of Piaget, agreed that cognitive development proceeds in stages which are characterised by different ways of thinking (Jarvis and Chandler, 2001); however, whereas Piaget emphasised the importance of a child's independent exploration of the world, Vygotsky believed that social interactions were essential for learning to take place. Piaget's theory advocated that a child would reach the appropriate stage of development at a time that was appropriate to the individual child and, as such, the practitioner should not 'push' the child, instead believing that the stage would be reached when the child was mentally ready. In contrast, Vygotsky believed that with the right social interactions the child could achieve developmental readiness earlier than they might otherwise, as such cognitive development was influenced by their interactions with more knowledgeable others.

Bruner too was influenced by both Piaget and Vygotsky, however he rejected the idea of developmental stages completely, instead suggesting that cognitive development was influenced by different modes of representation, relating to the forms in which information is stored in the mind. Bruner saw development as a continuous process rather than a series of stages and, like Vygotsky, believed that development could be advanced through interactions with others. Nevertheless, Piaget's theories are reflected in Bruner's work, particularly with regard to the natural curiosity displayed by children and in his assertion that children are active participants in their own learning.

CRITIQUING PIAGET

It cannot be denied that Piaget's work was a dominant force in child psychology for a significant part of the twentieth century, yet he was not without his critics and many have sought to identify flaws in his work which might disprove his theories. From the 1960s onwards comparative studies on his experiments were undertaken and, while early replications yielded the same results, researchers began to criticise his methods and modify his experiments (Kohler, 2008). For many it was his research methods which were called into question, particularly given that his early experimental work was carried out with his own three children. This in itself suggests an unreliable scientific method, in which generalisations cannot be formed and where researcher bias is a potential risk, particularly given the clinical methods applied. Even when Piaget widened his sample group this was with the children of well-educated professionals with high socio-economic status, making it an unrepresentative sample. It could be argued that this sampling resulted in an overestimation of the abilities of children in the concrete operational stage, since studies undertaken by Sutherland (1992) revealed that children of working or middle class background only reached the concrete operational stage at the age of 12, not reaching formal operational until the age of 16, thus operating a full stage behind that which Piaget theorised. A further criticism of Piaget's work is in the complexity of the tasks which the children were set, with the suggestion being that they did not fully understand what was being asked of them (Flanagan, 1998). Post-Piagetian research such as that of McGarrigle and Donaldson (1974) has sought to identify flaws in Piaget's theories related to conservation, and here it was identified that when questions were framed in a different way, children in the preoperational stage demonstrated an ability to conserve, which Piaget formerly suggested they were unable to do. Furthermore, studies have also shown that he grossly underestimated the abilities of children particularly in the formative stages (Kohler, 2008), for example he believed that children had no concept of object permanence during the sensorimotor stage (0–2 years), however studies undertaken by Bremner (1985) and Baillargeon (1991) showed that object permanence appeared in babies as young as three or four months.

Mitchell and Ziegler (2007) suggest that Piaget's theory requires some modification, observing that the essence of childhood itself has changed, with children reaching both physical and intellectual maturity much earlier now than his theory suggests. Likewise, Flanagan (1998) believes that a more fluid approach to the ages and stages should be applied, suggesting that there is no abrupt change in a child's capabilities at each stage. Rather, there is some degree of crossover between the stages, with aspects of the next stage being achieved while the child is still in the preceding stage.

Perhaps the main flaw in Piaget's work, practically speaking, is in his assertion that a child learns best in isolation, and while this is indeed a mode of learning encouraged in some settings, research and modern education practice advocate a less formal style of teaching, with children learning in groups, supported by the intervention of the adult or more knowledgeable other in the room. More will be said of this in the following section of this chapter.

APPLYING PIAGET IN THE CLASSROOM

Piaget never intended his research to be directly aimed at education (Jarvis and Chandler, 2001), however it is fair to say that his work has influenced American pre-school programmes for over thirty years (Mooney, 2000), while in England, following the highly controversial Plowden Report (1967), primary school teachers began to apply some of the Piagetian principles in their classroom practice – a legacy which has endured to the present day.

Prior to the Plowden Report a typical primary school classroom saw children sat in rows, learning by rote, with the assumption that all children had the capacity to learn in this way, and those who could not frequently found themselves left behind or, worse, punished. The Plowden committee, then, was set up to examine primary education and look for ways of improving it. Their investigations led them to explore the work of Piaget and when compiling their report, aspects of his work were incorporated into their recommendations, resulting in a shift from a didactic form of teaching to one which put the child at the centre.

The three main messages from the Plowden Report made implicit that:

- children need to be given individual attention and cannot all be treated in the same way
- children should not be taught things until they are developed enough intellectually to cope with them
- children mature intellectually, physically and emotionally at different rates, so teachers should be aware of the stage of development each child has reached and treat them accordingly.

(Jarvis and Chandler, 2001: 142)

Piaget's stage theory can be seen reflected clearly through these recommendations, with the recognition that children mature at different rates and that the teacher should account for this when facilitating learning. This was a significant move from the previous 'one size fits all approach'.

The Plowden Report also placed an increased emphasis on the role of play and discovery learning, stating that:

> We know now that play – in the sense of 'messing about' either with material objects or with other children, and of creating fantasies – is vital to children's learning and therefore vital in school. (1967: 193)

Piaget was a firm advocate of the importance of play as a vehicle for learning, suggesting that it is through their symbolic play that children make sense of the world around them, understanding how things work and what they are for (Mooney, 2000). Likewise, discovery learning was an important aspect of his theory, referring to children as little scientists, who develop as a result of their interactions with the environment; this too was a key theme of the Plowden Report, suggesting that '[the report] lays special stress on individual discovery, on first-hand experience and on opportunities for creative work' (1967: 187).

The direct impact of the Plowden Report was short-lived due to some hostility from the Labour government which came into power in 1976 and also some well-documented extremes in school practice for which Plowden was blamed. This led to the suggestion that the report had encouraged some undesirable trends, which far from improving the state of education had led to an actual decline in standards. While this resulted in an immediate change in education policy, to an outlook which was more focused on the curriculum, it was heartening to see that in developing the curriculum many of Piaget's principles championed by Plowden were reflected, and indeed were also present in subsequent curriculum developments.

The most significant influence that Piaget's work had on the curriculum is through the acknowledgement that children have different intellectual capabilities at different stages of their development; as such, the post-Plowden curriculum saw an increased focus on what should be taught to different age groups, with a specific focus on the four key stages which largely reflected Piaget's four stages of development. The primary curriculum particularly recognises the importance of making the transition from preoperational to concrete operational thinking, with Foundation Stage and Key Stage 1 offering children opportunities for play and discovery learning as a key vehicle for learning while at the same time facilitating learning experiences which recognise the child's stage of development and support them in moving to the next. At secondary level, when children should be in the formal operational stage, the emphasis should be on activities which involve abstract reasoning, allowing pupils to demonstrate their concrete thinking.

A further legacy of Piaget's influence on the early years curriculum is its child-centred nature, a feature which has remained central to the many iterations of the curriculum since Plowden. Of course, Piaget was certainly not the first to encourage a child-centred approach to early years education since such approaches had previously been posited by the likes of Rousseau, Pestalozzi and Froebel (Halpenny and Pettersen, 2014), however his influence lies in the formalisation of a curriculum which puts children at the centre, with the most recent Early Years Foundation Stage Curriculum stating that 'every child is a unique child, who is constantly learning and can be resilient, capable, confident and self-assured' (Department for Education, 2017: 6). The acknowledgement of each child as a unique being, with their own needs and interests, certainly reflects Piaget's notion that the child should be the main driver of their own learning, and encourages a curriculum which allows practitioners the flexibility to plan according to the needs of the child rather than according to a prescribed set of objectives.

A key feature of a child-centred approach is the importance of play, and we have seen previously that Piaget advocated this throughout his stages of cognitive development. Indeed, he suggested that each of his four stages of development could be typified by the types of play which children engage in. While the sensorimotor stage sees children engaged in play which is dictated by their developing mobility, restricted largely to the use of senses and the information gleaned from their immediate environment, it is at the preoperational and concrete operational stage when play really becomes important in supporting children's intellectual development. In the former, children engage in symbolic play, whereby they begin to make sense of objects and people around them, while in the latter stage, children begin to understand the rules of play and learn that they can alter the rules to change a situation. Play can then be seen to support a child's cognitive and emotional development alongside allowing engagement with problem solving and creative endeavours. Although Piaget did not see a direct correlation between play and early years pedagogy, practitioners and curriculum developers have been mindful that providing the appropriate play activities at the right time can have a direct impact on a child's development. As stated in the Early Years Foundation Stage Curriculum, 'play is essential for children's development, building their confidence as they learn to explore, to think about problems and relate to others' (Department for Education, 2017: 9).

REFLECTIVE TASK

Consider what you know of child development and children's abilities at different key stages. In view of this do you think that Piaget's stage theory still holds true today or, as others have suggested, do you think it is outmoded and that actually children are able to do more than he gave them credit for?

SUMMARY

We have seen that some aspects of Piaget's theory have been called into question, particularly when considering the methods he used to develop his theories. Yet it is a testament to the conviction in his work that many of his theories have stood the test of time, which makes him undoubtedly the best-known child development theorist of the twentieth century.

Prior to the evolution of his theories those working with young children merely assumed that the child thinks much the same as the adult, the only difference being that the adult has more knowledge on which to base their thought. Piaget was responsible for reversing this view and, rather than assuming that intellect develops gradually as the child matures to adulthood, he demonstrated that thought actually develops through a series of stages, with each stage having its own unique characteristics in relation to the development of thought.

Piaget's stage theory has inspired and influenced curriculum developers and practitioners for over fifty years and we can still identify areas of the modern-day curriculum which reflect his work. While his stage theory can be seen through the modern-day key stages, his writings on the role of play, the environment and role of the teacher are also reflected in our primary schools today. This in itself is noteworthy but made even more so when we consider that he trained as a biologist, having no formal qualifications in psychology.

It is without a doubt that Jean Piaget was a remarkable individual and it is through his theories that practitioners today are able to view children in an entirely different way than previously, thereby providing them with the support and guidance appropriate to their age and stage of development.

GLOSSARY OF TERMS

Accommodation

Piaget saw accommodation as part of the adaptation process, in which the child adapts an original schema in order to make sense of a new experience. New schemas may also be formed as part of the process of accommodation.

Adaptation

Piaget saw adaptation as being a key element in the process of cognitive development. Adaptation refers to the process of learning through adjusting to new information and experiences, and can proceed through either assimilation or accommodation.

Assimilation

Assimilation is the ability to take in new experiences and information, making sense of this through relating it to existing schema. Piaget observed that the ability to assimilate was not always seamless in children, and where experiences did not fit comfortably into an existing schema then it was necessary to apply the process of accommodation.

Cognitive development

Cognitive development refers to a process of development which includes intelligence, conscious thought and problem-solving ability. Starting at infancy Piaget believed that cognitive development occurred through the two processes of adaptation and equilibrium.

Concrete operational

The third stage of Piaget's cognitive development theory. He theorised that this stage occurred around middle childhood and was typified by a child's growing ability to develop logical thought. The child's thinking also becomes more organised and rational at this stage.

Conservation

Piaget believed that children had an understanding of conservation when they could recognise that a quantity remains the same even if its appearance has changed. One of his most well-known experiments involved showing children two identical tumblers containing liquid. Once the children had agreed that the tumblers contained the same amount of liquid he then poured the liquid from one into a taller thinner container. Children were then asked if the two containers still contained the same amount of liquid. Children not at the conservation stage would believe the taller container to contain the most liquid due to the water level being higher. Piaget discovered that children began to understand the concept of conservation at around seven years of age.

Disequilibrium

Disequilibrium occurs when children are unable to apply an exisiting schema to a situation or event; this causes an imbalance between what is understood and what is encountered which can only be resolved through developing new schema or adopting old ones until balance is restored.

Egocentric

This is a stage of development in which children are unable to see things from the point of view of others; the child will assume that others see, hear and feel things in the same way as themselves.

Equilibrium

When a balance between accommodation and assimilation is struck children achieve a state of equilibrium. Piaget suggested that this occurred through the process of equilibration in which children use exisiting knowledge to make sense of new knowledge. This is seen as an important stage in their development.

Formal operational

The final stage of Piaget's theory, occurring from twelve years upwards. At this stage children can apply abstract thought to a situation, and can use logic and deductive reasoning to solve hypothetical problems. Piaget also believed that at this stage children developed moral, ethical and social awareness.

Preoperational

Occuring in early childhood (2–7 years) this stage of development is typified by egocentricity. Children are, however, developing language and thinking skills, although thinking is still at a concrete level. Piaget observed that children learn through pretend play, and can use words and pictures to represent objects.

Schemas

Schemas refer to the stages of intellectual growth which children go through. Piaget believed that they developed schemas through their interactions with the environment, as they take in information and learn new things. Schemas are constantly modified or changed as new experiences happen.

Sensorimotor

The first of Piaget's stages of development, occurring from birth to two years. At this stage children rely on their senses to make sense of the world and learn through basic movements such as sucking, grasping and listening. At this stage they have no concept of object permanence, believing that if an object has been removed from sight then it ceases to exist.

FURTHER READING

Donaldson, M. (1987) *Children's Minds*. London: Fontana Press.

Donaldson presents a critique of Piaget's theory, offering her own perspectives on child development and child psychology.

Piaget, J. and Inhelder, B. (1969) *The Psychology of the Child*. New York: Basic Books.

A comprehensive account of each stage of Piaget's theory from childhood to adolescence, written by Piaget and his colleague Barbel Inhelder.

Singer, D.G. and Revensen, T.A. (1996) *A Piaget Primer: How a child thinks*. London: Plume Books.

Offers a practical guide to child development for practitioners working in early years settings.

Wadsworth, B.J. (2003) *Piaget's Theory of Cognitive and Affective Development* (Fifth Edition). Harlow: Pearson.

An introduction to Piaget's constructivist theory showing how pupils construct and acquire knowledge. The book offers new insights into his work, demonstrating how it can be applied in the modern day.

REFERENCES

Baillargeon, R. (1991) Reasoning about the height and location of a hidden object in 4.5 and 6.5 month old infants. *Cognition, 38*, 13–42.

Brain, C. and Mukherji, P. (2003) *Understanding Child Psychology*. Cheltenham: Nelson Thorne.

Bremner, J.G. (1985) Object tracking and search in infancy: a review of data and theoretical evaluation. *Developmental Review, 5*, 371–96.

Department for Education (2017) *Statutory Framework for the Early Years Foundation Stage: Setting the standards for learning*. London: Department for Education.

Flanagan, C. (1998) *Applying Psychology to Early Child Development*. London: Hodder & Stoughton.

Halpenny, A. and Pettersen, J. (2014) *Introducing Piaget*. Abingdon: Routledge.

Jarvis, M. and Chandler, E. (2001) *Angles on Child Psychology*. Cheltenham: Nelson Thorne.

Kohler, R. (2008) *Piaget*. London: Bloomsbury Academic.

McGarrigle, J. and Donaldson, M. (1974) Conservation accidents. *Cognition*, *3*, 341–50.

Mitchell, P. and Ziegler, F. (2007) *Fundamentals of Development: The psychology of childhood*. Hove, East Sussex: Psychology Press.

Mooney, C.G. (2000) *Theories of Childhood*. St Paul, MN: Redleaf Press.

Plowden Report (1967) *Children and their Primary Schools: A report of the Central Advisory Council for England*. London: HMSO.

Schaffer, H.R. (2004) *Introducing Child Psychology*. Oxford: Blackwell.

Sutherland, P. (1992) *Cognitive Development Today: Piaget and his critics*. London: PCP.

4
LEV VYGOTSKY

AN EARLY SOCIAL CONSTRUCTIVIST VIEWPOINT

LEARNING OUTCOMES

Having read this chapter you should be able to:

- take into consideration Vygotsky's background as a person and as an educator
- understand his philosophies as they relate to education
- understand how his theories have influenced more contemporary educational thinkers
- critically analyse his theoretical viewpoints
- consider how his theories could be applied in practice.

KEY WORDS

cultural–historical social activity theory; social constructivism; internalisation; zone of proximal development (ZPD); scaffolding

INTRODUCTION

Vygotsky's '**cultural–historical social activity theory**' originated during the 1920s and 1930s, although it only became widely accepted in the 1980s. He argued for a radical idea of learning, in which children thought for themselves. Similar to Dewey, this idea of learning was opposite to the rote-learning model practised at the time. This far-reaching idea was to have an overwhelming consequence for how educators thought about learning and teaching. Higher-level learning for Vygotsky was a developmental and dynamic process where children make sense of what they learn; he also argued that children learn differently from adults, hence the redundancy of didactic teaching (Scott, 2008). Vygotsky's ideas gave educators a theoretical foundation for their practice. He highlighted significant aspects of successful practice for educators: 'so that one can say to oneself, "Ah, that's why I'm doing it! That's what's happening inside the child's head!"' (Palmer and Dolya, 2004: 16).

Vygotsky's most prolific and yet problematic period of writing was produced in the first four years of the 1930s, during a time of increasingly oppressive ideology in Russia. His admired work, which explored his ideas of the importance of language and learning, *Thought and Language* (1986 [1934]), was his last to be published during his lifetime. However, the period was also one where the Communist Party stepped up its oppression of intellectuals and all psychological theories were required to be based upon Marxist thinking. Those intellectuals who did not comply were punished or were set less controversial and more compliant tasks. As Palmer and Dolya (2004: 16) observe, 'In Stalinist Russia, suggestions for teaching children – indeed anyone – to think for themselves were not acceptable'. Colleagues of Vygotsky suggested that it was possible that had he 'not die[d] of tuberculosis, his chances of surviving the Stalinist purges of 1936–37 were slim' (Ardichvili, 2001: 35). It was not until the 1950s that his works were reproduced or even allowed to be discussed in Russia (Palmer and Dolya, 2004: 16). When first translated into English the content and insight of his writings, despite containing many inaccuracies, amazed academics worldwide.

Vygotsky's ideas are firmly situated in **social constructivism**, which stresses the significance of both culture and environment in the way in which we understand the world around us; it is the systems and processes we employ to build knowledge from our understanding (MacBlain, 2014). As with the overarching concept of cultural-historical social activity theory, his notions centred on the belief that a child's own social and cultural background would shape their cognitive development and allow them to adjust and grow. According to Wertsch (1991, cited in Keenan, 2002) there were three aspects which Vygotsky felt were important for cognitive development. Firstly, that it is a historical process; secondly, it is social in nature; and thirdly, it is enabled by the idea of mediation by employing the 'tools' of language, numbers and symbols. In sum, Vygotsky contested that cognitive development was transformational and:

… results from processes which occur first *between* people and then occur *within* the individual. Vygotsky referred to this process of functions moving from the interpersonal to the intrapersonal as *internalisation*. (Keenan, 2002: 133)

These three aspects of cognitive development and the notion of **internalisation** are all evident in aspects of Vygotsky's theories that will be explored below. These are cultural–historical social activity, language and play, zone of proximal development and scaffolding.

LEV VYGOTSKY, THE PERSON

Lev Semyonovich Vygotsky was born in a small town in Russia, the son of a middle-class Jewish family, in 1896. His father worked in banking and insurance and became a bank manager in Moscow, his mother trained as a teacher but dedicated her energies to her home and her eight children. Both parents were keen to ensure he had the best possible education. However, in Russia anti-semitic sentiments have always been present and although academic opportunities were available to Jews, academic survival and progression were always insecure because of the one-party ambitions of the Soviet era (Van der Veer, 2014). Initially he studied medicine then law at Moscow University before enrolling at the private Shaniavsky University from which he graduated with a degree in history and philosophy. He then went on to teach in local schools in his home town of Gomal. During this time he was also an enthusiastic follower of literature, theatre and especially poetry and the use of language structures. In 1924 Vygotsky became a research fellow at the Institute of Psychology in Moscow, completing his PhD the following year on the psychology of art. His academic career as a psychologist was extensive, starting as an assistant lecturer and from 1931 as a professor. He taught and researched in a number of higher education institutes including universities in Moscow and Leningrad. Between 1924 and 1934 he completed his most influential works, which were the foundations for a school of Russian psychology. He died of tuberculosis at the age of thirty-eight in 1934 (Ardichvili, 2001; Palmer and Dolya, 2004; Van der Veer, 2014).

VYGOTSKY'S THEORY OF LEARNING THROUGH SOCIAL ACTIVITY

Vygotsky's ideas have had a significant influence on the approaches to, and the way educators think about, learning and teaching. Although his main sphere was that of developmental psychology, his writings also influenced the thinking behind aspects of speech and language and different sectors of learning, such as tertiary, adult and special education. It was Vygotsky's notion that an individual's mental action 'can only be understood by going outside the individual and examining the social and cultural processes from which it derives' (Ardichvili, 2001: 35). It is these social and cultural processes which he argued were vital for a child to build knowledge. He proposed that an individual child's social background played a crucial role in their construction of knowledge in a manner which is in tune with the culture within which they mature (Keenan, 2002). It is where Vygotsky stresses the difference between humans and animals: the historical and cultural sophisticated features of humans are missing from the social environment of animals (John-Steiner and Souberman, 1978).

Furthermore, Vygotsky asserted that the human trait of being able to use tools sets us apart from animals. Just like physical tools a child develops cultural tools which represent how to communicate and how to make sense of the world. These cultural tools are developed and nurtured in a child's culture, they are not inherited. Vygotsky's view was that these cultural tools, such as language, stories, works of art, signs and models, should be introduced to children in school. He believed that they should experience a variety of cultural tools, to help them achieve new learning through problem solving and interaction with others (especially those who are skilled in the use of cultural tools) and increase their confidence (Wood, 1998; Palmer and Dolya, 2004; MacBlain, 2014). It is contested that language is the most significant of all cultural tools employed by learners:

> The main premise of Vygotsky's most famous work [*Thought and Language*] is the inter-relationship between thought and that most universal of cultural tools – language. He maintained that thought is internalised language. (Palmer and Dolya, 2004: 16)

Although speech is very much a matter of individual development it is also an intensely social activity which is enhanced through interactions with others. It is through speech that children are able to reflect, make plans and help nurture behaviour and solve problems (John-Steiner and Souberman, 1978). Children often think aloud to try and make sense of an activity or a situation, which Vygotsky termed the external monologue. This then transfers into the internalisation of thought, and the sophistication of thinking is enhanced by the language development of the child. This internalisation is the manner by which a child constructs and understands 'the world through his or her collaboration in social activities, and this includes the talk that occurs between skilled and less skilled participants' (Urquhart, 2000: 61). Therefore, the linguistic skill of a child is not merely a function of language which helps create sentences; it additionally affects their thinking and learning. Similar to Piaget, Vygotsky noted that children speak out loud without actually talking to anyone in particular. This occurrence was termed 'egocentric speech' by Piaget. Vygotsky developed this concept to explain that children were giving themselves verbal directions when they met problems as a way of thinking through possible solutions and what they could do next. As such he argued that egocentric speech 'is the intermediate stage between the social, interactive speech of adult-child conversations and the "underground" stage of genuine, private thinking' (Van der Veer, 2014: 63) – the idea being that the child guides themselves through problems and that coherent thinking is further developed by conversations with adults. Moreover, Vygotsky considered 'speech as the most important mediating device in human behaviour' (Wertsch, 1991: 32). The significance of speech in a child's learning and development is best explained by Vygotsky:

> A child's thought, precisely because it is born as a dim, amorphous whole, must find expression in a single word. As his thought becomes more differentiated, the child is less apt to express it in single words, but constructs a composite whole. Conversely, progress in speech to the differentiated whole of the sentence helps the child's thoughts to progress from a homogeneous whole to well-defined parts. (1986 [1934]: 219)

The use of talk is increasingly being recognised in schools as a learning strategy to assist children to express their ideas and thoughts (Bartlett et al., 2001). The application of talk will be considered later in this chapter.

Vygotsky also emphasised the importance of play in a child's development. In their play, children as young as three can experience both gratification and develop skills for their future. He argued that before the age of three a sense of imagination is missing. Imagination he suggested originates from action and play (Vygotsky, 1978). During play, children copy the way that adults conduct themselves in their culture and in so doing prepare themselves for their future responsibilities and values. Therefore, in play they start to gain the attributes needed for involvement within a social environment which can only be truly obtained with help from other children and adults (John-Steiner and Souberman, 1978). Indeed, a child during play will 'behave beyond his average age, above his daily behaviour … as though he were a head taller than himself' (Vygotsky, 1978: 102). According to Vygotsky what is important in play is that the child's imagination works within a set of rules of behaviour. For example, if they are playing the role of a parent then parental behavioural rules are obeyed.

During play and games, children copy the behaviour of adults within a known and recognised cultural model and in doing so they create opportunities for learning:

> Initially, their games are recollections and re-enactments of real situations; but through the dynamics of their imagination and recognition of implicit rules governing their activities they have reproduced in their games, children achieve an elementary mastery of abstract thought. In this sense, Vygotsky argued, play leads to development. (John-Steiner and Souberman, 1978)

Play, he proposed, is a vital element for a child's intellectual development and acts as a precursor for what takes place in school. Learning in play and learning in school should be perceived as equally important and they should both generate a **zone of proximal development (ZPD)**. In each of these contexts children build upon cultural and social proficiencies and information that develops through internalisation and interaction with more knowledgeable others (Vygotsky, 1978).

ZPD endeavours to illustrate the difference between what a child of a certain '"mental age" can do without help, and what the same child can achieve with the benefit of adult assistance' (Moore, 2000: 16). Specifically, ZPD is:

> The distance between the actual development level as determined by independent problem solving and the level of potential development as determined though problem solving under adult guidance or in collaboration with more capable peers. (Vygotsky, 1978: 86)

Vygotsky contested the significance of 'mental age' in a child's intellectual development. He thought that there were two principal areas of importance for the concept of ZPD. The first area concerns the ways in which the more knowledgeable other person in the same cultural and social environment helps develop the child. Such help will involve working at a marginally higher level than the child's current level of competence. The other area of importance, and disquiet, for Vygotsky was how cognitive development was measured. For him what was important was the child's potential for learning with the assistance of an adult or with a more 'capable peer' rather than what the child can do on their own. However, this viewpoint of ZPD became quite contentious in the politics of communist Russia. Vygotsky argued that those children entering school from socially and culturally nurturing families where books and artifacts were common place were at an advantage over those children who were not exposed to the written word. This he contended was because those children from advantaged backgrounds had a head start when they begin school as they had already covered most of the ZPD required by the state school curriculum. He found that those from more priviledged backgrounds soon became bored because school did not challenge them, and hence he argued for differentiated teaching to cater for the zones of development for individual children. The controversial nature, then, was due to:

> Vygotsky's plea for instruction in the zone of proximal development essentially boiled down to advocating a practice that preserves cognitive differences between children that are based on social class. That would certainly have been a very unwelcome suggestion in the Soviet period. (Van der Veer, 2014: 86)

On account of his conviction regarding the significance of cognitive development being a process rather than an outcome he was against summative assessment, favouring assessment which was developmental and formative in nature. Although it is recognised that ZPD has had a great impact on understanding how children learn and what educators can do to provide a quality experience for their pupils, what Vygotsky did not stipulate was what happened within the ZPD for development to take place (Keenan, 2002). This application of ZPD, termed ***scaffolding***, was left for others, mainly Jerome Bruner, to develop further.

Scaffolding, therefore, is the nature of the assistance the child has from, and with, the adult or more 'capable peer' to undertake a task or solve problems (Scott, 2008). It is an active practice between the child and adult where the type and level of guidance given to the child will hopefully result in successful outcomes of learning. Once success has been achieved the child is then confident enough to undertake a comparable task without help. Adults should support and persuade the child to work at the peak of their capability. In short, Olson describes scaffolding as a 'kind of teaching by modelling, showing and telling' (2014: 45). Then once the child achieves success, the level of support and guidance from the adult is reduced but at the same time the child is urged to push ahead and try more developmental tasks. The process is one where there is a shift from the child being regulated by others to one of self-regulation, the idea being that the teaching involved in scaffolding is not just focused on filling the void of the ZPD, but rather creates new forward-looking opportunities for future development (Van der Veer, 2014). The vital aspect of successful scaffolding is that the adult should know the child and their capabilities and be responsive to their needs (Keenan, 2002). A significant element of successful scaffolding belongs to Vygotsky's ideas on the importance of language in a social and cultural context. As such, the language the adult uses with the child should be adapted to their needs but also stretch the child's thinking in a supportive way which takes them to the limit of their potential learning (Urquhart, 2000). After exploring Vygotsky's links with other theorists and then briefly critiquing his ideas, the chapter revisits these concepts by considering their application in practice.

LINKS WITH OTHER THEORISTS

There has been a large number of educational philosophers who have been influenced by the works of Vygotsky; many of these could be loosely termed 'social constructivists'. His own philosophy, however, was shaped by the writing of Friedrich Engels who argued that man evolved by using and adapting the tools of labour and, more specifically, the tools of intricate language systems which made humans intelligent, good-humoured and inquisitive (John-Steiner and Souberman, 1978). Perhaps the most celebrated link is with Piaget. Although there is a certain similarity between the ideas of Vygotsky and Piaget in that they both considered learning to be active, there are significant differences. Piaget considered that children move through a succession of age-related stages of individually constructed development and learn through teaching which is confined to the child's stage of development. Unlike Piaget, what was important for Vygotsky was not the age of the child, but the notion of cultural history and the use of speech and thought in a socially interactive environment to shape their thinking (Wood, 1998).

The idea that learning is socially interactive is very much aligned with Dewey who felt that teaching should not be didactic or based on the predetermined restrictions within a subject-specific curriculum (Scott, 2008). As we have already seen, Bruner applied the concept of ZPD and practical ideas for scaffolding. He stressed the value of communication and highlighted from research that the teacher's speech has a profound effect on the intellectual development of a child's learning in a classroom environment (Wood, 1998). Vygotsky's association between language and learning and cultural history has connections with the somewhat more contemporary thinkers, such as French sociologist and philosopher Pierre Bourdieu and the British sociologist Basil Bernstein. Bourdieu emphasised the importance of culture in driving the learning process, particularly for the privileged groups in society. He argued that the language used in the curriculum and by educationalists gave an advantage to those learners who were brought up in a culture where such language was in everyday use (Moore, 2000). Bernstein's work with language was more specific. He used the terms 'restricted' linguistic codes, which related to working-class language, and 'elaborate' linguistic codes, relating to middle-class language. He argued that this gave an advantage to middle-class children who were well versed in the 'elaborate' code used in school (Moore, 2000: 84). Although this appears to be quite a negative view, Bernstein stressed that the teacher–pupil interrelationship was the key to how the 'different class factions were able to access the curriculum in schools' (Scott, 2008: 82).

Vygotsky's belief that education should match the cultural and historic needs of learners was adopted by Paulo Freire in his drive to raise levels of adult literacy in Brazil and other developing nations. Freire urged teachers to adapt a pedagogy which complemented the learners' social, historical and cultural backgrounds (Freire, 1996 [1970]). There are also close links with Vygotsky's concept of ZPD learning in the support of more capable others within Lave and Wenger's notion of situated learning and how culture and observation were key to learners building skills as part of the process of apprenticeship. Vygotsky's thoughts on language and social and cultural history have had an ongoing influence on other educational thinkers, which have consequently had an impact on classroom practice.

CRITIQUING VYGOTSKY

Although Vygotsky's theories have had a significant impact on how educationalists think about and apply their practice, there are some aspects of his ideas which others have criticised. Mainly it is his notion of ZPD which many have misgivings about even though the general idea holds a degree of fascination. Measuring the extent of difference between what the child can do on their own and what it can do with the help of an adult is a complex and challenging undertaking. Furthermore, it is difficult to gauge whether the help of an adult can be accurately differentiated to meet the particular needs of the child's ZPD. Hence the danger could be that the adult may either go beyond, or indeed, undervalue the child's potential (Wood, 1998). There is also some disquiet about the notion of children's dependence on adults, or peers, in the solving of problems. For example, in a school setting this assistance could be misinterpreted as cheating; conversely, in many social environments not seeking help in problem-solving from a more 'capable other' could be considered as imprudent (Rogoff, 1990).

According to Vygotsky, assessment should focus on the development of the child with the assistance of a more 'capable other'. This is both an innovative concept and one which would be very difficult to implement in practice. His idea is that assessment should take into account what the child would be able to do alone, not at the time, but in the future. This in turn would bring the processes of teaching and assessment much closer together as part of the ZPD. However, the idea of the assessment for development in the future and hence a closer link between teaching and assessment would be very complex to standardise. This standardisation could be impractical in a classroom environment, because the nature and level of assistance to be provided to assess potential would be dependent on the needs of the individual child (Scott, 2008).

As we have seen Vygotsky did not offer much about the application of the ZPD apart from the notion of scaffolding, which involved the adult asking questions, giving demonstrations and offering possible solutions to problems. He did not stipulate what the role of the child would be in negotiating the scaffolding process with the adult. It is suggested, as the adult is designated as the expert, that the scaffolding process could become somewhat one-sided and directed by the adult. A preferable and more inclusive notion of scaffolding has been proposed by Rogoff (1990) who used the terms 'guided participation' and 'apprenticeship', which are more specific in as much as they emphasise the active involvement of the child in their cognitive development. Furthermore, Rogoff's adaptation of scaffolding has, unlike Vygotsky's original idea, the benefit of including not just one adult and one child but learning that takes place within a community. Both experts and children learn and support each other by exploring resolutions to problems in a shared social and cultural environment (Rogoff, 1990).

APPLYING VYGOTSKY IN THE CLASSROOM

Vygotsky's ideas, and those which have been developed since his death, have considerable practical implications in the classroom. Most writers indicate the child's (novice) learning develops because of the teacher's (expert) ability to resolve problems, their detailed knowledge and their sense of responsibility. Moore suggests there are four major implications for applying Vygotsky's theories:

- the importance of not waiting to teach something until the child is deemed able to 'absorb' it (this can apply to the use of reading schemes in primary schools just as much as to the development of scientific concepts with older students)
- an opposition to the use and typically limited or misleading results of diagnostic tests that forbid any help being given to students by other students or by the teacher
- an emphasis on the development of independent *processes of learning* rather than the memorising and regurgitating of facts or 'knowledge'
- the importance of perceiving learning, in all phases of schooling, from a genuinely cross-curricular perspective.

(2000: 19)

The main practical applications of Vygotsky's ideas, then, are laid out above, but for young children the importance of play cannot be underestimated. It is during play that they cultivate relationships with others to make sense of what is happening; they do this by using the cultural tools of language and acting by copying the ways of others. In this way they become secure in what they are doing, make up and abide by rules and are more likely to then play and learn independently. Therefore, it is argued that play between children should be encouraged as, although such play may not have definitive objectives, it can promote experimentation and creativity which may help resolve problems in the future (Rogoff, 1990; MacBlain, 2014).

The role and speech of the teacher are also significant factors in developing the child's cognitive development. The teacher's talk will at one time be repeated and internalised by the child, which in turn develops thought and makes sense of situations. However, what makes Vygotsky appealing for teachers is that he believed the manner of interaction between adult and child was a core factor in cognitive development. An experienced and sensitive teacher modifies their degree of help to match the needs of the individual child and would adapt their *instruction* (scaffolding process) from the reactions of the child. In this way it is not only the child's cognitive development that improves but the teacher also enhances their practice by refining their own communication to use with other children (Urquhart, 2000). The difficulty of teachers responding to each child's needs in a differentiated manner in a busy classroom setting is recognised. Moore, however, offers four models of differentiation, which are differentiation by 'outcome', 'response', 'task' and 'stimulus' (2000: 108), and it is considered that these could be adapted to reflect the significance Vygotsky placed on language, culture and the child's potential for development.

Vygotsky would have approved of teachers supporting children in solving problems at a level higher than they were currently assessed at. This approach would also encourage teachers to reach for the uppermost stages of the child's achievement and consequently offer a more knowledgeable assessment for potential. What is central to this process of scaffolding and reaching for the child's potential for development is the teacher's skill at indicating what the main aspects of the problem are. This is not a matter of telling the child how to solve the problem so they will be able to learn by rote and do it themselves next time. Rather, it is about pointing them in the right direction, so they can internalise and make sense of the task needs, so that in future they will be able to solve a similar problem. Therefore, it is the scaffolding skill of the adult to make the major points of a problem, or task, clear to the child which is paramount to teaching. From a Vygotskian viewpoint it is at the heart of how lessons are planned, how resources are selected, what learning and teaching strategies are employed, how questions are asked and how feedback is given (Urquhart, 2000). The value of questions within the scaffolding process is not to be underestimated. By the teacher asking challenging questions the child will build and refine their own understanding and thought processes, and this will help them in talking about the way in which they used these to give an answer and hence develop cognitive learning and language skills (Muijs and Reynolds, 2001).

For Vygotsky, purposeful assessment related to the child's potential with the help of an adult rather than measuring what the child can currently achieve on their own. Here we see a difference between a Piagetian approach to assessment, which would be summative in nature and measure against levels where a child should be, and Vygotsky's, which would favour formative assessment, concerned with *'working towards levels'* (Moore, 2000: 23). This preference for formative assessment, it is suggested, would also require teachers to reconsider their practice, with assessments being undertaken individually following discussions between teacher and child rather than the reliance on pre-set diagnostic assessments. Teaching itself would not be organised in age–ability levels, each child would be involved in individual goal setting and one-to-one and small group tasks would be preferred to teaching the whole class (Moore, 2000). All of which suggests a view of teaching which is actively constructed with others and not didactic rote learning where facts are offered as rigid interpretations of knowledge (Scott, 2008).

Such Vygotskian practice, much the same as Dewey's ideal, would further suggest a move away from a traditional subject-specific curriculum where knowledge is acquired in separate silos and structures. Even though the primary curriculum does set out to focus on themes and topics which involve cross-curricular aspects, there is still a bias towards subject-specific topics, such as literacy and numeracy, and in the secondary sector there is little evidence of cross-curricular learning. This, according to Vygotsky, divides teaching into a restricted specialist and behaviourist model for the acquisition of specific skills and a more developmental approach which transcends subjects. His preferred model, which has different connotations today, he termed 'instruction'. He argued this holistic and cross-curricular approach to teaching had much more value for cognitive development as it allowed the child to reflect with others on what they had learned and they would be able to transfer that learning to other tasks and subjects. Furthermore, this model gives the opportunity for children to talk through complex tasks and their solutions with fellow pupils and teachers with the possibilities of using them in an array of situations (Moore, 2000). The application of Vygotsky's theories has been taken up by Reggio Emilia pre-primary phase schools, which offer a project-based curriculum where learning is centred on discussion and enquiry between children, teachers and parents.

Finally, it is argued that teachers in all schools are very conscious of ZPD and the value of scaffolding in children's cognitive development. Understandably, however, there is perhaps an element of apprehension in using what might be perceived to be a more learner-centred and discursive teaching style, especially with the constraints of the National Curriculum and Standard Assessment Tasks (SATs) (Bartlett et al., 2001). Nevertheless, even today, Vygotsky's ideas have a number of positive implications for practice in the classroom. These implications focus on interaction, the use of language, the role of the flexible and sensitive teacher, a formative approach to assessment and the avoidance where possible of subject-specific teaching.

REFLECTIVE TASK

Vygotsky emphasised the significance of the child's cultural history for their cognitive development; to what extent, and in what specific ways, could teachers use this in their practice?

SUMMARY

Despite the fact that it is some eighty years since his death and despite the comparative paucity of his written output, Vygotsky's theories still have an impact on both academics and practitioners alike. Many of his ideas have been adapted and developed further by more contemporary thinkers and writers. His ideas, which were quite radical for his time, are still used in teacher education and considered to be the basis for high-quality teaching.

His thoughts on the importance of the cultural history of children and the use of language and speech have helped educators to better understand the processes of cognitive development. Vygotsky believed that cognitive development was a social and interactive process which began during children's early years with play. During play children begin to make sense of the world through imagination, the creation of rules and modelling the behaviour of others. Young children often think out loud, using an external monologue, trying to make sense of what is happening, which then develops or is internalised as thought. The development of thought, then, is closely linked with the linguistic skill of the child.

He also argued that the role of the teacher was vital in assisting children to carry out tasks within their ZPD, tasks which were slightly beyond their competence if alone, but which they could manage with guidance. This guidance by teachers through the scaffolding process is managed by prompting discussion through questions and answers, offering possible solutions to problems and demonstrating. The skill of the teacher within this socially constructed learning is to offer the child a problem within their ZPD and then support the child to successfully solve the problem. In doing this, Vygotsky's idea of teaching was very discursive and child-centred with an emphasis on a cross-curricular approach to learning. He also opposed the use of diagnostic and summative assessment and argued for the use of formative assessment as a truer reflection of a child's potential.

GLOSSARY OF TERMS

Cultural–historical social activity theory

Highlights the significance of how social and cultural backgrounds influence children's cognitive development. Broadly speaking cultural–historical social activity theory infers that cognitive development is dependent on the children's historical context, that learning is a collaborative process, and involves the use of various communication tools including symbols, numbers and language.

Internalisation

Children often think aloud to make sense of a situation. This then changes to the internalisation of thought, and the intricacy of thinking is further enriched by the child's language development. Internalisation is the way the child makes sense of the world through social interaction, where language skills enhance both communication competence as well as shape the way the child thinks and learns at a higher level.

Scaffolding

(See zone of proximal development below) According to Vygotsky this is the form of help from an adult, or capable other, which enables the child to solve problems or achieve given tasks that would have otherwise been beyond their level of competence. The intention being that when the child achieves success through scaffolding they are then sufficiently confident in attempting similar tasks on their own. Successful scaffolding requires the adult, or capable other, to be aware of the individual child's abilities and to be responsive to their needs.

Social constructivism

Emphasises the importance of both culture and environment in the manner in which children make sense of the world they experience, through social interaction. As such social constructivism is a series of practices, strategies and ways of thinking that children adopt to create knowledge from how they see the world around them.

Zone of proximal development (ZPD)

The gap between what a child can do without any help and what they can do with the help of an adult or capable other.

FURTHER READING

Bernstein, B. (1996) *Pedagogy, Symbolic Control and Identity*. London: Taylor & Francis.

A contemporary exploration of the impact of language, culture and class in learning.

Farnan, R. (2012) Education psychology. In: Arthur, J. and Peterson, A. (eds) *The Routledge Companion to Education*. Abingdon: Routledge.

A concise exploration of where Vygotsky sits in the development between the behaviourist, cognitive and psychoanalytical theories (pages 76–8).

Jarvis, P., Holford, J. and Griffin, C. (2003) *The Theory and Practice of Learning* (Second Edition). Abingdon: Routledge.

An overview of Vygotsky's theories and their impact as well as how they link with other contemporary cognitive thinkers (pages 36–8).

Kozulin, A. (1990) *Vygotsky's Psychology: A biography of ideas*. London: Harvester Wheatsheaf.

A seminal resource which explores the specifics of Vygotsky's psychological theories.

Kyriacou, C. (2010) Teaching. In: Arthur, J. and Peterson, A. (eds) *The Routledge Companion to Education*. Abingdon: Routledge.

A brief but informative application of 'scaffolding' in the classroom (page 111).

Van der Veer, R. and Vallsiner, J. (1994) *The Vygotsky Reader*. Oxford: Blackwell.

An overarching and authoritative review of Vygotsky's theories.

REFERENCES

Ardichvili, A. (2001) Lev Semyonovich Vygotsky, 1896–1934. In: Palmer, J. (ed.) *Fifty Modern Thinkers on Education: From Piaget to the present*. Abingdon: Routledge.

Bartlett, S., Burton, D. and Peim, N. (2001) *Introduction to Education Studies*. London: Paul Chapman.

Bruner, J. (1983) *Child's Talk: Learning to use language*. New York: Norton & Company.

Freire, P. (1996 [1970]) *Pedagogy of the Oppressed* (Revised Edition). London: Penguin.

John-Steiner, V. and Souberman, E. (1978) Afterword. In: Vygotsky, L. *Mind in Society*. Cambridge, MA: Harvard University Press.

Keenan, T. (2002) *An Introduction to Child Development*. London: Sage.

MacBlain, S. (2014) *How Children Learn*. London: Sage.

Moore, A. (2000) *Teaching and Learning: Pedagogy, curriculum and culture*. London: RoutledgeFalmer.

Muijs, D. and Reynolds, D. (2001) *Effective Teaching: Evidence and practice*. London: Paul Chapman.

Olson, D. (2014) *Jerome Bruner*. London: Bloomsbury.

Palmer, S. and Dolya, G. (2004) Freedom of thought. *Times Educational Supplement*, 30 July.

Rogoff, B. (1990) *Apprenticeship in Thinking: Cognitive development in social context*. Oxford: Oxford University Press.

Scott, D. (2008) *Critical Essays on Major Curriculum Theorists*. Abingdon: Routledge.

Urquhart, I. (2000) Communicating well with children. In: Whitebread, D. (ed.) *The Psychology of Teaching and Learning in the Primary School*. London: RoutledgeFalmer.

Van der Veer, R. (2014) *Lev Vygotsky*. London: Bloomsbury.

Vygotsky, L. (1986 [1934]) *Thought and Language*. Cambridge, MA: Massachusetts Institute of Technology Press.

Vygotsky, L. (1978) *Mind in Society*. Cambridge, MA: Harvard University Press.

Wertsch, J. (1991) *Voices of the Mind: A sociocultural approach to mediated action*. London: Harvester Wheatsheaf.

Wood, D. (1998) *How Children Think and Learn* (Second Edition). Oxford: Blackwell.

5

B.F. SKINNER

THE FATHER OF OPERANT CONDITIONING

LEARNING OUTCOMES

Having read this chapter you should be able to:

- understand the influence of Skinner on behaviourist theories
- recognise the difference between classical and operant conditioning
- apply principles of behaviourism to your practice
- understand the influence of his work on understanding the development of verbal communication skills.

KEY WORDS

operant conditioning; behaviour modification; positive reinforcement; negative reinforcement; punishment; classical conditioning

INTRODUCTION

B.F. Skinner is one of the most influential theorists of the twentieth century, building on the work of renowned behaviourists, including John Locke and John Watson. Skinner defined his own branch of behaviourism 'operant conditioning', a theory that supposed behaviour is determined by consequences, such as positive and negative reinforcers, and the application of these will increase the possibility of a behaviour occurring again. Skinner's work advocated the idea that a behaviour could be shaped through **operant conditioning** and, as such, his theories became popular as a means of modifying behaviours for those suffering from phobias or addiction or in schools and clinics.

Despite taking a somewhat unconventional path to behavioural psychology, Skinner worked relentlessly in developing his theories and publishing works to expound his beliefs. He wrote prolifically on all aspects of animal and human behaviour, using his laboratory experiments as a basis for his publications and, according to Smith (1994: 1), 'no issue seemed too large or too small for his observant eye and analytical insights'. Skinner believed that psychology should be approached scientifically and only that which was observable should be measured. As a result, he invented a 'Skinner Box' in which to undertake his experiments – a secure soundproof box which ensured the animal could not be distracted by outside influences, thereby ensuring scientific objectivity.

Although his experimental work was undertaken with animals Skinner saw no reason why this should not be applied to human behaviour too, and he had a keen interest in how human behaviour could be modified. This was reflected in his 1948 novel *Walden Two*, which saw him exploring a utopian approach to child rearing. He also applied his theories in a practical sense to the rearing of his own children through the invention of his 'baby-crib', a transparent, air-conditioned crib which required no blankets or sleep suits.

Skinner was a theorist who divided opinion and, despite having 'a large and loyal following' (Nye, 1979: 2), there were many who saw his theories as being too radical and he had 'many opponents who enthusiastically counter his views' (Nye, 1979: 2). Many people believed that his work on animals could not and should not be applied to human behaviour, and there were those who felt that his belief in individual freedom as an illusion was contradictory to the American ideal. However, he remained firmly committed to his beliefs, referring to himself as a radical behaviourist, and it is this commitment that has made him one of the leading figures in the school of behaviourism even today.

BURRHUS FREDERIC SKINNER, THE PERSON

Burrhus Frederic Skinner, known as B.F. Skinner, was born on 20 March 1904 in the town of Susquehanna, Pennsylvania. His father, a lawyer, and his mother, a housewife, were hardworking parents and Skinner had a traditional, old-fashioned upbringing.

He was an active youngster who loved the outdoors and enjoyed building things. Perhaps the most significant event in his early life was the untimely death of his only brother from a cerebral aneurysm at just sixteen years of age. This 'had a dramatic effect on the family, [although] Skinner remained fairly objective about it' (Nye, 1979: 11). However, his brother had always been closer to his parents and his death resulted in their shifting their focus to Skinner, a position which he never really felt comfortable with (Nye, 1979).

Skinner enjoyed school and was heavily influenced by one teacher, Mary Greaves, who taught him drawing and English. It was following a debate, in the eighth grade, with Miss Greaves, about whether or not Shakespeare had actually written *As You Like It*, that he got his first taste of scholarship, and it was later, through Miss Greaves' influence, that he became an English literature major in college and afterwards sought a career as a writer (Nye, 1979).

Skinner attended Hamilton College, a small liberal college in New York, majoring in English and taking other courses in Romance languages, public speaking, biology, embryology, cat anatomy and mathematics. He expressed that this was an absurd range of courses, but they served him well in his later career (Nye, 1979). He did not fit in to college life, enjoying neither fraternity parties nor football, a staple of college life in America. He did, however, write for the school newspaper, producing critical articles on the school and the faculty and, in one such article, attacking the esteemed national honorary society, Phi Beta Kappa. Despite being brought up a Presbyterian, and attending Presbyterian Sunday School classes run by the aforementioned Miss Greaves, by the time he reached his teens he had become disenchanted with God and became an atheist – a further challenge to his college career, which required daily chapel attendance.

Towards the end of his time at college Skinner decided he was going to pursue a career as a writer, a decision which he later acknowledged was 'disastrous' (Nye, 1979: 13). Setting up a study in his parents' home he decided writing a novel was too challenging, instead turning to short stories. He found, however, that he lacked the motivation to write and easily became distracted. After undertaking a variety of writing jobs, including writing newspaper articles and a digest of decisions reached by the Board of Conciliations, he began to reconsider what he wanted to do as a career.

Deciding that he would prefer to write about science than fiction he began to consider psychology as a possible route. Despite knowing nothing about the field he was influenced by Bertrand Russell's book *Philosophy*, which discussed Watson's work on behaviourism, which inspired him to buy Watson's book *Behaviourism* (Nye, 1979). That decision to turn to psychology was later reinforced after he read about Pavlov's work in an article written by H.G. Wells. This resulted in him applying to, and being accepted by, Harvard University in 1928 to study psychology.

Skinner was awarded his psychology Master's from Harvard University in 1930, followed by his doctorate in 1931. He remained a researcher at Harvard University until 1936, where he began undertaking a variety of animal studies influenced by the work of Pavlov, in which, according to Nye, 'he followed the principle of control the environment and you will see order in behaviour' (1979: 16), thus beginning his journey into behaviourism. It was during his time as a researcher at Harvard that he developed his so-called 'Skinner Box' – a device designed to allow him to observe the behaviours of animals and their interactions with the environment. By observing the interactions of both pigeons and rats in the Skinner Box he began to develop his theory of operant conditioning, which formed the basis of his first published work, *The Behaviour of Organisms*, in 1936. In this book he drew comparisons with Pavlov's work, but also expressed how responses to the environment could be learned, as opposed to the involuntary responses about which Pavlov theorised.

As his fellowship at Harvard came to an end he secured a teaching position at the University of Minnesota where, alongside a successful teaching career, he continued his research on pigeons. By this time he had also become a father and turned his research focus to education, initially designing a transparent baby crib for his second daughter Deborah and, later, as his children got older, turning his attention to teaching, designing a 'Teaching Machine' and publishing *The Technology of Teaching* in 1968.

Following a brief period as Psychology Department Chair at the University of Indiana in 1945, Skinner returned to Harvard University in 1948 as a lecturer in the psychology department. He was later made a professor and remained at Harvard for the rest of his career. He became a prolific writer, publishing over 200 titles (Richelle, 1993), including his work of fiction, *Walden Two* (1948), in which he presented a utopian vision of the future whereby people became good citizens as a result of **behaviour modification**. He later turned his attention to applying his behaviour theories to society, receiving criticism from his contemporaries for his published work *Beyond Freedom and Dignity* (1971).

Skinner continued to be active in the field of behavioural psychology up until his death from leukaemia in 1990. Despite many of his theories falling out of favour, he remains one of the most influential psychologists of the twentieth century. His views on the use of **positive reinforcement** as a means of shaping behaviour have had a significant impact on practices, most especially in educational settings.

☐ SKINNER'S THEORY

Skinner's theory is firmly entrenched in the field of psychology related to the science of behaviour, or behaviourism as it is more commonly known. Building on the theories of John Watson, his work followed Watson's basic principles of behaviourism more closely than any other psychologist, which led Skinner to refer to himself as a 'radical behaviourist' (Richelle, 1993) relating to his idea that behaviourism should be viewed as natural science (Baum, 2011). His theories were less extreme than Watson's, however, and while he acknowledged that the mind was important in behaviour modification, he also believed that it was more productive to study observable behaviour rather than attempt to discern internal, mental events, such as feelings, motives and intentions, which are not easily seen (Johnston and Nahmad-Williams, 2009).

Skinner introduced a new term into the field of behaviourism, that of 'operant conditioning' – a term which was coined following extensive research undertaken with rats and pigeons in his Skinner Box. Based on Thorndike's theory of law and effect, he observed that rats quickly learned when sufficient pressure was applied to a lever in the box, a small amount of food was dispensed. Hence, the food led to the action being repeated. From this, he deduced that a behaviour which is reinforced tends to be repeated, hence the behaviour is strengthened. He also discovered that when there was no food reward, the action would eventually die out and the behaviour was thus weakened. Skinner used these observations to develop his theory of operant conditioning, in which he proposed that behaviour could be changed by the use of reinforcement, given directly after a desired response. In the case of the rats in the Skinner Box, they learned to go straight to the lever since the consequence of pressing the lever, in this case the food, was something they found pleasurable.

In developing his theories further he introduced an electric current to the box, which the rats found uncomfortable. The current could be turned off by pressing a lever and, after several accidental knocks of the lever, the rats soon learned to switch off the electric current as soon as they entered the box. When he linked the switching on of the current to turning on a light the rats again learned to press the lever as soon as the light came on, so as to avoid the unpleasant experience. This he referred to as **negative reinforcement**, in which the removal of an unpleasant experience can strengthen a behaviour.

Care must be taken not to confuse the terms reward and **punishment** with positive and negative reinforcement, since Skinner argued that rewards and punishment do not necessarily reinforce a behaviour and, while utilising both may change a behaviour for a short period, the theory of operant conditioning relies on a behaviour being strengthened as a result of the positive or negative reinforcement. As Nye states:

> … although giving so-called rewards may be reinforcing, the important point is that they do not necessarily strengthen the behaviours they follow. (1979: 30)

Skinner also advocated the use of positive reinforcement over negative reinforcement, as a means of controlling behaviour, believing this was more likely to produce the desired result.

Skinner believed that psychology should be seen as a science and, as such, his work was conducted in strict laboratory conditions, which allowed him to change variables in order to ascertain the effectiveness of different reinforcers. Thus, he observed that a change in behaviour occurred if he varied the number of times in which the lever triggered a response, suggesting that behaviour could be modified further and over-reliance on the reinforcer is avoided. In addition, he also noted that reinforcers could be primary or conditioned. Positive reinforcers which are primary relate largely to biological functioning, such as food, water and sexual contact, and these have a significant effect on how we behave (Nye, 1979). Additionally there are negative primary reinforcers, which include extremes of temperature, hard blows and electric shocks. A conditioned reinforcer relies on a primary reinforcer to give it value, for example rewarding good behaviour with a token which can be exchanged for a primary reinforcer such as food. Eventually, if used frequently, a conditioned reinforcer will function independently of the primary reinforcer in controlling a behaviour.

While Skinner's theories were predominantly a result of his work with animals he saw no reason why they should not be equally applicable to human beings, believing that people could just as easily be controlled by the consequences of their actions. Although not likely to be controlled by food, Skinner argued that human behaviour is dramatically affected by reinforcers such as money, compliments and approval from others (Nye, 1979) and, likewise, actions are equally reinforced by the environmental changes they produce.

Although Skinner is best known for his theories on behaviour modification he also applied his radical behaviourism to the acquisition of language, putting forth a theory in his 1957 book *Verbal Behaviour*, arguing 'that language is like any other form of behaviour in that it is acquired through operant conditioning' (Keenan, 2002: 147). Skinner believed that babies learn language through behaviour reinforcement, a result of the child's imitation of others and the role of adult reinforcement (Johnston and Nahmad-Williams, 2009), and a baby's babblings were the beginning of speech that, when received positively by the adults, results in further attempts at using verbal language. The closer the babbles become to real words the more positive the reinforcement, with adults generally rewarding only those behaviours that sound like real words or grammatically correct utterances. According to Skinner children will gradually only use those words or utterances for which they have been rewarded, hence the adults are responsible for shaping a child's linguistic behaviour (Keenan, 2002).

In writing about language he made clear that he was not dealing with language as studied by linguists, but, rather, verbal behaviour, 'that is an individual's activity in speaking and/or listening' (Richelle, 1993: 123). Dissatisfied with previous attempts to categorise verbal behaviour he began to 'build his own functional classification of verbal behaviours' (Richelle, 1993: 124) through developing new labels to categorise speech types, these being:

- echoic – referring to repeated utterances of heard verbal behaviour
- mands – which is short for demands and refers to a verbal operant that is characterised by a previous response to the verbal utterance – this would normally require further reinforcement in order for it to be sated
- tact – which refers to verbal behaviour that provides information about the subject's immediate environment and requires no response from others

- intraverbal – which pertains to the interactive nature of dialogue, so a response will bear some relation to what has previously been said and is not designed to provide information
- autoclictics – which refers to internal speech or thought.

Skinner's work on verbal behaviour was, then, very much a means of describing how children chain together words to produce grammatically correct speech, utilising a variety of strategies reinforced by the responses of the adults around them. Unfortunately, his work on verbal behaviour received much criticism from his contemporaries, which will be explored later in this chapter, and as a result 'his theory of verbal behaviour has very few adherents' (Keenan, 2002: 149).

LINKS WITH OTHER THEORISTS

We have previously seen that Skinner was influenced by the works of John Watson and Ivan Pavlov, both of whom he credits with inspiring him to move from 'a philosophical approach to psychology toward an empirical, scientific approach' (Nye, 1979: 14). Both Watson and Pavlov experimented with observable behaviours and believed that humans have no free will; rather, they were moulded and shaped by the environment. However, a fundamental difference between Skinner and Pavlov and Watson lay in their beliefs as to how behaviour could be conditioned. Pavlov and Watson advocated **classical conditioning** – that is, learning which occurs as a result of an association between an environmental stimulus and a naturally occurring stimulus. In classical conditioning the subject has no control over the response, so in Pavlov's experiments, conducted with dogs, salivation occurred when a bell was rung at the same time as food was delivered. Eventually the food stimulus was no longer required for saliva to be produced, the bell alone triggered the salivation, hence the dogs had been classically conditioned. Watson, too, carried out experiments which resulted in a young boy called Little Albert being conditioned to be afraid of fuzzy white objects after loud noises were attached to the handling of a white rat. In both cases the responses had been conditioned by environmental factors.

Skinner, however, believed that responses could be moulded and shaped through operant conditioning. He explains it thus: 'the dog in the Pavlovian experiment salivates in anticipation of food, or because it expects food. In operant experiments a rat presses a lever because it anticipates that food will be delivered or expects food to be delivered when it does so' (Skinner, 2011 [1974]: 69). This suggest that the subject has more control over the response, so, rather than the reflex response that Pavlov and Watson theorised, in operant conditioning a level of choice is evident.

Skinner's work was perhaps influenced, then, to a greater degree by the work of Edward Thorndike. In his studies on animals, usually cats, Thorndike observed that when a behaviour was followed by a pleasurable consequence it would frequently be repeated. Thorndike's work was built around his puzzle box in which he would place the cat. He then timed how long it took for the cat to escape from the box to get to a piece of fish on the outside of the box. As with Skinner's experiments the cats needed to press a lever in order to escape from the box. The similarities between Thorndike's and Skinner's work are clear and not surprising given that Skinner built on Thorndike's theory of law and effect. While both Thorndike's and Skinner's theories recognise that responses can be conditioned through consequences, Skinner developed Thorndike's work by utilising a reinforcer, rather than just a positive or negative consequence.

CRITIQUING SKINNER

One of the biggest criticisms levelled at Skinner was the generalisation he made between animals and humans. Most of his work was undertaken in a laboratory experimenting with rats and pigeons and, despite the fact that there have been clear applications of his work to explain human behaviour, this is still an area which has led to many people disputing his ideas. The main issue is with relation to the complexity of human behaviour, which some say cannot be compared to the behaviour of animals as this works at a far more basic level. Nye (1979) acknowledges that common relationships between humans and animals can be observed, with the frequency of behaviours in both humans and rats increasing when certain consequences occur. However, he argues that humans have a far more rational approach, thinking things out before deciding what to do, whereas with rats the process can be seen as more mechanical.

A further criticism of Skinner's assumptions that animal and human behaviour is comparable is that this 'degrades the human condition' (Nye, 1979: 74), with some simply resenting the fact that he likened animals to humans. Indeed, when he published his book *Beyond Freedom and Dignity*, writers in both Europe and America criticised him for attacking the freedom of the individual, as quoted in Richelle (1993: 4):

> America as a society was founded on respect of the individual and an unshakable belief in his worth and dignity ... Skinner attacked the very precepts on which our society is based, saying that 'life, liberty and pursuit of happiness' were once valid goals, but have no place in 20th Century America or in the creation of a new culture as he proposes (Spiro Agnew).

Indeed, one such critic who disagreed with Skinner's theories on behaviour modification was Carl Rogers, the creator of non-directive counselling and client-centred therapy, who 'debated with Skinner on issues of freedom and control in human behaviour and action' (Smith, 1994: 7).

A further criticism of Skinner's work can be seen in his theories of verbal communication. Noam Chomsky, a linguist, wrote a critical review of Skinner's book

Verbal Behaviour. As a linguist Chomsky's theory lay in a belief that language acquisition is developed through a set of structures or rules which cannot be worked out by repetition. As such, a behaviourist position is inadequate to account for language acquisition (Richelle, 1993: 121). Chomsky also questioned the validity of extrapolating from animal behaviour something which was an inherently human activity and a highly complex one at that.

While not directed specifically at Skinner's work, there has been criticism levelled at the increasing use of reward systems in schools which, as we will see later in this chapter, can in part be attributed to Skinner's theory of operant conditioning. McLean (2009) observes that the rewarding of children with stickers, chocolate and in some cases games consoles reduces intrinsic motivators such as pride and satisfaction, a view supported by Professor Dennis Hayes, who, in an interview for the *Daily Telegraph*, observed that:

> People have lost the idea of doing anything because it is intrinsically worthwhile – you can only work when something has an external reward. It is anti-educational. (Paton, 2009)

A study undertaken by researchers from Manchester Metropolitan University (MacLure and Jones, 2009) also revealed weaknesses in the use of reward systems in schools. Their research, which was undertaken in the reception classes of four primary schools in Manchester, showed that in many cases the children did not understand why they had received rewards. Moreover, in a bid to ensure equity of praise and encouragement, the study showed that the overuse of rewards was in fact devaluing the sincerity of teachers' praise (MacLure and Jones, 2009). However, as we shall see in the next section of this chapter, rewards can be a powerful tool in helping teachers to manage classroom behaviour, and this should be considered alongside the criticisms as outlined here.

APPLYING SKINNER IN THE CLASSROOM

Skinner's theory contends that the 'likelihood of a child's behaviour reoccurring can be increased by following it with a wide variety of rewards or reinforcers' (Keenan, 2002: 24). It stands to reason, then, that the theory of operant conditioning can effectively be applied in a classroom situation in order to shape and modify behaviour.

Managing children's behaviour in school is an area which has been debated by governments past and present, and there are numerous reports which offer schools advice and suggestions on how behaviour should be managed, with schools utilising a variety of methods in order to shape behaviour. In a Department for Education report entitled 'Pupil Behaviour in Schools in England' (2012), it was identified that the most common misbehaviour in schools is low-level disruption which can result in up to a 30% loss of teaching time, thereby impacting on the education of other children within the classroom. It is desirable, therefore, that such behaviour is managed effectively in order to minimise the risk of children's education being compromised as a result of the misbehaviour of others.

In the past schools had at their disposal a range of extreme measures to discipline children, the most common being forms of corporal punishment, including the cane, whippings and beatings. While corporal punishment was abolished in all schools in the UK by 1998, schools have continued to use different forms of punishment, such as detentions, exclusions and loss of privileges, as a means of managing undesirable behaviour. However, according to Skinner's theory, such measures are counterproductive, only managing the behaviour temporarily while the effects of the punishment are still fresh in the child's mind. Government policy and legislation following the abolition of corporal punishment recommended that 'schools should provide a range of opportunities in which pupils can excel and be rewarded' (Steer, 2005: 18), and advised that an appropriate balance of rewards and sanctions should be utilised to manage behaviour. As such, schools began to adopt a range of strategies more in keeping with Skinner's operant conditioning theory, including a variety of different, and sometimes complicated, reward systems designed to moderate the behaviour of the individual, such as stickers and praise, as well as systems which reward whole groups, such as house points.

Since then teachers have become increasingly adept at applying such systems to eliminate undesirable behaviour through rewarding the desired behaviour instead, and reward systems in schools have become embedded in everyday practice with children who are seeking approval from their teacher complying with what is being asked in order to receive the praise or reinforcement given. Cowley posits that rewards should be used as a 'strategy in a potential toolbox of techniques' (2014: 80) and observes that rewards help to encourage good behaviour and hard work, and can motivate students who lack the intrinsic motivation to work hard. It is important, however, that the teacher has clearly communicated what behaviour they expect to see since it is far more effective to reinforce the acceptable behaviour than correct any misdemeanours once they have occurred. Returning to Skinner's work, he advocated that positive reinforcement was far more effective than negative reinforcement. As such, the success of any behaviour management programme is reliant on a consistent approach to managing positive behaviour, in order to minimise the likelihood of undesirable behaviour occurring.

Of course, it would be naïve to suppose that all undesirable behaviour can be eliminated solely by the consistent application of positive reinforcement. However, the theory of operant conditioning suggests that rather than punishing an undesirable behaviour, negative reinforcement is a far more effective means of preventing such a behaviour reoccurring. As previously stated, low-level disruption is the most common type of misbehaviour reported in classrooms, and this might include anything from children shouting out or getting out of their seats to interfering with other children who are trying to work. While this sort of behaviour may not be seen as particularly challenging it does have a negative impact on teaching and learning and must therefore be addressed. Bennett uses the following analogy to describe low level disruption:

> A stream cuts a score down a mountain until it becomes a ravine, and then a valley. It doesn't do this because it's powerful. It succeeds by persistence and patience, using the same weapon with which a weed splits a paving slab: time. A student can do the same to your lesson, and eventually your sanity, if they are allowed to drip, drip, drip away at you. (2010: 21)

However, it is highly likely that the children responsible for these low-level behaviours are seeking attention and by punishing such behaviours they are in fact being rewarded for their efforts. Therefore, in applying a negative reinforcement by, for example, ignoring the behaviour, children will soon learn that this type of behaviour is not gaining them the attention they crave, and they should eventually learn more desirable behaviours which will afford them the desired attention.

In many ways Skinner was ahead of his time when viewing the education system as a whole, arguing that extrinsic motivation to moderate behaviour should not be used at the expense of encouraging intrinsic motivation. He believed that 'one essential ingredient of successful teaching is leading students to find their own pleasure and satisfaction in learning activity proper' (Richelle, 1993: 173), and once this is achieved the acquisition of knowledge should become an intrinsic reinforcement; children who are motivated and enthusiastic to learn are less likely to require extrinsic reinforcement for learning to proceed. After observing a mathematics lesson at which his own daughter was present he commented that:

> Possibly through no fault of her own the teacher was violating two fundamental principles, the students were not being told at once whether their work was right or wrong (a corrected paper seen twenty-four hours later cannot act as a reinforcer), and they were all moving at the same pace, regardless of preparation or ability. (Skinner, 1983: 64)

This observation is reflective of work undertaken by Black and Wiliam (2001) in their research into the use of formative assessment in the classroom entitled *Inside the Black Box* (see Chapter 16). In this work they argue that 'teachers need to know about their pupils' progress and difficulties with learning so that they can adapt their work to meet their needs' (2001: 2). They also argue that any feedback undertaken by teachers or children should be used to inform the next steps of learning, and wherever possible feedback should be given instantaneously in order that children are aware of where they went wrong and can rectify this immediately. This work has seen a change in classroom practices, with an increased focus on the differentiation of work to meet the individual needs of the pupils and which involves pupils in assessment practices – something Skinner believed to be important in encouraging children to take responsibility for their own learning. Skinner urged teachers to be creative in their teaching, not adopting a 'one size fits all' strategy, but finding ways to tap into the specific learning styles of their pupils. As Smith (1994: 6) points out, 'if a teacher already has a broad range of teaching strategies and tactics, then he/she will always be on the look-out for additional elements to add to the intellectual and practical repertory'.

As discussed earlier in this chapter, Skinner applied his theory of operant conditioning to the development of verbal language, and despite his theories receiving criticism from others in the field, it should not be overlooked that practices in early years settings frequently adopt positive reinforcement to encourage language and communication. Key workers in early years settings exhibit natural behaviours when responding to the children in their care, such as waving and repeating 'ta ta' or repeatedly naming objects that the children are playing with, thus reinforcing language acquisition (Johnston and Nahmad-Williams, 2009).

REFLECTIVE TASK

It could be argued that the application of operant conditioning leads children and young people to become reliant on the extrinsic motivation of the reward and thereby minimises the chance for intrinsic motivation to be developed.

Think about when you have seen reward systems used in settings and consider what sort of effect this has had on the pupils.

SUMMARY

B.F. Skinner has been described as one of the most influential theorists of the twentieth century. He was a prolific writer, publishing his first scientific articles in the 1930s and continuing to publish articles and books for the next five decades. Not just a writer, Skinner should also be remembered for his scientific work, which formed the basis of his published work, in which he demonstrated how a psychological laboratory could be used as a tool for research. This is a tool still in common use today, not just in the experimental study of behaviour but also in those fields where behaviour is important at some stage of enquiry, such as in neurophysiology (Richelle, 1993).

Skinner's contribution to psychology was in the field of behaviourism, where he advanced many theories first put forward by renowned theorists Pavlov, Watson and Thorndike. However, he put his own perspective on this, developing his own strand of behaviourism: operant conditioning. Working initially with rats and pigeons, he boldly applied his theories of animal behaviour to mankind in his quest to gain a comprehensive world view (Smith, 1994). This he accomplished, but it did earn him a number of high-profile critics.

While the field of behaviourism is no longer a dominant school of thought, Skinner's work remains an influential force in schools and institutions, with operant conditioning being a common strategy for managing behaviour. It is perhaps the practical application of his operant conditioning theory which has allowed his work to remain at the forefront of the field, with rewards and sanctions being common strategies used in schools today, and while this does not strictly adhere to his theory its foundations can clearly be seen in his work.

Despite receiving some vehement criticism for his work and being frequently misunderstood and misrepresented, Skinner remained committed to undertaking work which would improve the human condition, and it is a testament to his hard work and commitment that he has left a legacy which makes him as well known today as when he was at the height of his career.

GLOSSARY OF TERMS

Behaviour modification

Based on Skinner's operant conditioning theory, behaviour modification refers to changing a behaviour through the application of external stimuli such as consequences or reinforcement.

Classical conditioning

Reflected through the work of John Watson and Ivan Pavlov, classical conditioning refers to learning a behaviour through the process of association. Classical conditioning proceeds with the linking of two stimuli resulting in a newly learned response from the subject.

Negative reinforcement

A form of behaviour modification in which a negative stimulus is removed after a desired behaviour is exhibited. Skinner believed this to be longer lasting than punishment since the desired behaviour will be repeated to avoid the negative stimulus, for example a child who is constantly badgered by their parent to tidy their room will do it to stop the badgering, and eventually the tidying of the room becomes habitual to avoid a recurrence of the badgering.

Operant conditioning

A means of understanding behaviour through studying the cause of an action and its resulting consequences. Skinner believed that an action which was rewarded was more likely to be repeated and thereby through the process of operant conditioning behaviour could be shaped.

Positive reinforcement

The rewarding of a behaviour by providing something which the subject values with the aim of encouraging that behaviour to be repeated and reinforced.

Punishment

Using an aversive or painful stimulus to prevent an undesirable behaviour.

 FURTHER READING

Benjamin, L.T. (2007) *A Brief History of Modern Psychology*. Malden, MA: Blackwell.

Chapter 8, Behaviourism, presents an overview of the history of the science and practice of behaviourist theory, including the work of Skinner.

Chomsky, N. (1959) Review of *Verbal Behaviour* by B.F. Skinner. *Language*, 35, 26–58.

A scathing review of Skinner's work on verbal behaviour written by Noam Chomsky.

Epstein, R. (1982) *Skinner for the Classroom: Selected papers*. Champaign, IL: Research Press.

A collection of papers by Skinner focusing on his laboratory work, some of his major theories and the application of his work to animal training, education and child-rearing.

Modgil, S. and Modgil, C. (eds) (1987) *B.F. Skinner: Consensus and controversy*. New York: Falmer.

A series of original papers presenting a theoretical analysis of Skinner's theories, including a paper written by Skinner himself.

Skinner, B.F. (1971) *Beyond Freedom and Dignity*. Indianapolis, IN: Hackett Publishing.

Skinner's controversial work in which critics suggested he called into question a person's free will and autonomy, suggesting it was all an illusion.

REFERENCES

Baum, W.M. (2011) What is radical behaviorism? A review of Jay Moore's *Conceptual Foundations of Radical Behaviorism*. *Journal of Experimental Analysis of Behavior*, 95(1), 119–26. Available from: www.ncbi.nlm.nih.gov/pmc/articles/PMC3014776/ [accessed 06/03/18].

Bennett, T. (2010) *Behaviour Guru: Behaviour management strategies for children*. London: Continuum.

Black, P. and Wiliam, D. (2001) *Inside the Black Box: Raising standards through classroom assessment*. King's College London School of Education. Available from: http://weaeducation. typepad.co.uk/files/blackbox-1.pdf [accessed 06/03/18].

Cowley, S. (2014) *Getting the Buggers to Behave* Fifth Edition. London: Bloomsbury.

Department for Education (2012) *Pupil Behaviour in Schools in England*. Education Standards Analysis and Research Division. Available from: www.gov.uk/government/uploads/system/ uploads/attachment_data/file/184078/DFE-RR218.pdf [accessed 06/03/18].

Johnston, J. and Nahmad-Williams, L. (2009) *Early Childhood Studies*. Harlow: Pearson Education.

Keenan, T. (2002) *An Introduction to Child Development*. London: Sage.

MacLure, M. and Jones, L. (2009) *Becoming a Problem: How and why children acquire a reputation as 'naughty' in the earliest years at school*. Available at: www.esri.mmu.ac.uk/resprojects/reports/becomingaproblem.pdf [accessed 06/03/18].

McLean, A. (2009) *Motivating Every Learner*. London: Sage.

Nye, R.D. (1979) *What Is B.F. Skinner Really Saying?* Upper Saddle River, NJ: Prentice Hall.

Paton, G. (2009) School reward culture is harming education. Available at www.telegraph.co.uk/education/6833871/School-reward-culture-is-harming-education.html [accessed 05/03/18].

Richelle, M.N. (1993) *B.F. Skinner: A reappraisal*. Hove, East Sussex: Lawrence Erlbaum.

Skinner, B.F. (1936) *The Behaviour of Organisms: An experimental analysis*. Michigan, IL: University of Michigan Press.

Skinner. B.F. (1948) *Walden Two*. New York: Macmillan.

Skinner. B.F. (1957) *Verbal Behaviour*. Upper Saddle River, NJ: Prentice Hall.

Skinner, B.F. (1971) *Beyond Freedom and Dignity*. Indianapolis, IN: Hackett Publishing.

Skinner. B.F. (1983) *A Matter of Consequences*. New York: Knopf Doubleday Publishing.

Skinner, B.F. (2003[1968]) *The Technology of Teaching*. Acton, MA: Copley Publishing Group.

Skinner, B.F. (2011[1974]) *About Behaviourism*. New York: Knopf Doubleday Publishing.

Smith, L.M. (1994) B.F. Skinner. *Prospects: The Quarterly Review of Comparative Education* (Paris, UNESCO: International Bureau of Education), *XX1V* (3/4), 519–32.

Steer, A. (2005) *Learning Behaviour: The report of The Practitioners Group on School Behaviour and Discipline*. Crown Copyright.

6
BENJAMIN BLOOM

LEARNING THROUGH TAXONOMIES

LEARNING OUTCOMES

Having read this chapter you should be able to:

- understand the impact of Bloom on the theories of evaluation and learning
- identify and understand his notions of mastery and the cognitive, affective and psychomotor learning domains
- apply principles of mastery learning and the three learning domains to your practice
- critically appraise his theories.

KEY WORDS

cognitive domain; mastery; affective domain; psychomotor domain

INTRODUCTION

> Benjamin Bloom was indeed a psychologist and authority, who influenced generations in their quest to improve educational quality. (Husen, 2001: 89)

He wrote seventeen books and numerous articles which had a significant role in shaping educational thought in the latter half of the twentieth century and today. His major theories were mostly a result of work conducted overseas, in particular India where he witnessed the widespread use of rote learning – learning which he considered was just the attaining of knowledge and was only retained long enough to pass examinations. As a result of this experience he created the first of his taxonomies (classifications) of learning – the **cognitive domain** – which was published in the *Taxonomy of Educational Objectives, Book 1: Cognitive domain* (1956). He later focused on enhancing '**mastery**' in learning rather than rote learning just to pass examinations. He went on to develop his work in the **affective domain** which considered feelings and behaviours. Unfortunately, Bloom did not finish his work on the **psychomotor domain** relating to manual and physical skills. However, this and his earlier works on mastery and the cognitive and affective domains have been explored and developed by others (Williams, 2004). Bloom's taxonomies have 'provided educators with one of the first systematic classifications of the processes of thinking and learning' (Forehand, 2010: 4). These three taxonomy domains will be examined separately later in this chapter.

Along with development of the domains of learning, Bloom's other important idea was his 1960s work on mastery learning. Within this notion, he argued, the vast majority of students could learn the fundamentals of skills and knowledge if they were allowed enough time to do so. He contested that academic achievement was not really about intellectual ability which was examined within time constraints. He suggested that those learners who came from advantaged social backgrounds were quite used to having the time to prepare and rehearse examinations. Therefore, they had an edge over those less socially advantaged. The differences are evident before children start formal education, but the gap between those who are advantaged in this way is widened as they progress through the levels of learning at school. It was through the work of Bloom, and contemporary educational thinkers such as Jerome Bruner, that the significance of cognitive activity for the very young was highlighted, thus prompting the US government to launch the Head Start programme (Goodlad, 2004). Head Start was a 1960s initiative to provide three- to five-year-old children from low-income families with medical and social enrichment 'to enable them to learn more effectively once they reach school' (Rowntree, 1981: 113). Prior to this the traditional perception was that the level of academic achievement was an inherent ability that individual children possessed, rather than a matter of social advantage or disadvantage.

Bloom, therefore, thought privilege and social class played a large part in deciding which children did well at school. Children benefited if they grew up in environments which fostered the behaviour, language and cognitive skills that were applicable for school. What was important was for children to be given time to develop and that the curriculum and associated pedagogy matched their learning needs. Bloom questioned the mainstream idea that some learners were superior to others, but he acknowledged some students were quicker than others in their learning. Furthermore, a favourable learning environment would enhance children's aptitude, motivation and speed of learning (Husen, 2001). For Bloom, education was embedded in a personal ethos of social justice and thus:

> Attainment was a product of learning, and learning was influenced by opportunity and effort. It was then, and is now, a powerful and optimistic conception of the possibilities that education provides. (Eisner, 2000: 4)

BENJAMIN BLOOM, THE PERSON

Benjamin Bloom was from a poor Jewish family who fled their native Russia because of religious persecution. He was born after their arrival in the United States, in Lansford, Pennsylvania, in 1913. His first position following his graduation from Pennsylvania State College in 1933 was as a research assistant, firstly with the American Youth Commission and then with the Cooperation Study in General Education. Perhaps his most formative role was working with Ralph Tyler who was the chairman of the School of Education at the University of Chicago on the seminal 'Eight-Year Study'. The purpose of the study was to revise the secondary school curriculum with a view to allowing greater numbers of students to access higher education. He was to have a very close relationship with the university throughout his career, becoming Professor of Education, completing his PhD and serving as a university examiner.

Other positions of esteem followed, which included being involved in the setting up of Research and Development Centers, he was elected chairman of the American Educational Research Association (AERA) and, in 1970, in recognition of his work in education he was given the AERA Phi Delta Kappa award. From an early point in his studies he became absorbed in a number of global projects, particularly in Israel and India, and in 1961 he was instrumental in the implementation of the International Association for the Evaluation of Educational achievement (IEA). Some of his major theories explored further on in this chapter were as a result of his international work.

In the 1960s Bloom was to play an influential role in the task force set up at the behest of President Lyndon Johnson's administration to research and develop ways to improve American school education. Bloom's main contribution to this task force was to recommend a programme of compensatory education. This was achieved by apportioning resources to schools in geographical areas with a high ratio of children who were considered to be living in poverty or children who did not have English as their first language. This programme was very much a part of the War Against Poverty campaign which sought to alleviate forms of social and cultural injustice in the United

States. His thoughts on these issues and for compensatory educational programmes were set out in *Compensatory Education for Cultural Deprivation*, published with fellow researchers Alison Davis and Robert Hess in 1965 (Husen, 2001).

Bloom's work was internationally recognised and his career was varied and included teaching and research which helped shape education policy. He wrote or edited eighteen books, and Bloom's taxonomy has been published in twenty-two languages (Forehand, 2010). The main areas he influenced were evaluation, compensatory education and curriculum design. However, for many teachers it is his ideas of taxonomies and mastery learning which are at the forefront. Benjamin Bloom died in 1999.

BLOOM'S TAXONOMIES AND MASTERY LEARNING

As a psychologist who was an expert on educational evaluation and measurement, Bloom's works have influenced a host of educational thinkers, particularly regarding education in early childhood. Moreover, his ideas have had an international impact on how we perceive the attainment of learning and in the way that schools are resourced, as well as the way their curricula are designed and organised. This section of the chapter will, rather than being strictly chronological, cover the major developments of his ideas. Firstly, an overview of the cultural and social aspects of Bloom's research will be made to gain an appreciation of what underpinned his ideas on education. Secondly, his taxonomies of learning – cognitive, affective and psychomotor – will be explored. Thirdly, there will be a consideration of his notion of mastery learning. Finally, and briefly, his thoughts on curricula design and organisation will be offered.

Bloom argued strongly that children who were culturally deprived were greatly hampered not only in their education but also in the quality of their lives after formal schooling. This, he thought, was exacerbated by a changing society where economic security was somewhat flimsy, an issue which is arguably reflected in our current times. He contested that where such deprivation affected the most basic of children's needs, such as insufficient rest, shelter and nutrition, there would be little hope of them achieving in school; their priorities would be to satisfy their basic needs rather than take an interest in school learning activities. Bloom censured both the school system and society for not providing children with these fundamental requirements:

> That children should struggle to learn under such handicaps [sic] should be regarded as a serious indictment of school regulations and community morality … If it is the school regulations which are at fault, they must be changed. If it is the lack of food and other provisions, action at the community, state, or national level should be quick and adequate. (Bloom et al., 1965: 10)

It is the cultural environment of the home which Bloom considered significant in the development of children's learning. He found that parents and grandparents from middle-class families were comfortable in talking and reinforcing the learning of language, which put these children at an advantage before starting school and as they progressed in their schooling. Consequently, they were advantaged because they were stimulated by a range of interactions and resources such as toys and games. Equally, his studies demonstrated that children who grew up without this stimulation were intellectually hindered. Nevertheless, on a more optimistic note he found:

> ... the culturally deprived child's intelligence at one point does not determine the upper limits of what he might be able to learn in the schools if more favourable conditions are subsequently provided in the home and/or the school. (Bloom et al., 1965: 12)

It is with this spirit of hope that he developed his domains of learning and the notion of mastery learning, which have transformed thinking about school curricula and pedagogy.

Bloom became interested in developing educational objectives which could be organised and ordered according to their cognitive complexity. This he argued would enable university examiners to reliably assess students and improve the validity of education practices. The result of this early work was the *Taxonomy of Educational Objectives, Book 1: Cognitive domain* (1956), which Bloom edited. The cognitive taxonomy stated that cognitive functions can be ordered into six progressively more difficult levels. Students needed to achieve at the level which came before to progress to the next higher stage of the taxonomy. Bloom also set out his ideas for a further two domains of learning in this text which were developed later: the affective and psychomotor, each with a hierarchical taxonomy similar to that of the cognitive domain. These taxonomies could be employed to evaluate tasks and offer a method of forming learning objectives (Eisner, 2000). This is accomplished by linking specific verbs or outcomes in the taxonomies with a level of attainment, which in turn has been helpful to educators in their lesson planning (Forehand, 2010).The cognitive domain taxonomy was concerned with knowledge and information and contained the following six hierarchical levels, from simple to more complex, which students may be asked to perform:

THE COGNITIVE DOMAIN TAXONOMY

- knowledge – facts, recall, categorisation, theories and abstractions
- comprehension – making sense of what things mean and how they relate to each other
- application – applying knowledge to different situations
- analysis – breaking down knowledge into its constituent parts to gain a clearer understanding of the whole
- synthesis – bringing together the separate constituents to create a new whole
- evaluation – reflecting on knowledge and making judgements.

This cognitive domain was followed by the affective domain which related to matters of attitudes and emotions – particularly important for working with people. This has a taxonomy of five levels:

THE AFFECTIVE DOMAIN TAXONOMY

- receiving – taking messages and responding to stimulus
- responding – taking responsibility by responding to and seeking to find out
- valuing – recognising that something is worth doing
- organising and conceptualising – the individual develops their own way of arranging responses to stimuli and develops particular attitudes based on a set of values
- characterising by value or value concept – bringing together ideas, beliefs and attitudes in a coherent whole.

The third and final domain was the psychomotor domain, which related to the acquisition of practical or physical skills. The purpose of this domain is specifically important for learners in fields such as performing arts and in the vocational subjects of engineering and construction. The psychomotor taxonomy has six levels.

THE PSYCHOMOTOR DOMAIN TAXONOMY

- reflex movements – in response to stimuli
- basic fundamental movements – build upon reflex movements
- perceptual abilities – used to interpret stimuli and behave accordingly
- physical abilities
- skilled movements – involve practice
- non-discursive communication – involves creative and artistic behaviour.

(Huddleston and Unwin, 2002: 125)

With each of these three domains Bloom was seeking to change the behaviour of learners: 'The distinction between the cognitive and the psychomotor domain can be related to the difference between *knowing that* and *knowing how*' (McLay et al., 2010: 83). Though there are criticisms that some teachers employ Bloom's taxonomies mechanistically, there is no doubt that they offer a valuable aid for the planning of lessons, assessments and programmes of study, as well as forming learning objectives, all of which will be explored when this chapter looks at the application of Bloom's work. His work on the domains of learning, particularly the cognitive and affective domains, played a large part in his thinking behind his research into the concept of mastery learning.

Bloom's idea of mastery learning was influenced by John Carroll's (1963) model of school learning. Bloom set out his thoughts on mastery learning in *Human Characteristics and School Learning* (1976), in which he suggested that mastery of any subject of knowledge is theoretically achievable for almost all learners if they are provided with the pedagogy apposite to their individual needs:

> ... central to the mastery learning strategies was the development of feedback and corrective procedures at various stages or parts of the learning process ... the key to the success of mastery learning strategies largely lies in the extent to which students can be motivated and helped to correct their learning difficulties at the appropriate points in the learning process. (Bloom, 1976: 5)

Bloom's assertion was that student achievement could be improved by teachers adopting three strategies during the schooling process. Firstly, by finding out, what he called, the cognitive entry behaviour of students – that is, what their level of ability was when given assignments to undertake. After establishing the differences between the learner's actual ability and the ability level required by the school, a differentiated pedagogy is then employed to match these differences. Secondly, by considering the affective entry behaviour it would allow teachers to counter early disappointments in the learning process by using motivating interventions and feedback. The final strategy is to modify the teaching and learning resources to the individual needs and interests of the student (Husen, 2001). As we will discover later on in this chapter, Bloom's claims regarding the value of mastery learning may appear a little over-optimistic. Nevertheless, his inclusive approach to learning cannot be faulted and he championed a non-elitist attitude to learning and achievement: 'Modern societies no longer can content themselves with the *selection of talent*; they must find the means for *developing talent*' (Bloom, 1976: 17).

Bloom's ethos of social justice was also evident in his ideas of curriculum design. Although his work is very closely connected with assessment and test score outcomes, he was very aware that these needed to be seen in light of the differences between resources, time allowed for the study of subjects and quality of learning experiences of the various schools. He felt that an understanding of the different regional environments mattered when trying to make sense of assessment outcomes. Although governments of the USA and UK appear not to have taken much notice of this element of Bloom's thinking, he did, however, have an international impact on the design of school curricula, particularly in nations that traditionally used methods such as rote learning. In 1971 he directed a UNESCO seminar in Sweden that promoted the inclusion of environmental aspects in curricula design, and included the differences in geographic locations and the adoption of pedagogic and assessment methods that matched national cultures (Eisner, 2000).

LINKS WITH OTHER THEORISTS

Bloom's work on education evaluation, objective setting and the curriculum was influenced by his mentor Ralph Tyler. Bloom was a researcher under Tyler's guidance during the notable 'Eight-Year Study' between 1934 and 1942, in which thirty secondary schools were given the opportunity to follow their own radical curricula and evaluation methods: 'The basic aim of the study was to provide the space needed for schools to function as educational laboratories, a concept first advanced by John Dewey' (Eisner, 2001: 55). As we have already seen, Bloom was further influenced by John Carroll's ideal style of school learning which helped shape his later notions of mastery learning. John Hattie's empirical research into the effectiveness of learning and teaching methods reflects much of Bloom's ideas of corrective feedback and challenging learners in both the use of mastery learning and the use of hierarchical taxonomies.

Bloom argued that their family, social and cultural backgrounds all have an impact upon children's achievement in school. This is certainly aligned with Bourdieu's views on social reproduction and cultural capital as well as the notion of 'habitus', which Bloom linked with the pre-entry cognition and affective domain levels of children starting in school. These ideas, which argued that culturally deprived children were at a disadvantage when compared with their middle-class peers, were outlined in *Compensatory Education for Cultural Deprivation* (Bloom et al., 1965). Like Vygotsky and his contemporary Bruner, Bloom stressed the significance of the use of language for learners in their early years:

> Most disadvantaged children ... spend less time in direct interaction with their parents than middle-class children do. In addition the parents in deprived homes usually do not have the skills or the language to effectively use the time they spend with their children to foster the language and cognitive development which will help children in school. (1965: 69)

Furthermore, the role of the family and the environment in nurturing language skills in preparation for schooling was also associated with Basil Bernstein and the ecological theory of Urie Bronfenbrenner, who we will encounter again in Chapter 10. Bronfenbrenner, with possibly the same degree of optimism as Bloom, argued that the role of the parent could have a great impact on altering their child's learning before school and during their schooling (Bloom, 1981). Such optimism, however, is underpinned by a realisation that children require their basic human needs to be met before they can perform at higher-level cognitive tasks. Like Maslow, Bloom felt that teachers, and indeed schools and society, should ensure that a child's basic human needs of food, shelter and safety should be met before learners could start to reach their ultimate goal of self-actualisation.

CRITIQUING BLOOM

Criticisms of Bloom's work generally focus on his over-optimistic inclusive stance on child development and the perceived predetermined and mechanistic nature of taxonomies and mastery learning. His ideas on compensatory learning which brought 'deprived' children up to the entry level standard at school, although laudable from a social justice viewpoint, are a somewhat hopeful aspiration rather than a practical proposition. Although Bloom's differentiated and progressive notion is evident in some initiatives in schools today, such as personal learning and assessment for learning, the idea of individual children having time to have formative learning teaching and assessment so they can all achieve in an already crowded curriculum is not a practical option. This is particularly the case in a school system which is becoming more competitive and reverting to a culture of summative assessment with end-of-year examinations.

Bloom's concept of using taxonomies to develop learning in the three domains of cognition, affection and psychomotor, are based on the idea that hierarchical objectives will change behaviour. This, some would argue, places too much stress on rigid outcomes, which in turn can lead to a perilously restricted and mechanistic manner of learning (Huddleston and Unwin, 2002; McLay et al., 2010). There is also a philosophical criticism of the meaning of the words used in the hierarchical taxonomies. For example, 'knowledge' could mean a number of things to a number of people, and 'how do we know that we know something[?]' (Matheson, 2008: 3). In an effort to be clearer about what is meant by words used in the taxonomies there is a natural tendency (and a dilemma) to be more prescriptive and detailed in framing the objectives so the outcomes of the learning can be assessed – which returns again to the criticism of a restricted and mechanistic approach to learning and teaching.

As we have seen, mastery learning is effective in that it can allow, time and resourcing permitting, for slower learners to achieve the same level as faster learners. Furthermore, mastery learning has a positive effect on the levels of learner persistence, motivation and self-esteem. Nevertheless, mastery learning has been censured because overuse, and a narrow application of mastery learning methods, could lead teachers 'to teach to the test'. Stenhouse also contests that mastery learning is 'predictive of the rate at which they [the students] can learn rather than the possible level of achievement' (Stenhouse, 1975: 64). It is further argued that some of the more important developmental outcomes of the affected domain are very difficult to measure, such as valuing, showing sympathy and awareness. So perhaps the notion of mastery learning is flawed when it comes to the deeper, developmental and creative nature of learning. Moreover, mastery learning in practice takes a huge amount of time and groundwork to prepare resources, plan sessions, organise the classroom environment, and give corrective summative feedback to learners (O'Donnell, 2007). Unfortunately, despite the best intentions not all teachers are afforded such conditions (Petty, 1998). However, in spite of these criticisms teachers can take a great deal from Bloom's work and apply this to their classroom practice.

APPLYING BLOOM IN THE CLASSROOM

Bloom's positive outlook regarding learning and development for the majority of children centred on the significance of an encouraging learning environment and the role and value of the teaching within it:

> Who can learn in schools is determined to a large extent by the conditions in the school; the quality of instruction is a major determiner of who will learn well – *the few or the many*. (1976: 138)

To begin with Bloom considered his taxonomies as not just a means to assess pupils' learning. He saw the three domains as providing a conventional set of terms which could be used by all teachers (and recognised by learners) in challenging learners from easier to more developmental tasks. These taxonomical terms could be used in setting learning objectives and employed in short-term planning for lessons and medium- and long-term planning such as schemes of work. Furthermore, they could be used for tasks which teachers do on a day-to-day basis, such as setting differentiated learning activities, questions and answers and providing formative and corrective feedback. However, for the most part the taxonomies provide an excellent basis for a developmental learning framework and the setting of objectives to be used in the planning, teaching and assessment activities mentioned. Many writers have given suggestions for learning objectives for each of the domains. Here are some offered by Petty (1998: 347).

THE COGNITIVE DOMAIN TAXONOMY

Knowledge: To be able to: state; recall; list; recognise; select; reproduce …

Comprehension: To be able to: explain; describe reasons for; identify causes of …

Application: To be able to: use; apply; construct; solve; select …

Analysis: To be able to: break down; list component parts of; compare and contrast; differentiate between …

Synthesis: To be able to: summarise; generalise; argue; organise; design; explain the reason for …

Evaluate: To be able to: judge; evaluate; give arguments for and against; criticise …

THE AFFECTIVE DOMAIN

to listen to … to appreciate the importance of …

to have an awareness of … to respond with personal feelings …

to have an aesthetic appreciation of … to have a commitment towards …

to recognise the moral dilemmas involved in …

THE PSYCHOMOTOR DOMAIN

to plane; to draw; to throw; to weld …

The taxonomies, particularly the cognitive domain, have been sequenced with the easiest first, starting with knowledge and ending with evaluation as the most complex. Petty (2009) suggests that the cognitive domain is divided into two categories of tasks, reproductive tasks and reasoning tasks. Reproductive tasks (knowledge, comprehension and application) require low cognitive effort, whilst reasoning tasks (analysis, synthesis and evaluation) involve a deeper learning experience for the student. Reproductive tasks are those which are given directly to the student by the teacher such as copying or recounting information. With reasoning tasks, on the other hand, 'the student must process and apply what they have learned, linking it with existing learning and experience' (Petty, 2009: 14). It is crucial that the more developmental and harder objectives (reasoning tasks) are also used in teaching, otherwise the criticism of the taxonomies being mechanistic becomes a reality and the learners will not develop their deep learning. So the taxonomies give teachers a framework to check that their planning and teaching actually help progress children's learning. The three different domains should be used accordingly. For example, practical and skill-based sessions should employ the psychomotor domain, group projects and activities the affective domain and classroom-based sessions the cognitive domain. Perhaps more importantly, all three could be used over a range of activities for the same subject matter – cognitive for the introduction of the subject and linking to previous learning, leading into the affective domain for group work in preparation for the psychomotor domain to practise and hone their skills, then back to the cognitive domain to make sense of and evaluate their learning.

Therefore, what is of note here is that although Bloom distinguished between the different domains, he did indicate that one domain influences the learning of the next domain and, as such, the learner develops as a whole. For example, the cognitive domain leads into the affective domain, which in turn leads into the psychomotor domain. As the pupil gains knowledge of their subject, their behaviour and awareness develop, which allows them to use and value the skills attained (Huddleston and Unwin, 2002). All of these activities range from the easier to the higher-order challenging outcomes of learning. Bloom's taxonomies also offer the chance to differentiate teaching to help reach the pupils who require more time to learn, so they 'can feel secure but stretched' (Williams, 2004: 11).

There are two aspects of teaching where differentiation and challenge can be very effective. The first is by the use of questions during lessons. These should be from the easier (using the verbs given above to ascertain knowledge and understanding) to the more developmental (to ascertain analysis, synthesis and evaluation) in the cognitive domain. The teacher, knowing the pupil, will be able to challenge them to help them develop. During this process what is important is how the teacher responds to the answers given by the pupils. As such, feedback to answers needs to be corrective for the future but also encouraging in its nature. The second aspect is the use of these encouraging and developmental comments in formative feedback on pupils' written work. Written feedback which is corrective, encouraging and allows time to achieve is central to Bloom's inclusive approach to teaching and education in general.

The uses of differentiated questioning and formative feedback are, as previously mentioned, recent examples of initiatives such as personalised learning and assessment for learning. Such personalised methods, as we discovered in the previous section of this chapter, take time, but it is argued that they are well worth the effort and with collaborative planning and sharing of practice are achievable activities. Moreover, apart from the advantage to the individual pupils, Bloom contests that the use of formative assessment and feedback (based on the use of objectives formed from the taxonomies) allows the teacher to discover what elements of the lesson the pupils as a group learned well and what elements were not so successfully learned (Bloom, 1981).

It is this appreciation of what went well and what not so well that gives teachers the opportunity to reflect and evaluate their practice. This reflection and evaluation has two purposes. The first is about evaluating the outcomes of pupils' work and ensuring that the formative feedback is both informative by giving direction for further improvement and encouraging to help motivate further engagement in the learning process. The second purpose of the reflection and evaluation is of a more personal and professional nature, in that it gives teachers a chance to see where they can improve their planning, assessment and teaching and hence further progress the pupils' learning (Kyriacou, 2012).

Although Bloom's ideas appear inclusive, valid, well meant and practical in terms of teaching and assessment, their application should be considered with a slight element of caution. The criticisms – for example, of the mechanistic dangers of teaching to predetermined hierarchical objectives and the possibility of an over-reliance on mastery learning – are valid. However, with a degree of flexibility, and individualised and negotiated planning, Bloom's ideas can lead to a progressive and deep learning experience for pupils and avoid the pitfalls of the aforementioned criticisms.

REFLECTIVE TASK

As we have seen, the affective domain is about emotions and changing beliefs and attitudes. From a teaching viewpoint some aspects of the affective domain are challenging. Therefore, in your own words, consider what types of teaching strategies could be adopted and suggest ways of assessing the following affective domain learning objective (give the reasons for your choices):

To have an aesthetic appreciation of a particular work of art.

SUMMARY

As a psychologist, Bloom has had a significant impact on the development of education as a whole. This impact was driven by his research experiences in countries such as India and Israel, as well as his idealistic yet optimistic desire for all children to have equal access to quality education systems regardless of their social background. His early work was mainly concerned with evaluation and assessment matters; his seminal ideas emanated from these studies. He held a number of prestigious educational and research positions. He was also at the forefront in campaigns such as the War Against Poverty in the United States, which explored ways of developing educational programmes to tackle the growing learning barriers for those children and families perceived to be educationally and culturally disadvantaged.

His initial interest came from helping universities become more confident and secure in their assessment practices, which would then enable them to evaluate the teaching and learning practices they employed. As a consequence of this interest Bloom developed and produced two taxonomies of learning objectives. The first two domains were the cognitive and the affective domains. A third taxonomy for the psychomotor domain was added later. The original notion was that these taxonomies could be employed to ensure a focus on the assessment tasks of programmes and avoid students just memorising facts. However, the taxonomies became a widely used means for teachers to formulate learning objectives, plan and develop lessons and even programmes of learning. They could also be used to challenge learners and differentiate teaching methods. The use of Bloom's taxonomies is widespread in many sectors of education. However, their function is not without some criticism, in that if the taxonomies were rigidly applied this could lead to a mechanistic approach to learning.

Bloom is also renowned for his concept of mastery learning, which emerged from both his optimism and his work on developing the taxonomies. This notion argued that almost all children can master any subject of knowledge given the time to do so and if they are provided with the appropriate pedagogy, and resources, which meet their individual needs. This is a worthy and inclusive idea and one which has the support of a number of other like-minded educational thinkers. Nonetheless, the practical implications of time and resources needed for mastery learning to work, for all children, would indicate that it is a difficult outcome to achieve.

What is important is that Bloom has left a functional set of ideas in his taxonomies and the notion of mastery learning which have been of benefit to numerous teachers who have applied these to their practice. He has also been a campaigner for children and communities perceived to be educationally deprived in the United States and internationally, but what is more noteworthy is that his ideas, driven by his deep belief in social justice, have advantaged numerous young people in accessing learning.

GLOSSARY OF TERMS

Affective domain

The area of learning relating to feelings, emotions and behaviours.

Cognitive domain

The area of learning concerned with intellectual ability such as knowledge and thinking skills.

Mastery

Mastery is more than just the recall of facts, it is the acquisition of the principles of the skills and knowledge of any given subject. Given enough time, appropriate pedagogy and resources all children can theoretically achieve subject mastery.

Psychomotor domain

The area of learning relating to the acquisition of practical or physical skills.

 ## FURTHER READING

Bloom, B. (1964) *Stability and Change in Human Characteristics*. New York: John Wiley & Sons.

This quantitative work explores how variations in the environment affect human characteristics such as physique, intelligence, interests, attitudes and personality.

Bloom, B., Hastings, J. and Madaus, G. (eds) (1971) *Handbook on Formative and Summative Evaluation of Student Learning*. New York: McGraw-Hill.

A comprehensive practical textbook for teachers regarding the evaluation of student learning. It covers both general processes of evaluation techniques and teaching, as well as how those techniques can be applied to specific subject areas.

Dixon, L., Harvey, J., Thompson, R. and Williamson, S. (2010) Practical teaching. In: Avis, J., Fisher, R. and Thompson, R. (eds) *Teaching in Lifelong Learning: A guide to theory and practice*. Maidenhead: Open University Press.

This chapter contains some practical ideas for the setting of general and specific learning objectives in lesson planning to enhance learner challenge and differentiation.

REFERENCES

Bloom, B. (ed.) (1956) *Taxonomy of Educational Objectives, Book 1: Cognitive domain*. London: Longman.
Bloom, B. (1976) *Human Characteristics and School Learning*. New York: McGraw-Hill.

Bloom, B. (1981) *All Our Children Learning: A primer for parents, teachers and other educators.* New York: McGraw-Hill.

Bloom, B., Davis, A. and Hess, R. (1965) *Compensatory Education for Cultural Deprivation.* London: Holt, Rinehart & Winston.

Carroll, J.B. (1963) A model of school learning. *Teachers College Record, 64,* 723–33.

Eisner, E. (2000) Benjamin Bloom 1913–99. *Prospects: The Quarterly Review of Comparative Education* (Paris, UNESCO: International Bureau of Education), *XXX*(3), 1–7. Available from: www.ibe.unesco.org/publications/ThinkersPdf/bloome/pdf [accessed 06/03/18].

Eisner, E. (2001) Ralph Winifred Tyler, 1902–94. In: Palmer, J. (ed.) *Fifty Modern Thinkers on Education.* Abingdon: Routledge.

Forehand, M. (2010) *Bloom's Taxonomy: Emerging Perspectives on Learning, Teaching and Technology.* University of Georgia. Available from: www.projects.coe.edu/epltt/index.php?title=Bloom's_Taxonom [accessed 06/03/18].

Goodlad, J. (2004) *A Place Called School: Prospects for the Future* (Revised Edition). New York: McGraw-Hill.

Huddleston, P. and Unwin, L. (2002) *Teaching and Learning in Further Education* (Second Edition). London: RoutledgeFalmer.

Husen, T. (2001) Benjamin S. Bloom, 1913–99. In: Palmer, J. (ed.) *Fifty Modern Thinkers on Education.* Abingdon: Routledge.

Kyriacou, C. (2012) Teaching. In: Arthur, J. and Peterson, A. (eds) *The Routledge Companion to Education.* Abingdon: Routledge.

McLay, M., Mycroft, L., Noel, P., Orr, K., Thompson, R., Tummons, J. and Weatherby, J. (2010) Learning and learners. In: Avis, J., Fisher, R. and Thompson, R. (eds) *Teaching in Lifelong Learning: A guide to theory and practice.* Maidenhead: Open University Press.

Matheson, D. (2008) What is education? In: Matheson, D. (ed.) *An Introduction to the Study of Education* (Third Edition). Abingdon: Routledge.

O'Donnell, M. (2007) *Maria Montessori.* London: Bloomsbury.

Petty, G. (1998) *Teaching Today* (Second Edition). Cheltenham: Nelson Thornes.

Petty, G. (2009) *Evidenced-Based Teaching* (Second Edition). Cheltenham: Nelson Thornes.

Rowntree, D. (1981) *A Dictionary of Education.* London: Harper and Row.

Stenhouse, L. (1975) *An Introduction to Curriculum Research and Development.* London: Heinemann.

Williams, J. (2004) Great Minds: Education's most influential philosophers. A *Times Education Supplement Essential Guide.*

7
MALCOLM S. KNOWLES

CONTEXTUALISING ADULT LEARNING

LEARNING OUTCOMES

Having read this chapter you should be able to:

- recognise Knowles' background as a person and an educator
- draw a clear distinction between pedagogy and andragogy
- recognise the distinctive features of adult learning
- critically evaluate his work in relation to its applicability to practice
- apply the theory of andragogy to your own learning experiences.

KEY WORDS

adult education; andragogy; lifelong learning; pedagogy; self-directing; active learning; learning society; knowledge-based economy

INTRODUCTION

Malcolm Knowles, a central figure in the United States education system during the second half of the twentieth century, can be credited with raising awareness of adult learning in America, reorientating **adult education** from 'educating people' to 'helping them learn' (Knowles, 1950: 6). Knowles is best known for popularising the term '**andragogy**' and conceptualising the way in which adults learn. Through his work with adult learners Knowles determined that when adults were taught in the same way as children they quickly became demotivated, particularly where the application of such teaching methods did not acknowledge the vast amount of practical experience which adult learners often possessed. As such, Knowles devised a model which was responsive to the distinctive characteristics of adult learning (Merriam and Caffarella, 1991).

Following his Master's studies in 1949 Knowles used his research as a basis for his first publication, *Informal Adult Education*, published in 1950. This was followed by a series of further works centring on the adult learner and their specific mode of learning. In searching for a 'coherent and comprehensive theory of adult learning' (Knowles, 1989: 76) he established six assumptions about adult learning which he suggested should be used as a basis for anyone involved in adult education. Rooted in a humanistic and pragmatic philosophy, and reflecting the work of theorists such as Maslow and Dewey, he proposed that knowledge should be developed through building on existing experience rather than through authority and recognised the importance of self-actualisation as a key factor in the success of an adult's learning experience.

Despite entering adult education by chance, originally aspiring to enter the Foreign Service, Malcolm Knowles will be remembered for his work in creating an identity for adult education and, up until his death in 1997, he remained an advocate for **lifelong learning**, ensuring that his writings were practically orientated and influencing adult educators worldwide.

MALCOLM KNOWLES, THE PERSON

Malcolm Knowles was born in 1913 and raised in Montana where he had a relatively happy childhood. Both of his parents played an influential role in his development as a young boy, albeit in different ways. Knowles recalled his father treating him as an adult from as young as the age of three, while he attributes to his mother inspiring him to be a 'tender, loving and caring person' (Knowles, 1989). As a result of such affirmation from his parents he developed a positive self-concept, leading to a successful school experience which eventually resulted in a scholarship to Harvard University. Throughout his time in school Knowles was a boy scout, which he claimed was as important in enabling him to gain knowledge and skills and perform a leadership role as any of his school experiences.

After graduating from university in 1934 Knowles' intention was to embark on a career in the US Foreign Service. However, having passed the entry exams, he was informed by the State Department that only the most urgent vacancies were being filled and that there was likely to be a three-year waiting list before any jobs became available. Having a wife to support it was necessary, therefore, for him to accept a 'holding job' as director of related training for the National Youth Administration (NYA) in Massachusetts. Having no formal training in the sector, he sought to find a book to support him in conducting such a programme. Having no success, he went on to enlist the help of associates who were directing similar adult education pro-grammes to form an advisory council to provide him with guidance. Acting on their advice Knowles carried out an informal survey of local employers to establish what skills they were looking for in potential employees and then developed courses to teach these skills. He found he was able to recruit to these courses and, more impor-tantly, many of the youths began getting jobs. It was from here his love of adult education was born, although he could not at this time give it a name:

> I loved what I was doing, but I didn't know that it had a name. Then around 1937, some-one asked me what I did. When I told him he said 'Oh, you are an adult educator.' So now I had an identity. (Knowles and associates, 1984: 2)

In 1940 he became Director of Adult Education at Boston YMCA where he organised an Association School for Adults. However, his time there was short-lived as he was drafted into the US Navy in 1943. During his time in the navy Knowles had the oppor-tunity to develop his knowledge of the adult education sector stating, '[I] had more time to read and think than I had ever had before in my life' (Knowles and associates, 1984: 4), and he devoured all the books in print about adult education with a view to developing his own comprehensive theory of adult learning. On leaving the navy he was able to resume his work in adult learning, becoming executive director of adult education for the YMCA in Chicago. He also studied for his Master's degree at the University of Chicago, which was quickly followed by a PhD, working with C.O. Houle (Jarvis, 1998), whose intellectual rigour and teaching style greatly influ-enced Knowles (Knowles and associates, 1984).

The period that followed was one which showed him continuing to develop his skills and expertise as an adult educator and, as a result, he became firmly entrenched in the academic world of adult education, being invited to become executive director of the Adult Education Association of the USA in 1951. Nine years later he commenced a new graduate programme in adult education as Associate Professor at Boston University, a post which lasted for fourteen years and allowed him to explore the application of the principles of adult education to university teaching.

Throughout his roles in adult education Knowles sought to find a means by which to conceptualise adult education, writing prolifically on the subject. His first book, published in 1950, was entitled *Informal Adult Education* and built on his Master's study. In developing a theory for adult education he rationalised that the closest he could come to an organising theme was 'informal education'. While informal education was an important component in adult education it is far from the core and he went on to identify further characteristics related to informal learning which would maximise the learning experience of the adult learner.

In his development of a theoretical framework for adult learning Knowles was introduced to the term 'andragogy' by a Yugoslavian adult educator, Dusan Savicevic, who attended a summer session on adult learning run by Knowles. Building on the concept of andragogy, which can be defined as 'the art and science of helping adults to learn' (Knowles, 1980: 43), Knowles published an article expounding how andragogy fitted with his own views on adult learning. The concept 'provided an important identity to adult education at a time when it desperately needed one' (Jarvis, 1998: 70) and led him to expand on his theory in his book *The Modern Practice of Adult Education: Andragogy versus Pedagogy* (1970). In this text Knowles provided a practical guide to adult education methods (andragogy), as a direct comparison to typical school education (**pedagogy**). Here he identified two dichotomous models of learning, but by 1980 the subtitle for this book was revised to *From pedagogy to andragogy* when it became evident that the learning styles could be interchanged depending on the needs of the learner.

Despite retiring in 1979, Knowles maintained his interest in the developments in adult learning, publishing his autobiography, *The Making of an Adult Educator*, in 1989. He explained how he had developed as an adult educator and recognised his own impact in the field of adult education. His work was not without its critics, which will be explored later in this chapter, but he accepted the criticism and continued to develop and build on his theories, particularly in the light of new innovations, up until his death in 1997.

KNOWLES' THEORY OF ADULT LEARNING

Knowles' theory was based around the concept of helping adults to maximise their learning experience. From his work with adults he identified that the pedagogical model typically used in educational settings, and which was typified by the transmission of knowledge and skills, was not appropriate for the adult learner. As discussed in the previous section, he based his work around the concept of andragogy, a term which has the literal interpretation of 'adult leading', as opposed to pedagogy, meaning 'child leading'. Knowles cannot be credited with originating the term 'andragogy' since it was first used by Kapp in the 1800s and later in the 1920s by Lindeman and Rosenstock (Hiemstra and Sisco, 1990), but popularising the term and bringing it to the forefront of adult education in America is attributed to him.

In developing his andragogical model it was necessary for Knowles to firstly consider the pedagogical model since, as he stated, '[the pedagogical model] is the only way of thinking that most of us know, for it has dominated all of education – even adult education until recently' (Knowles and associates, 1984: 8). He observed that one of the reasons why more is known about children's learning is that the study of learning was taken over by experimental psychologists using measurable variables, and while it is possible to control the conditions under which children learn, it is less easy to control the adult learning environment (Knowles et al., 2014). Indeed, the traditional pedagogical model of education dates as far back as the seventh century in the cathedral and monastic schools in Europe, and remained the sole educational model throughout the following centuries as secular and public education grew (Knowles et al., 2014).

In examining the pedagogical model Knowles identified a set of assumptions which he used as a starting point when developing the andragogical model. He saw this model as being one which was teacher-directed, with the learner as submissive following the direction of the teacher, and observed that the learner was a dependent, passive recipient of knowledge, allowing the teacher to take full responsibility for the content delivered, how it was delivered and when. Additionally, the teacher assumes the learner has no experience on which to draw, again leading to a transmissional approach to delivery, with the assumption that the teacher directs when students will be ready to learn in order to move on to the next stage or grade. Within a pedagogical model the curriculum is organised in a subject-centred way, allowing students to build on subject content as defined by the curriculum developers. Finally, the motivation to learn comes largely from a desire to pass exams, which is reinforced by external pressures from parents and teachers, rather than receiving any internal gratification from the learning process.

Given the long tradition of the pedagogical model it is not surprising, then, that early adult educators replicated this style of delivery in their programmes and, given that the adult learner has been conditioned to this mode of delivery based on past experience, then it is equally likely that the learner will assume the role of the learner as a dependent, passive recipient of transmitted content. Despite being **self-directing** in all other aspects of life, they would frequently change when embarking on educational endeavours to a mode of 'teach me' (Hiemstra and Sisco, 1990). Knowles, then, looked to the adult learner and devised an alternative set of assumptions inherent to the andragogical model which would encourage a move away from the dependency model and allow adults to learn in a way which better suited their characteristics.

Knowles identified six key assumptions which characterised the adult learner:

1. Self-concept

In defining the adult learner Knowles assumed that a level of self-concept has already been reached – that is, the adult is responsible for their own life and is already self-directing. The adult is also conscious of how others view them in relation to an ability to take responsibility for themself. In view of this Knowles believed that resentment and resistance could ensue if it was felt that others were imposing their will without taking the adult's views and feelings into consideration.

2. Role of experience

The assumption here is that the adult enters into education with a vast amount of experience, both in terms of quality and quantity. As such, the adults in question become an essential resource for learning, with discussion and problem solving playing a prominent role in the learning experience. Alongside this comes self-identity, since celebrating the adult's experience can in turn raise the esteem of the under-educated adult.

3. Readiness to learn

Knowles acknowledged in his third assumption that 'adults become ready to learn when they experience a need to know or do something in order to perform more effectively in some aspect of their lives' (Knowles and associates, 1984: 11). That is, something occurs which may trigger the adult to want to learn. Alternatively, this may also be achieved through career planning or a skills audit which may identify gaps between where they are now and where they want to be.

4. Orientation for learning

Unlike in the pedagogical model where the learner is subject-orientated, in the adult learner the focus is life-centred, task-centred or problem-centred. The adult learner is not learning for the sake of learning but has a clear goal in mind: 'to perform a task, solve a problem or live in a more satisfying way' (Knowles and associates, 1984: 12).

5. Internal motivation

Knowles identified that while the motivation to learn may well be a salary increase or better job prospects, more potent motivators come in the form of internal satisfaction, such as self-esteem, recognition, self-confidence and better quality of life.

6. Need to know

Knowles added the sixth assumption at a later date and in this case he acknowledged that adults must know the value of learning and what they need to learn.

In order for the andragogical model to be applied successfully, Knowles did however acknowledge that there was a need to initiate the adult learner into an alternative mode of learning that differs from their previous experience. We cannot assume that the adult learner will automatically fit into the andragogical model immediately and Knowles advised that some degree of orientation would need to be applied if the model was to prove successful.

Initially, Knowles et al. presented the two models, pedagogy and andragogy, 'as antithetical, that pedagogy is bad and andragogy is good', and that pedagogy is for children and andragogy is for adults (2014: 47). However, a decade after he published his original model teachers in elementary and secondary schools and colleges advised that they had been applying the andragogical model to teaching pupils with some success. Conversely some trainers and teachers of adults reported that the andragogical model was not working, resulting in Knowles revisiting his original model. Later revisions of his model saw Knowles conceive of the two models as parallel and interchangeable depending on the needs of the learner, advising that it is the responsibility of the educator to check which assumptions are realistic in a given situation and applying the appropriate pedagogical or andragogical assumption. For example, an adult learner who is learning an entirely new skill may need to begin with a pedagogical model as they do not yet have experience from which to draw, whereas some young people respond better if given a degree of autonomy in their learning. A key feature of Knowles' revised theory was, then, its flexibility. He considered that having the two discrete models should allow practitioners to make informed choices as to how provision should proceed.

LINKS WITH OTHER THEORISTS

As previously stated, Knowles popularised the term 'andragogy', but he was not the first to use it. In 1833 the German writer Alexander Kapp wrote about the practical necessity of the education of adults in his book *Platon's Erziehungslehre [Plato's Educational Ideas]*. Kapp saw andragogy as the normal process by which adults engage in continuing education. However, the term fell into disuse as Kapp's work lacked any theoretical underpinnings. Indeed, this is an overarching theme when viewing andragogy, since while few dispute the importance of adult education, it can be argued that a theory behind it is superfluous, a suggestion that will be unpacked in the next section of this chapter.

A number of theorists have, however, attempted to contextualise adult learning and one whom Knowles regarded as his mentor was Eduard Lindeman. Knowles states:

> … the single most influential person in guiding my thinking was Eduard C. Lindeman, whose book *The Meaning of Adult Education* (1926) enlightened me about the unique characteristics of adults as learners and the need for methods and techniques for helping them learn. (Knowles and associates, 1984: 3)

Lindeman was a firm advocate of informal learning and believed in using learners' experience as a starting point for education, particularly with regard to using small group work as a means of delivering adult education – a concept evident in Knowles' climates for learning, in which he expressed the importance of creating a learning environment conducive to learning through both the physical space and the psychological climate. Lindeman also developed central assumptions about adult education which influenced Knowles when formulating his own assumptions. However, Lindeman did not provide a tight definition for adult learning, suggesting that this could be too constraining, also reflecting the suggestion that adult learning is some-what difficult to determine.

Lindeman, himself, was influenced by the work of John Dewey, so it is not surprising that parallels can also be drawn between the work of Dewey and Knowles. Knowles' idea that adult learners were self-directing was not a new concept, since Dewey had previously recognised the self-directing capacity of learners in 1902. Dewey, too, advocated the role of the teacher as one of facilitator, guiding the learner rather than imposing their own ideas, although Dewey's work at this time was predominantly with children rather than adult learners. Another theorist who posited that the teacher be seen as a facilitator was Carl Rogers who theorised that 'we cannot teach another person directly; we can only facilitate his learning' (Rogers 1951: 389) and suggested that an over-reliance on a prescribed curriculum impeded the learner's ability to be self-directed. Rogers put forward a theory of experiential learning which addressed the needs of the learner through the building of mutual relationships, which arguably formed the basis for Knowles' assumptions of self-directedness, experience and problem-centered learning (Blondy, 2007).

In focusing on the specific needs of adult learners it might also be pertinent to look at some of the theories advanced at that time. Knowles' work can be positioned in the humanist theories of Abraham Maslow since the andragogical model 'predicates that the more potent motivators [of adult learning] are internal – self-esteem, recognition, better quality of life' (Knowles and associates, 1984: 12), all of which reflect Maslow's hierarchy of needs, which sees the learner aspiring to the uppermost layer of self-actualisation. Furthermore, behavioural and social psychologists at the time were looking at how stage transitions were related to adults' readiness to learn and considering how people changed their behaviour as a result of external and internal stimuli.

Blondy (2007) suggests that aspects of constructivism can be seen in Knowles' work, particularly in respect of Bruner's notion of learning as an active process, with the learner developing new ideas based upon knowledge already attained. Knowles (1984) advised that learning should build on the learners' past experiences through problem-centred and **active learning** strategies, both of which are reflective of Bruner's theory that a curriculum should build on past knowledge, while also identifying gaps in knowledge which should then become a focus for future learning.

It can be seen therefore that Knowles' work was strongly influenced not only by people he admired but also by the changing attitudes towards the adult learner at the time and developments in the social science genre.

CRITIQUING KNOWLES

A major criticism of Knowles' work is how far it can actually be considered a theory. Merriam states 'the 1970s and early 1980s witnessed much writing, discussion and debate about ... the validity of andragogy as a theory of learning' (2001: 3), a view supported by Hartree (1984: 205) who suggests that Knowles had merely presented a set of guidelines for what the adult learner should be like in the classroom, based solely on Knowles' own observations and not supported by any tried and tested theory of learning. McGrath (2009) observes that even Knowles (1989: 112) recognised that 'andragogy is less a theory of adult learning than a model of assumptions about learning or a conceptual framework that serves as a basis for emergent theory'.

Questions can also be asked regarding the assumptions Knowles made about adult learners and how far these were truly reflective of the student body. He made the assumption that adult learners were motivated to learn because they had chosen to undertake adult education, but the reality of this can be questioned as employers may, in some cases, have encouraged employees to undertake training or gain qualifications without fully investigating the relevance of the course. In such cases the adult learner may become demotivated and resentful, often feeling forced into education for job security rather than through any personal desire for self-improvement. This in turn can have a negative impact on self-concept which is another important assumption made by Knowles.

Merriam (2001) also questions how far there is a distinction between pedagogy and andragogy, suggesting that both adults and children can show elements of both models. She goes on to say it is equally likely that a child can be an independent, self-directed learner with self-concept, while adults can be highly dependent on their tutor for support, depending on the learning situation. Knowles himself eventually revised his own assumptions, observing that following his 1970 book *The Modern Practice of Adult Education: Andragogy versus pedagogy*, practitioners in the field of elementary and secondary education identified that students responded well to the andragogical model, while those working with adults suggested that in some cases a pedagogical model still needed to be applied. Hence, in the revised edition of his book in 1980 the subtitle was changed to *From pedagogy to andragogy*. This could lead us to question if it is necessary to put a label on adult learning or whether it is merely the case that a commonsense attitude needs to be applied – simply matching teaching style to the needs of the learner.

APPLYING KNOWLES IN THE CLASSROOM

Jarvis states that '[Knowles] writings were always practically orientated' (1998: 71) and as a result his works are easily translated into the adult learning environment. It could be argued that recent policy initiatives such as the promotion of a **learning society** and the drive towards lifelong learning (OECD, 2000) have seen a renewed interest in adult learning as a concept. The notion of a learning society promotes the idea that 'learning is an activity not a place and goes beyond the school and the university' (CISCO, 2010: i), The learning society is seen as a basis for lifelong learning which in essence supports the **knowledge-based economy**. Schuller sees lifelong learning as 'involving people of all ages learning in a variety of contexts (2017: 4) but with a specific focus on adults returning to organised learning. In his research he emphasises the importance of the quality and nature of learning particularly in respect of its appropriateness to the individual. Here we see echoes with the original intention of Knowles' work in which he sought to find guidance for educating adults which did not rely on techniques used with children.

Knowles originally observed that the adult learner comes to the learning experience with preconceived ideas of the educational experience, which fits largely with the pedagogical, rather than andragogical, model. As such, Knowles recognises that it is the role of the adult educator to help students make the transition from dependent to independent learner (Knowles and associates, 1984). It is easy to see how those adults returning to learning as a result of lifelong learning agendas may bring with them these fixed ideas of education, and for Knowles one of the biggest considerations was their understanding of the role of the teacher and how they perceive themselves in the learning environment, since this forms the basis of much of his work. In the andragogical model he views the teacher as a facilitator, believing that this term best fits with the specific role of the adult educator, and sees the facilitator as playing a dual role:

> … as designer and manager of processes and procedures that will facilitate the acquisition of content by the learners; and only secondarily the role of content resource. (Knowles and associates, 1984: 14)

Indeed, he also acknowledges the wide range of resources available to the facilitator, notwithstanding the experiences of the students themselves, who should therefore be presented with opportunities to share these experiences through, for example, workshops and discussions. This is, however, not without its challenges since students coming into learning entrenched in the pedagogical model of content delivery may become anxious about, or even feel threatened by, a learning experience which exposes them through direct questioning and discussion, requiring the facilitator to skilfully introduce this mode of learning.

It is necessary, therefore, when adopting an andragogical model to set a climate that is conducive to learning, of which Knowles identified two specific areas for consideration: physical space and psychological atmosphere. Regarding the physical space, Knowles observed that a classroom designed with chairs in rows facing a lectern automatically predisposes the learner to believe that the delivery style will be one of knowledge transmission and possibly reinforce their preconceptions of what constitutes a learning environment. While this arrangement presents a challenge in terms of undertaking workshop or group activities, it also encourages students to behave in a certain way, discouraging any form of participation. Knowles suggests, therefore, that the facilitator should arrange the classroom before the students arrive in a manner which reinforces a delivery style more conducive to group activity and discussion, such as having chairs in a circle or table groups, with furniture designed with adult learners in mind. In this way a clear message is given to the adult learner about how a session will be delivered, dispelling any preconceived ideas.

Of even greater importance, according to Knowles, is the psychological climate for learning, which he stresses should be 'one which causes adults to feel accepted, respected and supported' (1980: 47), believing that there should be a spirit of mutuality between students and facilitators as joint enquirers. This can be supported by the adult educator having a secure knowledge of the student body in order that any experiences can be valued and maximised throughout the session. Adults will thrive if they feel their views are respected and that others understand and value them as individuals. This in turn helps to raise self-esteem, which is an important component of effective learning.

Alongside mutual respect there also needs to be a strong element of trust in an adult learning setting. As Knowles suggests, people are more likely to learn from those they trust. This notion goes hand in hand with the importance of collaboration and removing some of the barriers which the competitiveness of early school experiences often creates. In this respect it is important that the adult learner sees the facilitator as non-judgemental. From their school experience the adult learner may recall the teacher as one who makes judgements, particularly in relation to grading assignments and commenting on performance. While it is of course necessary, by the very nature of their role, for the adult educator to assign marks and grade work, Knowles suggests that this should be done, where possible, in collaboration with the learner, giving them a greater sense of ownership of their work. In applying andragogical principles in practice, Birzer (2004, cited in Chan, 2010: 29) recommended involving learners in self-evaluation, suggesting that this helps to remove bias from a single judgement of the instructor. If an adult understands why a mark or grade has been awarded because criteria have been shared with them, then they are less likely to feel resentful of the person responsible for awarding that grade or mark.

Returning to the assumptions made by Knowles, one important area which differentiated adults from children in their approach to learning, he felt, was the 'readiness to learn'. Most adults in education have made the decision to return to learning based on a particular reason, such as to secure a job or for better career prospects, and it is when they are at the peak of their readiness to learn that a 'teachable moment' is presented, this being when the learner is the most receptive to learning. The adult educator should capitalise on this moment and present a curriculum which is reactive to learner requirements. Knowles recommends that a curriculum should be organised in such a way that it is in step with the adult learners' developmental tasks. For example, where possible, learning experiences should correlate with experiences in work placements. Alternatively, a diagnosis of needs may be carried out from the outset in order that sessions may be planned around learners' specific needs and requirements. Involving learners in the organisation of delivery and selection of content may increase student motivation, since, as Knowles states, 'people tend to feel committed to any decision in proportion to the extent to which they have participated in making it' (Knowles and associates, 1984: 17) – the reverse being that they are more likely to feel resentful if the decisions of others are imposed upon them.

In establishing a climate conducive to learning Knowles suggests that a climate of pleasure should also be aspired to. He reminds us that 'learning should be one of the most pleasant and gratifying experiences in life' (Knowles and associates, 1984: 16), enabling students to achieve their full potential. He also suggests that previous educational experience may have been a 'dull chore', warning that the adult educator would be doing the learner a disservice if they were to merely reproduce what had gone before. As such, it is important that adult education is an enjoyable experience. McGrath (2009) suggests that the very essence of andragogy is to examine how learning in the classroom can be made more attractive for the student, and teaching styles should be modified to ensure that adults gain maximum enjoyment from the learning experience alongside learning which directly correlates with their specific needs as adults. As such, the facilitator should look to ways of delivering content which engage the adult learner.

REFLECTIVE TASK

Knowles made six assumptions about adult learners:

1. Self-concept

   As a person matures their self-concept moves from one of being a dependent personality towards one of being a self-directed human being.

2. Role of experience

   As a person matures they accumulate a growing reservoir of experience that becomes an increasing resource for learning.

3. Readiness to learn

   As a person matures their readiness to learn becomes orientated increasingly to the developmental tasks of their social roles.

4. Orientation for learning

   As a person matures their time perspective changes from one of postponed application of knowledge to immediacy of application and, accordingly, their orientation towards learning shifts from one of subject-centeredness to one of problem-centeredness.

5. Internal motivation

   As a person matures the motivation to learn is internal.

6. Need to know

   Knowles added the sixth assumption at a later date and in this case he acknowledged that adults need to know the value of learning and what they need to learn.

Reflect on these in terms of how far you can apply them to your own learning or the learning of your students.

SUMMARY

Despite becoming an adult educator by chance, Malcolm Knowles very quickly established himself in the field of adult education and his writing on the subject made him one of the most well-known figures in adult education in America, his concept of andragogy having been adopted by adult educators around the world (Chan, 2010). Jarvis writes of Knowles, 'I do not think that he would have ever claimed to have been a great scholar – but his writings have been very influential in adult education worldwide' (1998: 71). It is perhaps this lack of a scholarly approach which has made his work so accessible to adult educators, since his works were written predominantly with the intention that they would be applied in educational settings.

Knowles had a genuine interest and concern for adults in education and, in identifying that there was little by way of literature on the subject, he made it his work to develop his own understanding of the needs of adult learners, utilising what he discovered to support others in the field. Knowles' work was not without its critics, but he used critical feedback as a means of further developing his work. He acknowledged that his distinction between pedagogy and andragogy may well have been oversimplified, but he remained committed both emotionally and practically to the distinction he had drawn (Jarvis, 1998).

It could be said that Knowles created a legacy which changed the face of adult education. He was the first to chart the rise of the adult education movement in the United States, from which he devised a statement of informal adult education practice, and later he developed a comprehensive theory of adult education through his own interpretation of andragogy. He was keen to advance his theories in view of the changing nature of education and continued to play an active role in the field of adult education until his death in 1997.

GLOSSARY OF TERMS

Active learning

A method of teaching which actively engages learners in the learning process, normally through practical learning activities and a reflection on their own role in the learning process.

Adult education

Any form of learning undertaken by adults, usually following a period of absence from education.

Andragogy

The theory and practice of educating adults. The term derives from the Greek language and is literally translated as 'man leading' or leader of man. Malcolm Knowles popularised the term in the 1950s in order to conceptualise how educating adults differed to educating children (see pedagogy).

Knowledge-based economy

To recognise the place of knowledge and technology in modern OECD economies. This sees a shift from the traditional economies, such as farming and industry, to one which centres on the production and use of knowledge.

Learning society

An educational philosophy which posits that learning should extend beyond that of formal learning into informal learning to build a knowledge economy. The learning society relates to the activity of learning rather than the place of learning and responds to a widening participation agenda in which lifelong learning is promoted.

Lifelong learning

Learning that is pursued throughout life for personal or professional reasons. Lifelong learning can be flexible and diverse and does not necessarily occur in the traditional educational setting. Lifelong learning has been promoted by politicians with a growing number of policies directed towards the creation of a 'learning society'.

Pedagogy

The art and science of helping children to learn, directly translated as child leading.

Self-directing

To direct one's own learning in relation to a predetermined set of aim and values. The self-directed learner knows what they want to achieve and will determine for themself the most effective way of reaching their goals.

FURTHER READING

Brockett, R.G. and Hiemstra, R. (1991) *Self-direction in Adult Learning: Perspectives on theory, research, and practice*. New York: Routledge.

An examination of aspects of self-direction in adult learning, including mention of andragogy as a foundational notion.

Cross, K.P. (1981) *Adults as Learners*. San Francisco, CA: Jossey-Bass.

Examines the strengths and weaknesses of the andragogical concept, which Cross believes is closer to a theory of teaching than to a theory of learning.

Darkenwald, G.D. and Merriam, S.B. (1982) *Adult Education: Foundations of practice*. New York: Harper & Row.

A guide for the novice reader to gain a better understanding of andragogy and self-directed learning.

Knowles, M.S., Holton, E.R. III and Swanson, A. (1998) *The Adult Learner: The definitive classic in adult education and human resource development* (Fifth Edition). New York: Heinemann.

Building on the work of Knowles, a theoretical framework for understanding adult learning issues in the workplace and educational settings.

REFERENCES

Blondy, L.C. (2007) Evaluation and application of andragogical assumptions to the adult online learning environment. *Journal of Interactive On-line Learning*, 6(2), 116–30.

Chan, S. (2010) Application of andragogy in multi-disciplined teaching and learning. *Journal of Adult Education*, 39(2), 25–35.

CISCO (2010) The Learning Society. *CISCO public information*. Available at: www.cisco.com/c/dam/en_us/about/citizenship/socio-economic/docs/LearningSociety_WhitePaper.pdf [accessed 07/03/18].

Hartree, A. (1984) Malcolm Knowles' theory of andragogy: a critique. *International Journal of Lifelong Education*, 3(3), 203–10.

Hiemstra, R. and Sisco, B. (1990) *Individualizing Instruction: Making learning personal, empowering, and successful*. San Francisco, CA: Jossey-Bass.

Jarvis, P. (1998) Malcolm Knowles (1913–97): an appreciation. *International Journal of Lifelong Education*, 17(2), 70–1.

Kapp, A. (1833) *Platon's Erziehungslehre*. Mindon and Leipzig: Verlag von Ferdinand Ofmann.

Knowles, M.S. (1950) *Informal Adult Education*. New York: Association Press.

Knowles, M.S. (1980 [1970]) *The Modern Practice of Adult Education: From pedagogy to andragogy* (Revised and updated). Chicago, IL: Association Press.

Knowles, M.S. (1989) *The Making of an Adult Educator: An autobiographical journey.* San Francisco, CA: Jossey-Bass.

Knowles, M.S. and associates (1984) *Andragogy in Action: Applying modern principles of adult learning.* San Francisco, CA: Jossey-Bass.

Knowles, M.S., Holton. E.F. and Swanson, R.F. (2014) *The Adult Learner: The definitive classic in adult education and human resource development.* London: Routledge.

McGrath, V. (2009) Reviewing the evidence on how adult students learn: An examination of Knowles' model of andragogy. *Adult Learner: The Irish Journal of Adult and Community Education,* (1), 99–110.

Merriam, S.B. (2001) Andragogy and self-directed learning: Pillars of adult learning theory. *New Directions for Adult and Continuing Education, 89,* 3–13.

Merriam, S.B. and Caffarella, R.S. (1991) *Learning in Adulthood: A comprehensive guide.* San Francisco, CA: Jossey-Bass.

OECD (2000) *Knowledge Management in the Learning Society.* Paris: OECD Publishing.

Rogers, C. (1951) *Client-centered Therapy: Its current practice, implications and theory.* London: Constable.

Schuller, T. (2017) What are the wider benefits of learning across the life course? London: Government Office for Science. Available at: www.gov.uk/government/uploads/system/uploads/attachment_data/file/635837/Skills_and_lifelong_learning_-_the_benefits_of_adult_learning_-_schuller_-_final.pdf [accessed 06/03/18].

8

JEROME BRUNER

AN EVOLUTION OF LEARNING THEORIES

LEARNING OUTCOMES

Having read this chapter you should be able to:

- appreciate Bruner's background and his contribution to education
- understand and identify his educational philosophies and evolution of thought
- appreciate how his theories influence other thinkers within education
- critically appraise his works
- recognise how his ideas could be applied in practice.

KEY WORDS

culture; spiral curriculum; Man: A Course of Study; constructivism; cognitivism; computation

INTRODUCTION

Jerome Bruner had a long, dynamic and esteemed career as a psychologist with a particular influence on education policy, learning and teaching and the development of the curriculum. His ideas have all been grounded in investigation and have affected both theory and practice. During the 1950s he concerned himself with the field of cognitive science, which he later came to argue against in favour of a constructivist approach (Bruner, 2009). To give an overview of how his ideas evolved we will briefly look at his major works.

In his early seminal text of 1960, *The Process of Education*, he set out his ideas regarding cognitive development and how children represent concepts, which in turn led him to consider the importance of **culture** and the environment in their learning. He argued against the traditional view that children should learn facts and systems and was in favour of children constructing knowledge in a scientific manner. In so doing, if the child comprehended the fundamental process in a particular curriculum area, they could then progress to think in a holistic way about newly introduced topics. He argued for a '**spiral curriculum**' where themes were initially presented to learners and then revisited later on in the programme to reinforce understanding and give added vigour. The child in Bruner's eyes was 'an active problem-solver, who had his or her own ways of making sense of the world' (Gardner, 2001: 92). Two years after the publication of *The Process of Education* Bruner planned and later managed the implementation of the **Man: A Course of Study (MACOS)** project. This was a radical venture to create a new, and refocused, school curriculum. The questions he and the planning team considered were what characteristics were involved in being a human: 'how people reach that state and how we might become more human' (Wragg, 2004: 16).

In later texts such as the *Toward a Theory of Instruction* (1966) and the *The Relevance of Education* (1971) Bruner offered his thoughts about how teachers help children construct modes of learning. He suggested there were three ways that children convert experiences into knowledge: through action, imagery and by symbols. The impact of Vygotsky is apparent in Bruner's ideas at this stage, as he contested that learning includes the notion of internalisation and uses symbols and cultural interaction between humans. Bruner's (1996) work *The Culture of Education* considered the function of schools and the school curriculum. In particular, he stressed the significance of culture, the interface between learners and teachers in the process of building knowledge together. In summary this work disputed the focus on the individual child and argued for the use of group work. The features of Bruner's theories, in the sequence they evolved, will be explored later in this chapter.

JEROME BRUNER, THE PERSON

Jerome Bruner was born in New York City in 1915. He attended Duke and Harvard universities. He worked as a social psychologist during the Second World War in producing the broadcasting of public information. Following the war he emerged as one of the eminent thinkers about human cognition. He and his fellow social psychologists became involved in work relating to children's use of modes of representation at the Center for Cognitive Studies at Harvard University. Arguably, his greatest national role was to be chosen to chair the science commission which effectively set about reorganising the school system in the United States with a curricular emphasis on science and technology. This was largely in response to the perceived advances in technology by the Russians and in particular the launching of the first Sputnik satellite in 1957. In the 1960s he was influential in the Head Start project, which looked to provide a just foundation for disadvantaged young children before they began their formal schooling, and the project was replicated worldwide. Bruner transferred from Harvard to the University of Oxford in 1970, where he studied child agency and children's language. In the early 1980s he returned to the United States where he became drawn to the idea of cultural psychology and its application for education (Gardner, 2001; Wragg, 2004; Olson, 2007: Bruner, 2009).

Bruner was driven by a deep sense of social justice in his efforts towards educational change, especially relevant in the mid- and later twentieth-century United States – a point he underlined in the preface to *The Culture of Education*:

> It was the 'discovery of poverty' and the civil rights movement in America that woke most of us from our unthinking complacency about reforming education – specifically, the discovery of the impact of poverty, racism, and alienation on the mental life and growth of the child victims of these blights. (1996: xiii)

Jerome Bruner died in 2016.

BRUNER'S EVOLVING THEORY: COGNITIVISM, CONSTRUCTIVISM AND CULTURALISM

As a psychologist Bruner had an extraordinary and significant impact on educational policy, theory and practice. Although his body of work changed over a period of time, as a whole it can be seen as an alternative to the behaviourist approach with its emphasis on reward and punishment. Bruner's ideas, particularly as they evolved, stressed a more human approach to learning, where interests, motivation and culture were at the fore. Even though his theories changed, all still have varying degrees of significance today. This section will sequentially explore these shifts in Bruner's theoretical standpoints which are, generally, introduced and elucidated in his major works. It is a journey from his early experience in cognitive science and curriculum development to **constructivism** and infant development and, finally, to his notions of the importance of social and cultural factors in education and learning.

Bruner's earlier work focused on the development of the curriculum. There were two particular major projects launched in the 1960s which were the product of his research into the curriculum. Both it is suggested were influenced by his quest for social justice. The first, and internationally imitated, was the Head Start Program, which set out to give young children a positive beginning before they started school. The second was Man: A Course of Study (MACOS), which was a bold attempt at creating a complete curriculum derived from the then latest research into cognitive science. Overall MACOS set out to find out, 'What is uniquely human about human beings? How did they get that way? How could they be made more so?' (Gardner, 2001: 92). What was significant with these two major projects, especially the latter, was Bruner's notion and application of the 'spiral curriculum' explored in *The Process of Education* (1960). While the spiral curriculum was a major product to come from this seminal work, the book also explored four main and important aspects, which were: the structure of learning and how it may be made central in teaching; readiness for learning (and the spiral curriculum); intuitive and analytical thinking; and motives for learning. The notion of a spiral curriculum has been the mainstay of numerous policy edicts on curricula design. According to Bruner what was important was not:

> ... *coverage* but *depth* ... It was a short step from there to the idea that the shape of the curriculum be conceived as a spiral, beginning with an intuitive depiction of a domain of knowledge, circling back to represent the domain more powerfully or formally as needed. The teacher, in this version of pedagogy, is a guide to understanding, someone who helps you discover on your own. (1996: xii)

The idea of a spiral curriculum considers that knowledge is refreshable and needs revisiting to further develop. This in turn has implications for the previous notions from thinkers, such as Piaget, that learning is a process where children pass through a series of predetermined stages. The spiral curriculum considers that the child builds upon knowledge by revisiting topics and, hence, gives greater depth to their learning and 'makes sense of that body of knowledge in terms of their current concerns, preoccupations and states of mind' (Scott, 2008: 91).

Unlike Piaget's sequential and predetermined stages of learning, such as the sensorimotor, preoperational, concrete and formal operational stages, Bruner considered three modes whereby children develop their experiences into learning. These are the enactive, iconic and symbolic modes. The *enactive mode* relates to where children do things for themselves through action and play. The *iconic mode* happens when children can comprehend images, pictures and numbers. The *symbolic mode* is where children can understand abstraction, language and reason. Bruner stressed that the acquisition of these modes was not a sequential process but was reliant on being developed with other people. Furthermore, he argued that there might be one mode which would be overriding at any specific phase of a child's development (Wragg, 2004; Scott, 2008).

Bruner (1996) appears to admit in his later works that his earlier theories regarding **cognitivism** were too focused on the individual child and processes of learning. His idea of **computation**, for example, considered:

... learning as comprising coded unambiguous information about the world being sorted, stored, retrieved and managed in the same way that a computer processes data. The mind is a blank sheet ... the individual is treated as a passive reflector of the way the world works; correct or incorrect views of the world are understood as a function of the efficiency with which these processes are conducted. (Scott, 2008: 92)

The significance of this notion of computation is that information is processed once gathered and is unchanging and of no personal worth to the gatherer. It could be construed that such computation considers the mind as some sort of computer which needs to be programmed in a particular way for it to operate in a competent and economical manner. This is a troubled notion because computation in this sense does not take into account the varieties, uncertainties and ambiguities which are present in contextualised learning, which as an activity is constructed socially (Bruner, 2009).

Bruner's ideas evolved from the perceived singularity of computation and information processing, which favoured a didactic approach to learning, towards stressing the importance of children actively constructing their knowledge. This knowledge and meaning-making, he argued, was constructed from children's current and previous experiences as well as with others. Not only do children build their knowledge with others but also by interacting with their environment. For Bruner, this constructivist phase was rooted in problem solving and discovery learning. Discovery learning, for Bruner, assisted learners to make their own meaning by engaging 'in discussions and the use of concrete materials, which causes learners to gain insights into the processes of knowledge' (O'Donnell, 2007: 134). An approach which adopts discovery learning is scaffolding, which is akin to the ideas put forward by Vygotsky. Bruner based his pedagogical application of scaffolding on an engineering model, where a teacher creates a scaffold 'to support the efforts of the learner to construct his or her own understandings' (Olson, 2007: 45). Scaffolding is further explored in the following sections, and in the Vygotsky chapter (Chapter 4). Rather than the pedagogy being didactic, it was in favour of practical and activity-specific teaching. *Toward a Theory of Instruction* (1966) was considered as having significant influence on the application of constructivism in curriculum design and practice in the classroom (Wragg, 2004). Moreover, in *The Relevance of Education* (1971) Bruner argued that such constructed learning should be of social significance in addressing some of the difficulties in the world and also 'self-rewarding', 'real', 'exciting' or 'meaningful' (1971: 114). His views of constructivism are seen as a link between the individualistic notion of cognitivism and computation to his more recent theory, which stressed the importance of culture in learning.

Bruner's emerging ideas of the value of culture and the environment began with his emphasis on the importance of the home environment and the function of the mother in regard to the linguistic progress of the child. These ideas then moved on to trying to understand, from a cultural point of view, the differences between learning that took place in school and outside school. His seminal *The Culture of Education* (1996) marks his focus on how culture shaped the way that children learned. It is argued that this swing of emphasis, from a cognitive and constructivist approach, was brought about because of his increasing disquiet with issues of social injustice. *The Culture of Education* included much of his previous work with linguistic and literacy development. It was intended to help educators recognise:

> That when children do badly at school the reasons might lie not in some kind of 'independent' development that can be characterised and analysed outside of any socio-cultural context, but rather in the social *conditions* in which the child lives and grows up. (Moore, 2000: 24)

Bruner's earlier work with language centred on how children gained their skills in literacy. This he considered was developed when children were occupied in using written symbols and abstract ideas to make sense of the world. However, in his later works he argued for the use of narratives in education. Narratives, for Bruner, were both written and spoken and could be in the form of family discussions and observations of life and how children interact with each other. Involvement in narratives assisted children in expressing their worries and aspirations; narratives also helped them question accepted knowledge, reason and make sense of the world and create theories of their own in the relative safety of their own culture (Wood, 1998; Hutchings, 2013): 'Narratives, for Bruner, provide a source of newness, innovation and critical reflection on existing ways of understanding' (Scott, 2008: 101). These refreshing and innovative ways of understanding were shared by many other educational thinkers.

⟳ LINKS WITH OTHER THEORISTS

It would be a mammoth task to give a comprehensive account of Bruner's links with other educational thinkers. He became increasingly inspired by the works of Vygotsky which emphasised that most learning is developed by the use of cultural tools and formed over time by others. However, even though Vygotsky stressed the significance of the social and cultural aspects of learning, unlike Bruner's ideas, 'it is largely devoid of any overt political or "ideological" dimension' (Moore, 2000: 22).

Bruner's three modes of learning – enactive, iconic and symbolic – have been construed and expanded into the visual, auditory and kinaesthetic (VAK) learning styles, phenomena used when planning differentiated teaching and learning activities. Perhaps more importantly these modes have also enlightened Gardner's multiple intelligence theories, and these have been developed to design curricula to engage these different and individual 'intelligences'.

Bruner's ideas about the 'child-centred' approach to teaching underline the value of constructing a relationship between teacher and pupil. This approach calls for a pedagogical mode very much aligned with Dewey's thoughts on transferability and non-subject-specific teaching, and 'more concerned with interpretation and understanding than with the achievement of factual knowledge or skill performance'

(Bruner, 1996: 57). This is also evident in the works of Gardner, who in his book *The Unschooled Mind* (1991) argued against the testing of knowledge and towards a notion of how children 'think about their thinking' and how they perceive the world around them. It was important, then, to utilise the cultural assets of the child's family and community together with the values and beliefs held by that culture in the teaching and learning designed and employed. Similar to Bruner, Loris Malaguzzi also considered that children should focus on developing a shared language which is derived from experiences gained from the community as well as school (Farnan, 2012). There are also comparable connections between Lawrence Stenhouse's Humanities Curriculum Project and Bruner's MACOS, in that they both are aimed at constructing curricula relating to the social sciences and diverse cultures (Aubrey and Riley, 2017).

It is interesting to note that more contemporary educational, and social, thinkers have also adopted and developed Bruner's ideas, especially his later thoughts on the implications that cultures have had on learning and the role that schools and language play in that process. People like the Latin American and radical educational philosopher Paulo Freire contested that schools disadvantage, and indeed fail, those who do not conform to what society expects. Such conformability which schools require (schools turning out what they perceive is needed in society and the marketplace) is also contested by the French social thinker Bourdieu. Such conformability may well be at odds with the cultural norms, or what he calls 'habitus' – 'the stuff of daily life that gives shape to our biases and predispositions' (Bruner, 1996: 79). The criticisms of educational establishments that were espoused by Bruner were also echoed by Bernstein, who argued that the school assessment and curriculum favoured those learners whose home cultures 'match those cultures validated within the education system … [who] will enter that system already in possession of what Bernstein and others call "cultural capital"' (Moore, 2000: 98). Both Bourdieu and Bernstein argue that there would need to be a dramatic change in the school curriculum and assessment criteria to encompass those who do not fall within the category of the main social group.

Scaffolding is very closely associated with the concept of apprenticeships as explored by Lave and Wenger (1991) in their *Situated Learning: Legitimate peripheral participation*. Olson clearly makes the connection between scaffolding and apperenticeships:

> A novice would be given small tasks at the margins of a complex task and, as mastery increased, be given greater and greater responsibility for more and more complex tasks. (2007: 46)

Furthermore, Wenger in his seminal *Communities of Practice: Learning, meaning, and identity* (1998), like Bruner, presents his own theory in which he argues that learning is a social and cultural activity and involves matters of community, social practice, meaning and identity. Although many others have followed and developed his ideas, Bruner's theories throughout are not uncontentious.

CRITIQUING BRUNER

When we seek to critique Bruner's works it must be done with an understanding that his ideas changed and evolved over a long period of time and that he himself recognised with some misgiving the frail aspects of his earlier ideas and claims. Therefore, it is quite fitting that this section starts with Bruner's own criticism of his declaration that any subject can be taught to any child at any point of their development in some form that was honest. This was an exciting possibility yet one that could never be proved or disproved as he never really explained what he meant by 'honest'. In his own words, '"honest" was left undefined and has haunted me ever since!' (Bruner, 1996: xii). Even though much of his work has been adopted in education policy and curriculum design, it is somewhat doubtful as to whether or not some of his ideas on socially, culturally and creatively acquired learning are truly practicable for teachers in busy classrooms and within an increasingly performative environment which seeks continuous grade improvement. For example, how realistic is it for teachers to modify and make changes to the cultural contexts of their own settings?

Bruner's ideas on discovery learning have also been criticised, insofar as children may misconstrue meaning, which may in turn be unobserved by teachers. In addition, discovery learning would not suit those children who would prefer a more didactic style of learning and there is a growing perception that children should be involved in a more traditional form of teaching and learning, particularly when schools are increasingly driven by reaching targets and doing well in examinations (MacBlain, 2014). In particular, David Ausubel was highly critical of Bruner's concept of discovery learning. As a foil to discovery learning Ausubel argued for the use of reception learning, because young children needed to learn by direct instruction from the teacher first and there was too much to learn at school with too little time for discovery. With Ausubel's reception learning 'children were presented with the content to be learned and did not need to discover on their own' (O'Donnell, 2007: 133). Ausubel also censured the belief that discovery resulted in a deeper level of learning and that it was not a credible alternative to the direct teaching involved in reception learning (Bartlett et al., 2001: Olson, 2007).

Although the notions of scaffolding and spiralling are both exciting and have practical application regarding enhancing deep learning, they are still dependent on having knowledgeable and confident teachers. For such notions to be productive, both scaffolding and spiralling require teachers who know when to help, when to let go, how to motivate and, possibly more importantly, know the individual needs of the children. With this in mind, it is also important to recognise that Bruner's own research regarding scaffolding only involved working with children on a one-to-one basis. In this situation it was much easier for him to be appreciative of the needs and the comprehension of an individual student, unlike a teacher who has to cope with a whole class and check levels of understanding and make teaching adjustments for each child (Olson, 2007).

Furthermore, the idea of culturalism, by Bruner's own admission, 'is in principle interpretive, fraught with ambiguity, sensitive to occasion, and often after the fact' (2009: 163). It could also be argued that the notion of culture itself is shifting with the impact of globalisation, making geographically regional cultures less influential in learning and the design of curricula. In tandem with globalisation, ever-increasing advances in technology have also had a bearing on the degree of impact that culture has on learning.

APPLYING BRUNER IN THE CLASSROOM

Before we set out to explore how Bruner's ideas could be applied in the classroom it is pertinent at this point to remind ourselves of his influence on how we think about learning and the function of schools and indeed education. Bruner disputed the traditional reason for both schools and education. For him the role of schools 'is part of the process through which culture inducts children' (MacBlain, 2014: 118). It is with this radical understanding that the purpose of education and schooling should be embedded in the cultural context of the child that we should consider how Bruner's theories could be put into practice.

One of his deep-seated notions was that teachers should reflect on how they engage with their learners. Here, he argued, is where theories of learning should be intersubjective instead of objectivist in their nature. He notes that objectivist theory acts as a division between the teacher as the theorist and the learner as the subject. This suggests that the teacher, or the theorist, makes a 'culture-free judgement about the subject [learner], including their learning needs' (Moore, 2000: 25). Equally, he states that the intersubjective theorist should apply the same theories to themselves as to the learner. This intersubjectivity is 'reflexive, seeking to use self-understanding as a way of understanding the minds of others, and vice versa' (Moore, 2000: 25). It implies that teachers should be aware of their own practice and opinions when a learner seems to waver, instead of seeking reasons wholly from the learner.

In line with this notion of intersubjectivity, Bruner's earlier work with pedagogy highlighted the need for the teacher to act as a motivator and a catalyst for learning. He certainly argued against a didactic and routine pedagogical manner of teaching which might stifle any inherent motivation in the learner. He called for teachers to allow learners to explore and discover in the learning process. As such, teaching needs to be more than the presentation of facts and explanations, it needs an injection 'of excitement about discovery – discovery of regularities of previously unrecognised relations and similarities between ideas' (Bruner, 1960: 20). Discovery learning could be seen as a way that the internalisation of 'meaning can be strengthened along with the conceptualisation of new information into already existing knowledge' (MacBlain, 2014: 56).

Scaffolding, a pedagogical practice linked with Bruner's idea of discovery learning, involves the learner being helped by an adult or another child (who possess a greater level of knowledge) by starting tasks, simplifying problems and highlighting errors to a point where the child can do tasks by themselves. Successful scaffolding is evident when there is a shift of responsibility from the teacher (or other) to the child. Vygotsky felt that learning was a social activity where children's learning developed through interaction with other children, teachers and parents. Bruner extended the idea of scaffolding even more, because he considered that scaffolding was flexible and evident in all aspects of a child's learning:

> Grandparents or teachers may actively break down tasks into smaller more manageable parts and model to the child how the tasks or problems can be solved, or teachers may put children together in groups to solve a problem and find that the weaker children are learning from the more able through, for example, observation, imitating and using language. (MacBlain, 2014: 56)

Bruner argued that children should be encouraged to use written symbols to develop language to explore and question new phenomena and to enable them to make links with knowledge previously gained. Later in his research, he urged teachers to encourage children to use narratives based on their cultural environment to interact with others, both teachers and other learners, to help solve the problems they encounter in the classroom.

The use of language in discovery learning is evident in one of Bruner's most influential notions, which considered the shape of the curriculum – a shape which he thought should be spiral in form, starting with an initial description of the subject, then returning to the same area with greater depth. The role of the teacher within the spiral curriculum, similar to scaffolding, is to assist the child to develop a deeper understanding and help them discover on their own (Bruner, 1996). The spiral model is not just applicable to the 'curriculum' but is also an influential tool that can be used in single and groups of sessions to give depth to the learning process and fits well with enhancing discovery learning. The application of the concept of 'spiralling' moves away from the notion of a steady build-up of knowledge as the teacher allows and encourages the child to reflect on understandings and revisit these understandings if needed. Children use new knowledge, understanding and experiences to look again at what they have already learned.

For such spiralling to be effective, especially in the teaching of specific subjects, Bruner encouraged teachers to create organisational structures which enable children to understand the subject in relation to the broader context of learning. Not making these links to the broader picture he felt was both detrimental and uneconomical to the learning process. However, building these links into teaching helps children generalise and comprehend general principles, which in turn make learning a subject exciting and rewarding. He further argued that by having structures in place which help children make links to other learning, as well as structures which enable them to see the bigger picture, skills which enhance memory are developed (Bruner, 1960). This concept of seeing how the individual elements of a subject fit into the wider aspects of learning is aligned to a deeper and more lasting approach to learning. The benefits for the learners are that their thoughts are 'on the meaning of a topic as a whole, coming to see its critical features and recognise the interrelationships between them' (Entwistle, 2009: 77).

Bruner's ideas on teaching and learning may appear somewhat radical, particularly in a climate of overly prescriptive education policy. Wragg, however, urges teachers to:

Use his ideas as a spur to shake off dependency and apprehension, to have the confidence to exercise more of your own professional judgement about where children are, how they can think and act better, what they need to construct their own meanings and understandings, with not a tick box in sight. (2004: 16)

REFLECTIVE TASK

Consider the following quote:

Bruner emphasises the need for teachers to think about their own learning and development as well as their students', and to make constructive connections between the two. (Moore, 2000: 30-1)

Reflect upon your own practice and the cultural context of an education setting with which you are familiar with regard to such matters as supporting learning and teaching and the language used in communicating with your particular students. From this make a list of your own learning and development needs which could enhance the students' learning.

SUMMARY

During Bruner's long and distinguished career he had a significant impact on many areas of education. All his ideas have emanated from his drive for social justice, stimulated by what he considered was the 'blight' of poverty, racism and the inequities of social life. He held a considerable number of positions of importance which included the reorganisation of the school curriculum in the United States and implementing the Head Start programme.

Bruner's thinking evolved over the years from cognitivism to constructivism and then to culturalism. These thoughts and theories are evident in his major works. The first was *The Process of Education* (1960) which argued for curriculum reform, especially for the early years, and set out his thinking for the spiral curriculum which gave educators an innovative notion of pedagogy and the learning process. Following this he set up and led the MACOS project. The next influential texts which highlighted the shift of his thinking were *Toward a Theory of Instruction* (1966) and *The Relevance of Education* (1971). These considered how teachers can help children construct modes of learning and how children convert experiences into knowledge through action, imagery and by symbols. Probably his most influential work was *The Culture of Education* (1996) which explored the function of schools and the value of culture in the learning process.

It is clear that Bruner was influenced by the works of Vygotsky, especially in his notions of scaffolding, the spiral curriculum, interactive and exploratory learning and the dismissal of subject-specific teaching. It is telling that a considerable number of renowned thinkers on education could also be linked with the ideas of Bruner, particularly the value he placed on language and culture, including Freire, Bourdieu, Bernstein and Wenger. Most of the criticisms of his work focus on his earlier and more idealistic notions, but these were accepted by Bruner himself. Otherwise, the criticisms relate to teachers being unable to be as creative as he would have wished because of the constraints and overprescribed nature of government-imposed curricula. Nevertheless, there are still many aspects of his concepts that are applicable in classrooms today where teachers can 'Make the principle of social justice a reality. Assert what is human about humanity. What are you waiting for?' (Wragg, 2004: 16).

GLOSSARY OF TERMS

Cognitivism

A theoretical position which stresses that thinking and understanding are fundamental to the learning process. Learning and teaching should be focused on the needs of the individual student, and also be structured according to those needs.

Computation

Is concerned with information processing once it is gathered. It considers the brain as having a similar function to a computer which needs to be programmed in order to make sense of the world. This is a contested concept because it fails to recognise the complexities and diversities inherent in learning as a socially constructed activity.

Constructivism

Stresses the significance of students constructing their knowledge and understanding by being interactively involved in the learning process, building upon what they already know. Constructivism, for Bruner, is the link between the individual concept of cognitivism and his emphasis on culture in the learning process.

Culture

The notion that the social background and environment has a significant effect on students having a meaningful learning experience. It is through culture that children, from an early age, make sense of the world around them. The role of the family, home environment and community has a particular influence in relation to the linguistic development of children.

Man: A Course of Study

A far-reaching project which developed from the latest cognitive science research to construct a new radical and transformed school curriculum. The project's aim was to discover what was distinctive about a human being, and how to become more human, then design a new school curriculum which took into account the findings.

Spiral curriculum

A concept whereby students are introduced to topics and then revisit these later to reinforce their understanding. Each time the topic is revisited students improve their depth of understanding and their confidence in applying that knowledge.

FURTHER READING

Bruner, J. (2006) *In Search of Pedagogy Vol. 1: The selected works of Jerome S. Bruner.* Abingdon: Routledge.
Bruner's critical analytical examination of his own works.

Carr, D. (2003) *Making Sense of Education.* London: RoutledgeFalmer.

Chapter 6 – Learning: behaviour, perception and cognition – gives an overview and criticism of Bruner's notions of cognitivism.

Illeris, K. (ed.) (2009) *Contemporary Theories of Learning: Learning theorists … in their own words.* Abingdon: Routledge.

A critical review of some of the contemporaries of Bruner and their thinking, including a chapter by Bruner himself.

McLay, M., Mycroft, L., Noel, P., Orr, K., Thompson, R., Tummons, J. and Weatherby, J. (2010) Learning and learners. In: Avis, J., Fisher, R. and Thompson, R. (eds) *Teaching in Lifelong Learning: A guide to theory and practice.* Maidenhead: Open University Press.

A concise yet informative review of Bruner's cognitivism and the application of the spiral curriculum shown in a scheme of work, taken from a lifelong learning perspective.

REFERENCES

Aubrey, K. and Riley, A. (2017) *Understanding and Using Challenging Educational Theories.* London: Sage.
Bartlett, S., Burton, D. and Peim, N. (2001) *Introduction to Education Studies.* London: Paul Chapman Publishing.

Bruner, J. (1960) *The Process of Education*. Cambridge, MA: Harvard University Press.

Bruner, J. (1966) *Toward a Theory of Instruction*. Cambridge, MA: Harvard University Press.

Bruner, J. (1971) *The Relevance of Education*. New York: Norton.

Bruner, J. (1996) *The Culture of Education*. Cambridge, MA: Harvard University Press.

Bruner, J. (2009) Culture, Mind and Education. In: Illeris, K. (ed.) *Contemporary Theories of Learning*. Abingdon: Routledge.

Entwistle, N. (2009) *Teaching for Understanding at University*. Basingstoke: Palgrave Macmillan.

Farnan, R. (2012) Educational Psychology. In: Arthur, J. and Peterson, A. (eds) *The Routledge Companion to Education*. London: Routledge.

Gardner, H. (1991) *The Unschooled Mind: How children think and how schools should teach*. New York: Basic Books.

Gardner, H. (2001) Jerome S. Bruner, 1915–. In: Palmer, J. (ed.) *Fifty Modern Thinkers on Education*. Abingdon: Routledge.

Hutchings, M. (2013) Arriving in a New Place: The Ecology of Learning. In: Ward, S. (ed.) *A Student's Guide to Education Studies* (Third Edition). London: Routledge.

Lave, J. and Wenger, E. (1991) *Situated Learning: Legitimate peripheral participation*. Cambridge: Cambridge University Press.

MacBlain, S. (2014) *How Children Learn*. London: Sage.

Moore, A. (2000) *Teaching and Learning: Pedagogy, curriculum and culture*. London: RoutledgeFalmer.

O'Donnell, M. (2007) *Maria Montessori*. London: Bloomsbury.

Olson, D. (2007) *Jerome Bruner*. London: Bloomsbury.

Scott, D. (2008) *Critical Essays on Major Curriculum Theorists*. Abingdon: Routledge.

Wenger, E. (1998) *Communities of Practice: Learning, meaning, and identity*. Cambridge: Cambridge University Press.

Wood, D. (1998) *How Children Think and Learn* (Second Edition). Oxford: Blackwell.

Wragg, T. (2004) An icon of the mind. *Times Educational Supplement*, 6 August.

9
ALBERT BANDURA

LEARNING THROUGH OBSERVATION

LEARNING OUTCOMES

Having read this chapter you should be able to:

- Understand the life and work of Albert Bandura
- Recognise his contribution to the development of social learning theory
- Compare his work with that of other learning theorists
- Recognise how his work can be applied in practice.

KEY WORDS

Bobo doll; self-regulation; modelling; social learning theory; self-efficacy; social cognitive theory; vicarious reinforcement; vicarious punishment; identification; reciprocal determinism

INTRODUCTION

In their 2002 study of twentieth-century psychologists, Haggbloom et al. ranked Albert Bandura as the fourth most eminent psychologist in the twentieth century, behind Sigmund Freud, Jean Piaget and B.F. Skinner (Haggbloom et al., 2002). This is not surprising given his contributions as a major force in contemporary psychology (Ferrari, 2010) through a long and illustrious career which has spanned over half a century.

Bandura's early work, which centred on understanding aggression in children, formed the precursor to his most famous experimental work, a series of studies using a **Bobo doll** to ascertain how children learn aggressive behaviours through imitation. Through this work Bandura and his colleagues advanced theories on social learning, first developed at the Yale Institute of Human Relations in the 1930s (Ferrari, 2010), and to this day he is considered a leading proponent of this theory.

His early work was influenced by the behaviourist tradition, however his later studies into personality development saw his theories drawing from a more cognitive perspective as he began to acknowledge that there was more to personality than the influence of the environment. He began to study **self-regulation** as a part of personality development, considering how people managed their own behaviour. For him, the idea that all behaviour could be modified through the use of rewards and sanctions as suggested by behaviourist traditions was too simplistic, and he began to question how children learned through a process of observation rather than through the direct experience of being rewarded for a behaviour.

His work on self-regulation resulted in a therapy technique referred to as self-control therapy which has proved successful in helping people overcome simple problems such as smoking, overeating and study habits (Boeree, 2006 [1998]). He later developed a **modelling** therapy which was designed to support people with psychological disorders deal with their problems through observation and modelling techniques.

Bandura's work has had enormous impact in the field of psychology, specifically in the areas of **social learning theory** and in personality theory and therapy. Boeree suggests that this in part may be due to, 'his straightforward behaviourist-like style [which] makes good sense to people', and that 'his action-orientated, problem-solving approach likewise appeals to those who want to get things done' (Boeree, 2006 [1998]: 8).

Throughout his career he has sought to explore how **self-efficacy** and self-regulation can support people in various aspects of their lives and utilised advances in technology to show the effect of media and culture on the development of self-efficacy, with his most recent work examining how cultural tools can be used to shape individual consciousness (Ferrari, 2010). This ability to respond to advances in technology has ensured that his work continues to have currency in a fast-paced world.

ALBERT BANDURA, THE PERSON

Albert Bandura was born in the town of Mundare in Northern Alberta, Canada, in December 1925. He was the youngest of six children to parents who were Eastern European immigrants; his parents were family orientated, but also placed a lot of emphasis on the importance of education which Bandura (2006) suggests was because of the education they themselves missed.

His early experience of education was in a small, but successful, elementary and high school, in his hometown of Mundare. The school had only two teachers and limited educational resources meaning the pupils became responsible for their own education. As Bandura recalls:

> We had to take charge of our own learning. Self-directed learning was an essential means of academic self-development, not a theoretical abstraction. The paucity of educational resources turned out to be an enabling factor that has served me well rather than an insurmountable, handicapping one. The content of courses is perishable but self-regulatory skills have lasting functional value whatever the pursuit might be. (2006: 45)

During school vacations his parents encouraged him to seek paid work which helped to fund him through college; he worked in a furniture manufacturing factory as well as spending one summer after high school 'filling holes on the Alaskan highway in Yukon' (Boeree, 2006 [1998]: 3). This work enabled him to meet people from all walks of life, something which he had been somewhat sheltered from previously in his small home town. Reflecting on this experience Bandura (2006) observes that it provided him with a uniquely broad perspective on life.

On leaving high school, he enrolled at the University of British Columbia in Vancouver, a decision he puts down to the search for warmer climes. Ironically his choice of psychology as a course was by chance, since the classmates he car-shared with had courses with early starts. Leafing through course leaflets as he waited for an English class to start he noted that the introductory psychology course ran early enough to fill the time as he awaited his next class. Thus, he commenced a course which was the start of his future profession (Bandura, 2006).

After graduating with his Bachelor's degree in psychology in 1949, he sought to further his education in this field. On asking where he might find the 'stone tablets' of psychology, he was advised by his academic advisor to seek a position at the University of Iowa where some of the leading figures in social psychology, including Kenneth Spence and Kurt Lewin, were building on Clark Hull's theoretical and experimental analyses of learning (Ferrari, 2010). While at Iowa Bandura became heavily influenced by Neal Miller and John Dollard's studies of modelling and imitation, an area of study he later built upon in his own work.

He received his master's degree from the University of Iowa in 1951, followed by a PhD in clinical psychology in 1952, and was then recruited by Robert Sears to join the psychology department at Stanford University, a position which he still holds at the time of writing.

Bandura's early work centred on identifying the reasons for aggression in children. This included field studies of social learning which were undertaken in collaboration with his first doctoral student Richard Walters. Their findings revealed that modelling influences could help to explain aggression in children, even those from advantaged backgrounds, and led to their first published work, *Adolescent Aggression*, in 1959. This work was unconventional as it did not simply focus on individuals from disadvantaged backgrounds, and led to further research into the determinants and mechanisms of observational learning (Pajares, 2004). Bandura continued his work into aggression with his now famous Bobo doll experiments, collaborative work undertaken with Walters, and Dorrie and Sheila Ross which resulted in a second book, *Social Learning and Personality Development*, published in 1963.

Despite initially being given only a year's appointment at Stanford University, as an acting instructor (Pajares, 2004), Bandura was made a full professor in 1964 and since then has continued to focus his research around aspects of social modelling and how it relates to human motivation, thought and action. Additionally, a further major area of research which Bandura has contributed to is that of self-regulation in children. Collaborating with Walter Mischel, he has sought to establish how children develop the ability to self-regulate their behaviour, leading to a theory that views people as 'self-regulatory and self-reflective beings who create and do not merely react to environmental influences' (Ferrari, 2010: 14) – this was in stark contrast to the behaviourist theories which were still prevalent at the time.

Pajares (2004) observes that Bandura's research interests vary widely, and as such he is often pursuing several lines of enquiry concurrently. His academic career has seen him elected Fellow of the American Psychological Society in 1964, and Fellow at the Centre for Advanced Studies in the Behavioural Sciences between 1969 and 1970, and he was awarded an endowed chair by Stanford in 1974, becoming the David Starr Jordan Professor of Social Sciences. He has developed a number of theories, including a **social cognitive theory** of human functioning in the mid-1980s, and has published numerous books and articles. In a career that spans almost six decades it is not surprising that Bandura has received accolades which include the Distinguished Scientific Contribution Award of the American Psychological Association, the William James Award of the American Psychological Society for outstanding achievements in psychological science and the Distinguished Scientist Award of the Society of Behavioural Medicine. He has also received honorary degrees and awards from the University of Athens and the University of Catama, and a lifetime achievement award from the Western Psychological Society.

Alongside his commitment to research Albert Bandura is a family man who was married for fifty-nine years to Virginia Varns. He has two children, Mary, a clinical psychologist and Carol, the director of a clinic for adolescent children of migrant workers and the neglected poor; he also has twin grandchildren. He credits his late wife and children with ensuring that he had a good work–life balance, stating:

> We hiked the Bay Area ridge trails, camped amidst the stately redwoods, worked in grass-roots conservation movements, explored the regional culinary shrines, cheered the melodious operatic divas and philharmonias, applauded the baroquers at the Carmel Bach festivals, sampled the noble grape in the bucolic Napa Valley, and explored the grandeur of the High Sierras. (Bandura, 2006: 53)

Bandura continues to teach and research at Stanford University, and reflecting on his life as he reached the age of 80 he observed, 'I am reminded of the saying that it is not the miles travelled but the amount of tread remaining that is important. When I last checked, I still have too much tread left to gear down or conclude this engaging odyssey' (2006: 72).

THE THEORY

Bandura is most well-known for his work on *social learning theory*, expressing that – according to the social learning view – 'man is neither driven by inner forces nor buffeted helplessly by environmental influences' (1971: 2), rather he believes behaviour can best be explained by 'continuous reciprocal interaction between behaviour and it's controlling conditions' (1971: 2). Bandura was writing in response to the behavioural theories of the time which posited that behaviour was a direct response to the consequences experienced as a result of a particular behaviour, for example through rewards and sanctions. For him, learning was more complex than this, and through his experimental work he concluded that learning behaviour occurred on a vicarious basis, as a result of individuals observing the behaviour of others and the subsequent consequences (Bandura, 1971). He theorised that since humans have 'superior cognitive capacity' (1971: 2) they are able to internalise what they have observed symbolically, and then later use this information to make decisions based on these internal representations. It is for this reason that Bandura later referred to his theory as social cognitive theory, which he explains is a more fitting appellation:

> … the social portion of the title acknowledges the social origins of much human thought and action; the cognitive portion recognises the influential contribution of cognitive processes to human motivation, affect and action. (2006: 65)

In applying his work to learning in children Bandura was interested in how behaviours are learned. He did not accept that children simply learned a behaviour through being rewarded or punished as the theory of operant conditioning suggested. He questioned how children learned new behaviours when they had not been personally rewarded for that behaviour. He suggested instead that children learned through observational learning – the child did not have to be rewarded personally for the behaviour, it was enough to see someone else being rewarded for the child to imitate it, either immediately or at a later date.

Bandura's theory regarding observational learning originated from studies with a Bobo doll, a large inflatable egg-shaped clown which was weighted in the bottom so that it bounced back up once hit, which he carried out in collaboration with Dorothea Ross and Sheila Ross in 1961. In their now famous studies they created various scenarios in which kindergarten children witnessed adults acting physically and verbally aggressively towards the Bobo doll. Various iterations of the experiment were carried out with varying levels of aggression, utilising different tools such as mallets and dart guns. Having witnessed the adults interacting with the Bobo doll the children were then left in the room with the Bobo dolls and a variety of toys, including aggressive and non-aggressive toys. The children were then observed as they interacted with the objects in the room.

The observers were initially looking specifically at the aggressive responses made by the children, including aggressive behaviours which directly imitated the adults they had observed, aggressive behaviours that were similar to the adults and aggressive behaviours that were entirely different from that of the adults. Their findings showed that the children not only copied physical and verbal aggression, but also developed their own forms of aggressive behaviour based on what they had seen, for example they would hit toys other than the Bobo doll with the mallet. They also developed non-imitative forms of aggressive behaviour, for example gun play and use of aggressive vocabulary not previously heard from the adults.

Variables were introduced into the study including the levels of aggression observed by the children, the gender of the children and the gender of the aggressor. Their observations showed that:

- Children who observed the aggressive models made far more imitative aggressive responses than those who were in the non-aggressive or control groups.
- There was more partial and non-imitative aggression among those children who had observed aggressive behaviour, although the difference for non-imitative aggression was small.
- The girls in the aggressive model conditions also showed more physical aggressive responses if the model was male but more verbal aggressive responses if the model was female (however, the exception to this general pattern was the observation of how often they punched Bobo, and in this case the effects of gender were reversed).
- Boys were more likely to imitate same-sex models than girls. The evidence for girls imitating same-sex models is not strong.
- Boys imitated more physically aggressive acts than girls. There was little difference in the verbal aggression between boys and girls.

(McCloud, 2011)

Bandura et al. (1961) later went on to introduce other variables to their experiments including rewarding and punishing the models, rewarding the children for imitating a behaviour, and even introducing a video of a model acting aggressively towards a live clown when critics suggested that Bobo dolls were meant to be hit (Boeree, 2006 [1998]).

Bandura et al. concluded that 'observation of cues produced by the behaviour of others is one effective means of eliciting certain forms of responses for which the original probability is very low or zero' (1961: 580), determining that children only needed to see a behaviour in order to imitate it, and did not, as previous theories suggested, have to be offered incentives to do this. However, there were also factors which could influence the success of observational learning, such as the attractiveness of the model to the observer, whether the model received rewards or punishments for their actions (which Bandura referred to as **vicarious reinforcement** and **vicarious punishment)**, and whether or not the observer has the capabilities to carry out the action at that specific moment in time.

Bandura concluded that for observational learning to be successful four separate processes need to occur. In the first instance, the observer needs to be paying *attention* to the model and what is happening around them. The experimental work showed that children are more likely to pay attention to a model they are attracted to or identify with, for example someone of the same gender. Secondly, *retention*, since once observed the observer must be able to retain what they have seen so as to repeat it later. The observer needs to be able to structure, or code, the information in a way in which it can be easily retrieved. The observer then needs to be able to *produce* the action which requires the observer to be mentally or physically capable of reproducing what they have observed. This stage is the most complex of the processes, since it is highly likely that the observer may not yet have perfected the skills needed to reproduce the action in its entirety. Finally, *motivation*, the observer must have a reason for wanting to perform the action, and motivations might include past reinforcement, promised reinforcement or vicarious reinforcement. Equally, motivation might well be in the form of a punishment, although Bandura, like behaviourists, would argue that reinforcement is always more effective than punishment when encouraging certain behaviours (Boeree 2006 [1998]).

The motivations as identified by Bandura show similarities with the behaviourist tradition, not surprisingly given that both behaviourism and social learning theory are theories built on the experiences of children. However, he expanded on traditional behaviourism by suggesting that there was a more complex relationship between the environment, behaviour and personal factors, and then drew on the cognitive abilities of children, 'acknowledging that children's abilities to listen, remember and abstract general rules from complete sets of observed behaviour affect their imitation and learning' (Berk, 1991: 15). In this respect children did not need the immediate reinforcement or punishment which behaviourism proposed.

Developing this thinking Bandura later went on to examine self-regulation in children, suggesting that people were self-regulatory and self-reflective beings who were not just reactive to environmental influences (Pajares, 2004). This then resulted in another strand to his social learning theory which saw him identify how individuals controlled their own behaviour via three steps:

- Self-observation – looking at our own behaviour and monitoring it.
- Judgement – comparing ourselves with a standard; this might be a fixed standard or one that the individual creates for themselves. Judgement can then be comparing the self with others or with a personal goal.
- Self-response – this is in response to the standard set at the judgement step and would be a rewarding or punishing response depending on how far standards were met. Responses might range from feelings of pride or shame, through to more physical rewards; for example, treating or denying oneself.

Bandura saw self-regulation as being closely linked to self-esteem or self-efficacy, an important concept in psychology (Boeree, 2006 [1998]). A person who consistently meets the standards they set themselves will have high self-esteem, whereas those who fail to meet their own standards will suffer from low self-esteem. Bandura identified some of the dangers of low self-esteem as being compensation, inactivity and escape (Boeree, 2006 [1998]) and this will be discussed further in the next sections.

↻ LINKS WITH OTHER THEORISTS

Comparisons can be made between the work of Bandura and Skinner since Bandura's early career was very much influenced by the operant conditioning theory put forward by Skinner (Ferrari, 2010). Both Skinner and Bandura were interested in how environmental stimuli could influence behaviour in children, however while Skinner theorised that the environment was solely responsible for behaviour through reinforcement, Bandura developed this theory by suggesting that the child does not have to be personally reinforced for the behaviour for it to be imitated. He instead posited that behaviour was learned through observation and was not immediate; the child could internalise what they had observed and reproduce it at a later date.

Bandura's work, then, highlighted the importance of environmental influence on a child's cognitive development and behaviour which resonates with the work of Lev Vygotsky who was a social constructivist. Both Bandura and Vygotsky emphasise the importance of language construction in the development of human consciousness, which allows the individual to take control of the social potential of their environments. Additionally, both Vygotsky and Bandura developed theories on self-regulation and self-mastery with an emphasis on how 'people take charge of their own behaviour' (Ferrari, 2010: 17), although Bandura was more interested in how a person's self-belief could influence personal agency.

His early years at Iowa meant that he was directly exposed to some of the most influential theorists of the time in the fields of behavioural and social learning theories;

this included Clark Hull, Kenneth Spence and Kurt Lewin. Later at Stanford he was influenced by Robert Sears who was researching familial antecedents of social behaviour and identificatory learning, which inspired the aforementioned collaborative work with Richard Walters studying antisocial behaviour in boys. It was this work which saw him reject the ideas put forward by Clark Hull who suggested that if parents used aggression to punish their children it would reduce that behaviour. Bandura and Walters found that aggressive forms of punishment were more likely to result in further aggression.

Bandura's theory of observational learning suggested that a child identifies with the person they are modelling. The idea of **identification** has some parallels with Freud's Oedipus complex since both rely on the internalisation or adoption of another person's behaviour. However, Freud theorised that the child would only identify with the parent of the same gender as them whereas Bandura suggested that identification could occur with a much wider field of potential models.

CRITIQUING THE THEORY

Bandura's experimental work with the Bobo dolls received criticism for its unethical nature, with a suggestion that the children were manipulated to behave in an aggressive manner. The sample of children used in the study were all from Stamford Nursery which critics suggest created a bias towards the white upper-middle class. Hart and Kritsonis (2006) suggest that an overview of the sample was never acknowledged in the documentation of the work, and instead sweeping statements were made about lower socio-economic communities. Additionally, because the work was carried out under laboratory conditions critics suggest that this was not representative of a 'real-life' situation, and as such it would be wrong to assume that this behaviour would be repeated under normal conditions. A further suggestion in relation to the Bobo doll experiments is that the children's motivation to show aggression to the doll came from wanting to please the adult rather than a display of aggressive tendencies (Gauntlett, 2005; Ferguson, 2010).

Critics of social learning theory argue that the theory is too simplistic in its nature to fully explain the complexities of human behaviour and learning, and while it can be used to explain some behaviours it does not explain how thoughts and feelings are learned. Bandura responded to this criticism when he renamed social learning theory as social cognitive theory, acknowledging that individuals are able to apply cognitive processes to their decision making, for example they may observe violent behaviour but they are able to make the decision as to whether or not to replicate that behaviour. Bandura states that modelling is not a simple case of mimicry but that through using abstraction individuals are able to 'generate new versions of the behaviour that go beyond what they have seen and heard' (2006: 56). He has responded to a further criticism of modelling which suggests that it is antithetical to creativity.

Here he points out that individuals will respond differently to observing the different models and will in fact amalgamate what they have observed, thereby producing new and individual behaviours.

Finally, McLeod (2016) observes that social learning theory cannot fully explain all behaviour, particularly in cases where there is no apparent role model in a person's life to account for a specific behaviour. Likewise, social learning theory does not account for maturation and development stages over the lifetime of an individual in which personality and motivation are likely to have changed and developed.

⚙ APPLYING SOCIAL LEARNING THEORY TO PRACTICE

Bandura's theory of social learning is highly applicable in the classroom, and can be incorporated into the classroom routine relatively seamlessly. He identified through his Bobo doll experiments that children's learning is influenced by observation, with children modelling people around them, stating that:

> Most of the behaviours that people display are learned either deliberately or inadvertently through the influence of example. (Bandura, 1971: 5)

Arguably, a key influence – and role model – for children are the people they come into contact with on a daily basis through schools and early years settings. Bashir et al. observe, 'teachers have long-lasting impacts on the lives of their students, and the greatest teachers inspire their pupils to greatness' (2014: 9). The notion of the teacher being a positive role for the children in their care is reflected in the Teachers' Standards for England (DfE, 2011: 10) which state that teachers must 'demonstrate consistently the positive attitudes, values and behaviour which are expected of pupils'. These standards must be met by all newly qualified teachers and are also used as a basis for teacher appraisal, setting out the professional roles and responsibilities of the classroom teacher. Children will look to the adults around them for cues as to how to behave appropriately, so as a role model it is essential that teachers demonstrate professional behaviours at all times, for example in the manner in which they interact with colleagues, parents and pupils. Additionally, as stated in the standards, 'teachers must have proper and professional regard for the ethos, policies and practices of the school in which they teach, and maintain high standards in their own attendance and punctuality' (2011, 10). It is imperative that school staff lead by example in order that pupils might themselves be encouraged to respect the ethos and policies of the school setting.

The influence of peers should not be overlooked when considering role models in settings, and children will model those peers they hold in esteem such as older peers or siblings, according to social learning theory. Teachers and educational practitioners can capitalise on this using Bandura's ideas around vicarious reinforcement and punishment, for example, rewarding those pupils who are demonstrating a desired behaviour is likely to result in other children imitating that behaviour with the anticipation that they too will receive said reward. Conversely, if children see others being punished for a behaviour then they are less likely to copy that behaviour themselves for fear of receiving similar reprisals.

McDonald (2016) observes that:

> Several research studies, spanning nearly 15 years, have illustrated the significant role that peers play not only in forming supportive networks, but also in enhancing learning and personal development.

To this end, it can be seen that a more formal application of peer role models is being used in educational settings to support young people. In recognition of the important role peers can play in supporting learning, formal peer-mentoring programmes have been seen to prevent the escalation of issues for young people and to bolster the efforts of school principals and teachers to identify and respond to bullying incidents (Cowie and Smith, 2010). In addition, Stader and Gagnepain (2000) identified that peer-mentoring schemes enhanced the climate in schools and reduced incidences of pupil drop-out. Houlston et al. explain that 'Peer support involves school programmes which train and use students themselves to help others learn and develop emotionally, socially or academically' (2009: 328). While many of the advantages of peer mentoring appear to be in respect of the pastoral benefits of peer support, studies have also shown improvement in attainment for pupils involved in peer-mentoring schemes. The Mentoring and Befriending Foundation (MBF) worked with schools during 2009/10 to monitor peer mentoring schemes and found that:

- 80.6% of mentees improved their attainment compared to 78% of the control group of non-mentees
- the average mentee improved their attainment by 14.2% compared to the average non-mentee's improvement of 11.9%.

Additionally, schemes had advantages for the mentors where:

- 68.8% of peer mentors improved their attainment compared to 58.0% of the control group of non-mentors.

(MBF, 2010: 12)

One school principal involved with peer-mentoring schemes suggested that the success of the scheme may well be attributed to the fact that 'some students benefit by hearing positive messages about performance and conduct, not from parents and teachers, but from other students whose experiences give them some wisdom and credibility' (MBF, 2010: 9). It can be seen then that social learning theory can be applied to the support which both peers and practitioners can offer to support learning in settings.

Following his work on observational learning Bandura turned his attention to self-efficacy, which he defined as 'people's beliefs about their capabilities to produce designated levels of performance that exercise influence over events that affect their lives' (1994: 2). Bandura identified those with positive self-efficacy having high confidence in their abilities, being able to:

- approach difficult tasks as challenges to be mastered
- set challenging goals and maintain a strong commitment to them
- heighten or sustain their efforts in the face of failures or setbacks
- attribute failure to insufficient effort or deficient knowledge and skills which are acquirable
- approach threatening situations with the assurance that they can exercise control over them.

(Weibell, 2011)

On the other hand, those with poor self-efficacy, doubt their capabilities and:

- shy away from tasks they view as personal threats
- have low aspirations and weak commitment to the goals they choose to pursue
- dwell on personal deficiencies, obstacles they will encounter, and all kinds of adverse outcomes, rather than concentrating on how to perform successfully
- slacken their efforts and give up quickly in the face of difficulties
- are slow to recover their sense of efficacy following failures or setbacks
- fall easy victim to stress and depression.

(Weibell, 2011)

Bandura identified the school as having a key role to play in supporting children in the development of cognitive competences, and posited that as they master cognitive skills they begin to develop a sense of their intellectual efficacy (Bandura, 1994). He advised that this can be reinforced through factors such as:

> … peer modelling of cognitive skills, social comparison with the performances of other students, motivational enhancement through goals and positive incentives, and teachers' interpretations of children's successes and failures in ways that reflect favourably or unfavourably on their ability also affect children's judgments of their intellectual efficacy. (Bandura, 1994: 11)

The role of the teacher in supporting children in the development of self-efficacy cannot then be understated and Bandura (1994) identifies four main sources of influence for supporting self-efficacy development. The first of these sources is *mastery* which advocates that success supports self-efficacy while failure undermines it – the practitioner can then ensure that work is matched to allow pupils the appropriate level of challenge but which allows for success to be achieved. Settings will often achieve this through the use of ability groups and sets, or ensuring that work is suitably scaffolded to maximise success rate.

The second source identified by Bandura (1994) was through the *vicarious experiences* provided by role models. If pupils see peers achieving success on an activity it is likely that they will gain the confidence to try this for themselves, alternatively failure by peers is likely to act as a deterrent. Using his earlier findings he also suggested that vicarious experience was particularly powerful if the learner could identify with the model – if they could do so they would be more confident of their own success. This also strengthens some of the theory behind ability grouping and sets in classrooms, as well as the aforementioned application of peer mentoring.

Thirdly, Bandura (1994) sees *social persuasion* as a means by which a person's belief in themselves might be strengthened. He suggests that if an individual is persuaded by others that they can achieve something they are more likely to increase their efforts and persevere than if they doubt themselves or dwell on personal deficiencies. Sewell and St George (2000), however, believe that this is one of the least effective means by which a teacher raises self-efficacy, suggesting that 'unrealistic boosts in efficacy via persuasion are quickly deflated by failure, especially if it happens after hearing: "Come on, you can do it"' (2000: 60). Nonetheless, Bandura would dismiss this criticism, suggesting that people who are successful efficacy builders are more likely to create situations which allow success to be achieved, and will measure success in self-improvement rather than through competition with others. For the classroom teacher then the use of social persuasion should be employed with caution, building on their knowledge of individual pupils.

Finally, Bandura identifies an individual's physiological and emotional stress reactions as informing their self-efficacy – this might include trembling, sweating or 'butterflies in the stomach' (Sewell and St George, 2000). Sewell and St George (2000) identify these as the most subtle of processes and which might be open to interpretation, for example as Bandura suggests, 'it is not the sheer intensity of emotional and physical reactions that is important but rather how they are perceived and interpreted' (1994: 3). Bandura observes that for a person with high self-efficacy the physical signs of anxiety may act as an energising facilitator of performance, whereas those with low self-efficacy may find the physical reactions a debilitating force (Bandura, 1994).

It can be seen then that social learning theory is highly relevant to classroom situations, whether this is through the use of modelling to achieve a desired behaviour, or through supporting pupils in the development of self-efficacy in order to impact on both attainment and the development of life skills.

REFLECTIVE TASK

Bandura's work opened up the debate on how far violence through media could impact on behaviour (Anderson and Bushman, 2002; Anderson et al., 2007; Ferguson, 2010). What are your views on this – do you think that over-exposure to violent television programmes or video games can lead to aggressive behaviour in children?

SUMMARY

With a career which has spanned six decades Albert Bandura is considered to be one of the most influential psychologists of all time (Haggbloom et al., 2002). Bandura continues to make contributions to the field of psychology, however as this chapter shows he is best known for the influential work undertaken in the field of social learning theory, specifically observational learning, motivation and personality development. At a time when the prevalent theories included the behaviour theories of B.F. Skinner and the psychoanalytical theories of Sigmund Freud, Bandura set out to demonstrate how children's behaviour was influenced by the people around them, showing a correlation between learning theory and cognitive approaches.

His experimental work with Bobo dolls saw a shift from behaviourism to cognitive psychology as he demonstrated how learning did not necessarily result in an immediate change in behaviour, and children could internalise what they had observed and use this at a later date. He was also one of the first theorists to explore the importance of motivation in the development and learning of young children (Gray and MacBlain, 2015).

Bandura's work opened up much debate on the impact of television violence in the 1970s, with him warning that 'children and adults acquire attitudes, emotional responses, and new styles of conduct through filmed and televised modelling' (1977: 2). This is a debate which has continued to rage as technology has developed, and with a growing market for violent and aggressive video games, resulting in high-profile copycat cases, such as the Columbine High School shootings, his social learning theory continues to have relevance to date.

Bandura has dedicated a lifetime of work to understanding human motivation: his later work on self-efficacy was hugely influential in supporting people with phobias, and has also successfully helped people to overcome post-traumatic stress disorders through developing a sense of control. His current research continues to examine human motivation, particularly in respect of how people can exercise control over their own motivation and behaviour.

GLOSSARY OF TERMS

Bobo doll

An inflatable blow-up character, weighted at the bottom, which bounces back when hit.

Identification

Identifying with, and imitating, a specific individual with characters the observer deems desirable.

Modelling

A process whereby learning occurs through observing and imitating the actions of others. Bandura proposed that individuals are more likely to model those people they can identify with, such as people of the same gender, or people they look up to as role models.

Self-efficacy

The confidence an individual has in themselves to produce a desired result.

Self-regulation

The ability a person has to regulate their own behaviour, emotion and thought responses in particular situations.

Social learning theory

A theory first advanced by academics at the Yale Institute of Human Relations in the 1930s, but which was popularised by the work of Bandura, Ross and Ross in the 1960s through their Bobo doll experiments. The theory proposes that behaviours are learned through observing and imitation.

Social cognitive theory

The name which Bandura later gave to his own social learning theory which takes account of the thought processes which he theorised were key to learning.

Vicarious punishment

A learning process advanced by social learning theory in which undesirable behaviour is avoided through observing others being punished for that behaviour. An observer is unlikely to repeat a behaviour if they see someone else being punished.

Vicarious reinforcement

A learning process advanced by social learning theory in which a behaviour is learned through observing others being rewarded for that behaviour. An observer is likely to repeat a behaviour in anticipation of being rewarded.

FURTHER READING

Bandura, A., Ross, D., Ross, S. and Webb, D. (eds) (2013) *Psychology Classics All Psychology Students Should Read: The Bobo Doll experiment*. Retrieved from www.all-about-psychology.com

A full account of the Bobo Doll experiment with bonus material 'Transmission of Aggression Through Imitation of Aggressive Models' which built on Bandura's earlier work.

Evans, R.I. (1989) *Albert Bandura, The Man and His Ideas: A dialogue*. Santa Barbara, CA: Praeger.

A dialogue with Albert Bandura tracing his early work on modelling and subsequent theories and ideas on aggression, moral development and self-efficacy.

Kumpulainen, K. (2001) *Classroom Interaction and Social Learning: From theory to practice*. London: RoutledgeFalmer.

A case study approach to examining how social interactions in the classroom can lead to meaningful learning experiences for pupils.

REFERENCES

Anderson, C.A. and Bushman, B.J. (2002) The effects of media violence on society. *Science*, *295*(5564), 2377–79.

Anderson C.A., Gentile D.A. and Buckley, K.E. (2007) *Violent Video Game Effects on Children and Adolescents: Theory, Research, and Public Policy*. New York: Oxford University Press.

Bandura, A. (1971) *Social Learning Theory*. New York: General Learning Press.

Bandura, A. (1977) *Social Learning Theory*. New York: Prentice Hall.

Bandura, A. (1994) Self-efficacy. In: V.S. Ramachaudran (ed.) *Encyclopaedia of Human Behaviour*. New York: Academic Press. pp. 471–81.

Bandura, A. (2006) Autobiography. In: Lindzcy, M.G. and Runyam, W.M. (eds) *A History of Psychology in Autobiography* (Vol. *IX*). Washington, DC: American Psychologial Association. pp. 42–75.

Bandura, A. and Walters, R.H. (1959) *Adolescent Aggression: A study of the influence of child-training practices and family interrelationships*. New York: The Ronald Press Company.

Bandura, A. and Walters, R.H. (1963) *Social Learning and Personality Development*. New York: The Ronald Press.

Bandura, A., Ross, D. and Ross, S.A. (1961) Transmission of aggression through imitation of aggressive models. *Journal of Abnormal and Social Psychology*, *63* (3), 575–82.

Bashir, S., Bajwa, M. and Rana, S. (2014) Teacher as a role model and its impact on female students. *International Journal of Research Granthaalayah*, *1* (1), 9–20.

Berk, L. (1991) *Child Development* (Second Edition). Boston, MA: Allyn and Bacon.

Boeree, C.G. (2006 [1998]) *Albert Bandura: Personality theories*. Available at: www.ship.edu/%7Ecgboeree.perscontents.html [accessed 09/03/18].

Cowie, H. and Smith, P.K. (2010) Peer Support as a Means of Improving School Safety and Reducing Bullying and Violence. In: Doll, B., Pfohl, W. and Yoon, J. (eds) *Handbook of Youth Prevention Science*. Routledge: New York. pp. 179–95.

Department for Education (2011) *Teachers' Standards: Guidance for school leaders, school staff and governing bodies*. Crown Copyright.

Ferguson, C.J. (2010) Blazing Angels or Resident Evil? Can violent video games be a force for good? *Review of General Psychology, 14* (2), 68–81.

Ferrari, M. (2010) Wundt, Vygotsky and Bruner: A cultural-historical science of consciousness in three acts. *History of the Human Sciences, 23* (3): 95–118. jounals.sagepub.com.

Gauntlett, D. (2005) *Moving Experiences: Media Effects and Beyond* (Second Edition). Luton: John Libbey.

Gray, C. and MacBlain, S. (2015) *Learning Theories in Childhood* (Second Edition). London: Sage.

Haggbloom, S.J., Warnick, R., Warnick, J.E., Jones, V.K., Yarbrough, G.L., Russell, T.M., Borecky, C.M., McGahhey, J.L., Powell, J.L., Beavers. J. and Monte, E. (2002) The 100 most eminent psychologists of the twentieth century. *Review of General Psychology, 6* (2), 139–52.

Hart, K.E. and Kritsonis, W.A. (2006) Critical analysis of an original writing on social learning theory: Imitation of film-mediated aggressive models by Albert Bandura, Dorothea Ross and Sheila A. Ross. *National Forum of Applied Educational Research Journal, 19* (3), 1–7.

Houlston, C., Smith P.K. and Jessel, J. (2009) Investigating the extent and use of peer support initiatives in English schools. *Educational Psychology, 29* (3), 325–44.

McCloud, S. (2011) *The Bobo Doll experiment*. Available at: http://deannawatts.cmswiki.wikis paces.net/file/view/Bobo+Doll+Experiment.pdf [accessed 09/03/18].

McDonald, K. (2016) *Building an effective peer mentoring scheme*. Available at: www.sec-ed.co.uk/best-practice/building-an-effective-peer-mentoring-scheme-1/ [accessed 09/03/18].

McLeod, S. (2016) *Bandura: Social Learning Theory*. Available at: www.simplypsychology.org/bandura.html [accessed 09/03/18].

Mentoring and Befriending Foundation (2010) *Peer mentoring in schools: A review of the evidence base of the benefits of peer mentoring in schools including findings from the MBF Outcomes Measurement Programme*. Available at: www.mandbf.org/wp-content/uploads/2011/02/Peer_Mentoring_in_Schools.pdf [accessed 09/03/18].

Pajares, F. (2004) *Albert Bandura: Biographical sketch*. Available at: http://des.empory.edu/mfp/bandurabio.html [accessed 08/03/18].

Sewell, A. and St George, A. (2000) Developing efficacy beliefs in the classroom. *Journal of Educational Enquiry, 1* (2), 58–71.

Stader, D. and Gagnepain, F.G. (2000) Mentoring: the power of peers. *American Secondary Education, 28* (3), 28–32.

Weibell, C.J. (2011) *Principles of learning: 7 principles to guide personalized, student-centered learning in the technology-enhanced, blended learning environment*. Available at: https://principlesoflearning.wordpress.com [accessed 09/03/18].

10

URIE BRONFENBRENNER

THE ECOLOGY OF HUMAN DEVELOPMENT

LEARNING OUTCOMES

Having read this chapter you should be able to:

- understand Bronfenbrenner's theory related to the ecology of human development
- recognise how that theory might be applied to the workplace
- understand how human development can be influenced by environmental factors.

KEY WORDS

ecological systems theory; bioecological; microsystem; mesosystem; exosystem; macrosystem; chronosystem; proximal processes

INTRODUCTION

Urie Bronfenbrenner can be credited with breaking some of the barriers which prevailed in the social sciences, encouraging practitioners involved in the study of child development to view children and their families in an increasingly holistic manner, through his **ecological systems theory**. Prior to the development of Bronfenbrenner's model, human development was viewed in a predominantly fragmented manner, with each fragment having its own agenda and level of analysis. In essence: the child psychologist studied the child, sociologists studied the family, anthropologists examined society, economists studied the economic framework and political scientists looked at the structure of society. What then prevailed was a somewhat disjointed view of human development from which no clear picture emerged. Bronfenbrenner argued for a mode of study which encompassed all of these lenses, with family to economic and political structures all viewed as part of a life study, embracing childhood through to adulthood, thus his concept of *the ecology of human development* was born.

In Bronfenbrenner's theory the environment was viewed as an essential component in human development. He identified layers within the environment, each interconnecting and playing its own role in the growth of the child into adulthood. He did not understand the rationale behind investigating human development under laboratory conditions and stated that:

> Much of contemporary developmental psychology is the science of the strange behaviour of children in strange situations with strange adults for the briefest possible periods of time. (Bronfenbrenner, 1977: 513)

Bronfenbrenner firmly believed that the developing child should be studied within their own natural environment, undertaking tasks which were familiar to them amongst people they were comfortable with, suggesting that it is through these interactions that the true nature of the child can be revealed.

Through his work with children and their families Bronfenbrenner influenced how the child was viewed in society and highlighted the importance of working together in the best interests of the child. His work led to the introduction of the Head Start programme in the United States, a readiness for school scheme which saw practitioners increasing support for socially disadvantaged families. This was the forerunner to similar policies in the UK, such as Sure Start, which were arguably influenced by Head Start.

Up until his death in 2005, Urie Bronfenbrenner remained an advocate of the family, firmly believing that the child did not develop in isolation, but within the foundations of family, school, community and society, and argued that stronger ties between these structures aided human development. However, he also recognised that some of the processes which make us human were breaking down in modern society, suggesting that, now more than ever, practitioners should be looking to the forces which act on the developing child and, as Danner (2009) states, 'Perhaps his most enduring legacy will be his insistence that people must not only strive for a more accurate picture of human development but also act on this knowledge to improve the lives of children'.

URIE BRONFENBRENNER, THE PERSON

Urie Bronfenbrenner was born in Moscow in 1917. His family moved to the United States when Bronfenbrenner was six years of age and he spent the rest of his life as an American citizen. His father, Dr Alexander Bronfenbrenner, was a clinical pathologist and research director at the New York State Institution for the Mentally Retarded, which may in some way explain his son's later interest in developmental psychology.

On graduating from Haverstraw High School in New York, Bronfenbrenner went on to major in psychology and music at Cornell University, where he graduated with a Bachelor's degree in 1938. He then went on to study for a Master's degree in education at Harvard University, followed by a Doctorate in developmental psychology, which he gained from the University of Michigan in 1942. Immediately after being awarded his doctorate Bronfenbrenner was inducted into the US Army where he remained until the end of the Second World War, working as a psychologist on a number of assignments and, on completion of his officer training, working in the US Army Medical Corps.

At the end of the Second World War Bronfenbrenner spent a brief period working for Administration and Research for the Veterans Administration as Assistant Chief Clinical Psychologist before taking up the position of Assistant Professor of Psychology at the University of Michigan. He remained there for just two years before returning to Cornell University as a faculty member in 1948, where he stayed for the rest of his life.

For much of his professional career Bronfenbrenner sought to change the way in which human development was viewed, encouraging his contemporaries to build bridges between the separate disciplines of human development. He was fascinated by what made human beings human and centred his work on the idea that human development was influenced by the social structure that the individual was a part of. He placed great emphasis on the family and proposed that the study of human development should be undertaken within the context of the immediate family, but he also acknowledged that other parts of the larger social system should not be overlooked and reinforced the importance of culture, faith, economic policy and adult employment as key factors in child development (Lindon, 2007).

Bronfenbrenner's work had a significant impact on social policy in the 1960s and he was a strong advocate for family values. His ideas were influential in the introduction of the Head Start programme in America in 1965. This federal child development programme remains one of the most successful and longest-running programmes in the United States. Designed to stop child poverty, Head Start enabled families with low incomes to access advice and support in areas related to health and nutrition and increased parental involvement in the education of their children. Head Start was designed to increase school readiness for those children living in poverty, with the intention that if these children had the same start in life as more affluent children, then the cycle of poverty would be broken. Bronfenbrenner asserted that the programme would be most effective if the whole community were involved in providing for the needs of the child at a time when parental involvement in the school environment was minimal. This has now become a cornerstone of the programme.

Following the success of Head Start, Bronfenbrenner went on to investigate further the factors which influenced human development, resulting in his theoretical work centred on ecological systems. In his 1979 book, *The Ecology of Human Development*, he identified four (later five) systems, each interlinking and having its own unique but interrelated impact on development. This will be covered in greater detail in the next section of this chapter, but in essence his **bioecological** approach changed the way in which psychologists and social scientists studied human beings.

Bronfenbrenner began to see how the changing nature of society was impacting on young people, raising concerns that the hectic pace of modern life posed as big a threat to children as poverty and unemployment (Lang, 2014). He saw these trends as disruptive and potentially damaging to the next generation of adults in America. Speaking to a US congressional committee in 1969, Bronfenbrenner pointed to scientific evidence which testified to the fact that a societal breakdown threatened the processes which made human beings human (Keating and Hertzman, 1999), stating:

> … the signs of this breakdown are seen in the growing rates of alienation, apathy, rebellion, delinquency and violence we have observed in youth in this nation in recent decades. (Bronfenbrenner, 1969: 1838)

Bronfenbrenner remained committed to researching the impact of family on human development and in his later years studied the impact of modern family life and culture on development. In his 1986 article, 'Ecology of the Family as a Context for Human Development', he drew together research studies on a range of factors impacting family life and values. In this article he raised the concern that at a time when external factors, such as unemployment and poverty, were at an all-time high, policy makers were focusing on organisational issues and were failing to address the bigger issues affecting the nation.

Urie Bronfenbrenner had a long and illustrious career, producing over 300 articles and chapters and writing fourteen books, including *Two Worlds of Childhood: US and USSR* (1974 [1970]), *The State of Americans* (1996), *Making Human Beings Human* (2007), and his most influential text *The Ecology of Human Development* (1979). His most enduring legacy, however, must surely be the impact he had on the study of human development, changing the face of this area of study to one which saw all aspects of the child being examined in one context.

BRONFENBRENNER'S THEORY

In his study of human development, Bronfenbrenner looked to the factors which directly impact on the developing child – namely, the environment in which the child resides and the system of relationships within that environment. In developing his Ecology of Human Development theory, he observed that:

> A broader approach to research in human development is proposed that focuses on the progressive accommodation, throughout the human lifespan, between the growing human organism, and the changing environments in which it actually lives and grows. (Bronfenbrenner, 1977: 513)

He defined the ecological environment as 'a nested arrangement of structures, each contained within the next' (Bronfenbrenner, 1977: 514), initially identifying four such structures, adding a fifth in a later iteration. Each layer, or structure, has an effect on the developing child and the interactions between the structures will steer the child's development, thus creating a unique experience for each individual. In his theory Bronfenbrenner identified that a change or conflict in any one layer will have a direct impact on the other layers within the system (Paquette and Ryan, 2001).

In studying child development, then, it is necessary to look at the child in the context of their immediate environment, but within their wider environment also. According to Bronfenbrenner's theory the environment is structured as follows:

- The **microsystem** – the environment closest to the child, the most common examples being the home and the classroom. These environments provide interactions with family, friends, peers, teachers and neighbours who can be seen to directly influence the social interactions with which the child engages. It is through the microsystem that the child learns early rules of behaviour and social norms. Bronfenbrenner identified that at this level relationships can exist in two directions, both towards and away from the child. He referred to this as *bidirectional influences* and showed that while the parents can directly influence the beliefs and behaviour of the child, the child can also impact the parents' behaviour. While Bronfenbrenner acknowledged that bidirectional influences could occur within any level, they were at their strongest in the microsystem.
- The **mesosystem** – the relationships formed between the different components within the microsystem and the quality and frequency of the interactions between these. Bronfenbrenner advocated that children's development was optimised when the links between the microsystems were strong. For example, their educational attainment increased if there was effective communication between teachers and parents. Alternatively, if parents showed a poor attitude towards school because of their own experiences, then this could adversely affect children's development.

- The **exosystem** – a part of the child's environment which they are not a direct part of, but which nevertheless influences their development. Bronfenbrenner (1977) saw the exosystem as an extension of the mesosystem and suggested that these might include the world of work, the neighbourhood, mass media, government agencies and communication and transport facilities (Bronfenbrenner, 1977). While the child is not contained directly within that environment, according to Paquette and Ryan (2001) this layer impacts on the child because it interacts with some structure in the mesosystem. For example, a child may be positively or negatively impacted by the parents' work schedules.

- The **macrosystem** – this forms the outermost layer of the child's environment. Bronfenbrenner explained that the macrosystem is fundamentally different from the other layers, 'in that it refers not to the specific contexts affecting the life of a particular person, but to general prototypes, existing in the culture or subculture, that set the pattern for the structures and activities occurring at the concrete level' (Bronfenbrenner, 1977: 515). This, then, includes the laws, customs and cultural values of the society in which the child belongs, which will have a direct impact on the interactions within the other layers. Bronfenbrenner saw this layer as a 'blueprint' in which settings of a similar nature are governed by the same rules or principles; however, he also acknowledged that while many of these are explicitly defined by laws, regulations and rules, macrosystems can also be more informal, in which customs develop as part of everyday life (Bronfenbrenner, 1977).

- The **chronosystem** – this final layer was added at a later date and, within this layer, Bronfenbrenner acknowledged that human ecology changes over time. Such changes can be external, such as the separation of a child's parents, or internal, such as the physiological changes which naturally occur as the child grows older.

In his later work Bronfenbrenner revised his ecological systems theory of development, redefining it as the *bioecological model*. His rationale for making this revision followed his observations that in the original theory he had omitted to take account of the individual person as being key to how interactions with the environment influenced development. Bronfenbrenner and Morris (2007) saw the new model as a transition from a focus on the environment to one of ***proximal processes***, and in this model identified four primary components – *processes*, *person*, *context* and *time* (PPCT).

The first of the four components and the core of his model was processes which encompassed the interaction between the organism and the environment (Bronfenbrenner and Morris, 2007), Bronfenbrenner identified that human development occurs over a series of increasingly complex interactions, with the complexity arising as a result of the child's physical and cognitive structures growing and maturing (Paquette and Ryan, 2001). He also acknowledged that, to be effective, interactions need to occur on a regular basis over an extended period of time (Bronfenbrenner, 1993). He referred to these interactions as proximal processes and suggested that these could be found in parent-to-child and child-to-child activities, 'through group or solitary play, reading, learning new skills, studying athletic activities or performing complex tasks' (Bronfenbrenner, 1993: 38). For Bronfenbrenner the emphasis was on the reciprocal nature of the interactions. These were not just restricted to the interactions between two individuals but were also determined by interactions with objects and symbols in the environment, thus setting the context (Griffore and Phenice, 2016). Additionally, he also observed that proximal processes could not be assumed by the mere presence of people in the environment, this would only occur if interactions ensue.

Bronfenbrenner identifies that the proximal processes affecting development will vary significantly depending on the characteristics of each individual – the person – and both the immediate and wider environment in which the processes are taking place – thus reinforcing once again the idea that those factors influencing human development are very much dependent on the characteristics of the individual and their unique interactions with the environment. In his original theory Bronfenbrenner overlooked the unique characteristics of the individual, so in the bioecological theory he took account of features of the child such as physical appearance, age and gender, as well as genetic disposition, how a person responds to stress, temperament and age span in considering reciprocal responses.

In considering the final components of the bioecological model Bronfenbrenner referred back to his original ecological systems theory and the five elements related to the environment as described above. However, in this revised model the first four elements he referred to as the context, while the final element, the chronosystem, he categorised as time. We will see in the following section how his work has influenced how the child is viewed. He encouraged practitioners to view the child through the multiple contexts which impact on their development and, in so doing, he demonstrated how the child could be enabled to live up to their biological potential through the shared responsibility of all those who were active within that child's environment, or, as seen above, through the successful application of proximal processes.

LINKS WITH OTHER THEORISTS

While Bronfenbrenner is predominantly viewed as an ecological theorist, it should be noted that his work can be seen to complement other theories and parallels with other theorists can be drawn.

Proponents of attachment theory, such as Bowlby and Ainsworth, suggest that a child's relationship with the main caregiver, most often the mother, is essential to a child's social, emotional and cognitive development. Both Bowlby and Ainsworth observed that the infant becomes increasingly distressed when separated from the main caregiver, and that if attachments are not secure in the early years then this can have an impact on the child's ability to form bonds and maintain relationships in later life.

Through longitudinal studies, Bowlby observed that delinquency or behaviour problems in adolescence could be linked to some form of separation experience in childhood (Smith et al., 2011). This very much reflects Bronfenbrenner's emphasis on the importance of relationships in the microsystem as setting the foundation for all subsequent relationships.

Bronfenbrenner's work can also be seen reflected in the work of social learning theorist Albert Bandura. The premise of Bandura's work is that people learn from one another, through observation, replication and modelling. Bandura posited that most human behaviour is learned, thus he emphasised the importance of a child having positive role models. Like Bronfenbrenner, Bandura suggested that it was the child's interactions with the environment and those within it which impacted on behaviour. He referred to this as *reciprocal determinism*, positing that an individual's behaviour influences, and is influenced by, both the social world and personal characteristics.

Bronfenbrenner acknowledged the work of Glen Elder on life course development as influential in the formation of the original ecological model (Damon and Lerner, 2006). According to Damon and Lerner (2006), Elder's theory had four defining principles, the first three of which can be seen reflected in Bronfenbrenner's outermost layer, the chronosystem. Elder's first principle related to historical time and place, as he theorised that people are shaped by events in history and the events they experience in their lifetimes. In his second principle, timing in lives, he explains that the timing of an event will directly influence the effect it has on an individual. Bronfenbrenner, too, acknowledged this, suggesting that in the event of parental separation, the age of the child will directly correlate with the effect the separation has on their development.

Elder's third principle of 'linked lives' centred on the idea that 'lives are lived interdependently and social and historical influences are expressed through this network of shared relationships' (Damon and Lerner, 2006: 822). The interdependency of relationships was of course integral to Bronfenbrenner's theory. Interestingly, Elder's fourth principle related to human agency and the individual's construction of the life course. Elder believed that individuals had control over the choices they made and actions taken and, as we shall see in the next section, this is one area that was underrepresented in Bronfenbrenner's theory.

CRITIQUING BRONFENBRENNER

Tudge et al. (2009) acknowledge that Bronfenbrenner's theory is in a continual state of development and, due to the ever-changing nature of society and its influences on the developing child, it is necessary to apply his earlier theoretical assertions with some degree of caution. Indeed, Bronfenbrenner himself could be seen as one of his biggest critics, stating that:

> I have been pursuing a hidden agenda: that of re-assessing, revising and extending – as well as refining and even renouncing – some of the conceptions set forth in my 1979 monograph. (1989: 187)

While Bronfenbrenner is best known for his ecological systems model, his later amendments were perhaps more reflective of the evolving society in which he lived. In these later iterations he placed more emphasis on how the developing child should be viewed, through the Process–Person–Context–Time model (PPCT) as explained above, and, as observed by Tudge et al. (2009), on replicating Bronfenbrenner's work, each of these aspects should be equally represented. Tudge et al. (2009) also observe that numerous researchers have used Bronfenbrenner's work as a basis for their studies, but they caution that these should be carefully considered with regard to whether the studies have utilised the earlier outmoded model, which Bronfenbrenner himself questioned, or whether all aspects of the PPCT model have been used as he intended.

A further critique which Bronfenbrenner himself added was that his early work discounted the role the person plays in their own development, placing far too much emphasis on the context, such as the influence of the environment and people within it. As observed by Christensen (2010), Bronfenbrenner stressed the negative impact of the environment and took little account of the resilience of the individual in dealing with the hardships they may encounter. This is further supported by MacBlain (2014), who suggests that Bronfenbrenner failed to pay sufficient attention to the individual psychological needs of the child.

Doherty and Hughes (2009) extend this idea yet further, suggesting that his theory takes little account of the different ecologies which the child is likely to encounter, particularly in an increasingly globalised society, and more attention should be paid to the interactions of a range of people within the child's environment who will impact the individual throughout their lifespan.

Within a theory that places so much emphasis on the child and family and their whole environment it is easy to see how the work can become outmoded. When Bronfenbrenner first began developing his theory he could not have contemplated the rapid changes which have since occurred in society, particularly the enormous influence of technology. However, his work should not be underrated and, providing it is seen in the context of its time, still has value in helping us to understand the ecology of human development.

APPLYING BRONFENBRENNER IN THE CLASSROOM

Bronfenbrenner asserted that:

> … a child's ability to learn to read in the primary grades may depend no less on how he is taught than on the existence and nature of ties between the school and the home. (1979: 51)

He goes on to say that 'it requires us to look beyond single settings to the relationship between them' (1979: 51). Bronfenbrenner's theory can be seen as extremely relevant to the classroom, and the importance of home and school working together in the best interests of the child cannot be understated.

The transition which the child makes from home to school or early years setting is a significant one and marks a change in the role of the child from a member of a family group into a participant in a more formal setting, which for the most part is populated by strangers (MacBlain, 2014). It is important that this first transition from home to school is a positive one, since potentially this can set the tone for all future transitions and the child's future engagement in educational settings. As such, it is essential that home and school work together in the best interests of each individual child.

As we have seen previously, Bronfenbrenner defined the mesosystem as the relationships which develop between the immediate environments of the child, and if this interrelationship is both frequent and of a high quality, then this will have a direct impact on the development of the child (Foley and Leverett, 2008). So, when considering transitions, we can see how the role of the key worker in early years settings can impact on the effectiveness through close interactions with the parent. The 2017 Early Years Foundation Stage (EYFS) statutory guidance explains the role of the key worker as ensuring 'that every child's care is tailored to their individual needs' (Department for Education, 2017: 22) and offering 'a settled relationship for the child and building a relationship with their parents' (2017: 23). This may be as straightforward as the practitioner having an understanding of the child's likes and dislikes, favourite toy and so forth, which can be used as a means of engaging with the child, particularly in times of distress. Likewise, it is important that schools keep parents abreast of progress and attainment, which allows for parents to continue with a child's education in the home environment. There has, in recent years, been an increased focus in the primary age range on the importance of homework, which extends beyond reading with children to being more actively involved in other aspects of the wider curriculum.

Of course, transitions do not just occur between home and school and, as the child grows older, transitions within the school environment, from class to class or school to school, can be equally difficult for some children. Such transitions can be eased significantly if communications within educational settings are made. For example, it is common practice for a child's attainment record to be passed between settings, ensuring that educational needs can be met. Likewise, other relevant information passed between settings can help to ease the transition, thereby increasing the child's chances of educational success.

A child's success in school can also be impacted by systems within the wider environment, the exosystem, and here schools may look to these to gain a better understanding or appreciation of why a child might be behaving in a certain way. In his later studies Bronfenbrenner saw the instability and unpredictability of family life as being particularly harmful to a child's development (Addison, 1992). Addison expresses that where relationships in the immediate mesosystem break down, the child will lack the stability required to successfully interact with the wider environment. Equally, if there is a lack of positive affirmation from the closest caregivers then the child will look for that affirmation elsewhere, in some cases forming inappropriate relationships, particularly in the adolescent years. Practitioners can look, then, to what might be happening within the direct mesosystem in order to account for a possible change in behaviour. Indeed, Paquette and Ryan (2001) suggest that it is increasingly the role of the school and teachers to provide the stable, long-term relationships which are so important for healthy development and which, in modern-day society, can sadly be lacking in the home environment.

Bronfenbrenner would, however, caution against this type of relationship, suggesting that in order to be effective such relationships need to be consistent and enduring, something which schools and teachers are unable to effectively accommodate. Instead, Bronfenbrenner advocates home and school working together, with schools particularly providing a nurturing and supportive environment. He urged the creation of policies which would support the primary caregiver in their role in the child's development. We have already seen how this led to the Head Start programme in the United States, but we should at this juncture mention a similar programme in the UK – namely Sure Start, which was also intended to provide a supportive network for parents.

Introduced in 1998, its remit was to provide a supportive network for parents from pregnancy through to children reaching school age. Housed in Children's Centres, predominantly in socially deprived areas, parents could access a range of services, bringing together health, education and parenting support services in a coordinated way. As with Head Start, policy makers recognised that children from deprived areas did less well in school than their more affluent peers and, as such, in order to redress the balance, support needed to be provided in the formative years, before it became too late. Reflecting Bronfenbrenner's work, Sure Start was aimed at educating parents and improving the chances of success through strengthening family values and ensuring that all stakeholders took full responsibility for the developing child.

The importance of the interactions between family and school can also be seen reflected in the latest revision of the Early Years Foundation Stage, which clearly states in its introduction that 'good parenting and high quality early learning together provide the foundation the children need to make the most of their abilities and talents as they grow up' (Department for Education, 2017: 5). The document also advocates 'partnership working between practitioners and with parents and carers' (2017: 5). Likewise, keeping parents informed of their child's progress is also an important component of the document, particularly regarding the two-year progress check. In fact, the importance of parents as partners is a consistent theme throughout and is highly relevant when considering the importance that Bronfenbrenner placed on the mesosystem as a firm foundation on which the other layers are built.

Educational practitioners can then take much from his work, particularly when we consider how society is evolving and changing. In an increasingly global society it is important that teachers have an awareness of the cultures and values which may be dictating the child's lifestyle, as well as understanding how wider issues affecting family life may have an adverse effect on a child's development. It is only through an appreciation and understanding of these that the setting can meet the best interests of the child.

REFLECTIVE TASK

Bronfenbrenner is frequently quoted as saying:

It can be said that much of developmental psychology is the science of the strange behaviour of children in strange situations with strange adults for the briefest possible period of time. (Bronfenbrenner, 1977: 513)

What do you think Bronfenbrenner meant by this – can you think of any examples? Do you think this is still the case or is the study of human development now carried out in a more naturalistic environment – can you find any examples?

SUMMARY

Bronfenbrenner is viewed as one of the leading figures in the study of human development, and his *ecological systems theory* not only changed the way in which human development is viewed but also spearheaded a significant number of studies in the field of human development. Later known as the *bioecological systems theory*, Bronfenbrenner's theory outlined the importance of the child's own biological environment as the key to their development, and stressed that it was the quality and context of these environments which will have the most significant influence on their development. He stated that the child's interaction with their environment is a complex one, a complexity which increases as the child matures and develops.

Besides his ecological systems theory, a lasting legacy left by Bronfenbrenner is the US Head Start programme, of which he was a co-founder. This programme arguably changed the lives of children and families living in poverty in the United States and was also responsible for the inception of similar programmes in other countries.

Bronfenbrenner used his ecological model to raise awareness of the potential problems which exist in an ever-changing society and provided a model by which those working with young people could begin to pre-empt these and, in doing so, provide an environment more conducive to healthy child development. He was a firm advocate of the family and their individual values and believed that the way forward was to nurture the developing child within the family structure. However, he also encouraged the notion that home and school should work closely together, suggesting that 'schools and teachers should work to support the primary relationship and to create an environment that welcomes and nurtures families' (Paquette and Ryan, 2001: 3).

Bronfenbrenner recognised that to fully understand human development it was important to consider the ecological system in which growth occurred, thus changing the nature of studies from a fragmented one to a holistic one. He urged all those who were part of a child's development to work together in the best interests of the child, and worked tirelessly to address some of the harmful influences which he believed modern-day society had encouraged.

GLOSSARY OF TERMS

Bioecological model

A model of human development proposed by Urie Bronfenbrenner and Stephen J. Ceci in 1994 as an extension of Bronfenbrenner's original ecological systems theory. The model examines the relationship between organisms and their interactions with the environment. The key focus for the work was on the individual which Bronfenbrenner believed had been overlooked in his original model.

Chronosystem

The final tier of Bronfenbrenner's ecological system's theory which encapsulates the key events that happen during a child's development, including life transitions and major historical and environmental events. According to Bronfenbrenner experience of such events will influence how the child interacts with future events.

Ecological systems theory

Theory developed by Urie Bronfenbrenner which attempts to explain how children are influenced by a range of different environmental factors as they grow and develop. Presented as a series of five consecutive circles with each one showing aspects of the environmental factors which influence development to different degrees.

Exosystem

The environmental setting which the child does not have active involvement in, but is influenced by nevertheless. For example, a parent may be forced to take a job away from home in times of high unemployment which might adversely affect the child.

Macrosystem

Relates to aspects of a child's culture which might influence growth and development. This usually relates to a child's heritage or identity as being part of a larger group with shared beliefs and culture.

Mesosystem

The second level of Bronfenbrenner's ecological system's theory which looks at the interactions between two microsystems. For example, a child's parents interacting with their teachers would be a mesosystem, thus building a bridge between two key aspects of a child's life.

Microsystem

This is the smallest part of the ecological systems theory, and the one which is the closest to the child. This then is the most influential in terms of the developing child and has the most direct influence. The microsystem includes family, schools, religious institutes, neighbours and peers.

Proximal processes

Reciprocated interactions between a child and their immediate external environment. According to Bronfenbrenner this might include interaction with people, the physical environment or objects within the environment, with such transactions driving development and contributing to the child's competences and general well-being.

 # FURTHER READING

Bronfenbrenner, U. (1974 [1970]) *Two Worlds of Childhood: US and USSR.* London: Penguin.

In this Bronfenbrenner compares two aspects of childhood, in Russia and America, showing how cross-cultural research can be used to gain a better understanding of childhood.

Bronfenbrenner, U. (ed.) (2005) *Making Human Beings Human: Bioecological perspectives on human development.* London: Sage.

A series of works which present Bronfenbrenner's own thoughts on the bioecological theory of human development.

Frost, N. (2011) *Rethinking Children and Families: The relationship between children, families and state.* London: Continuum.

An examination of the complex relationship between children, families and the state. The book draws on contemporary research to examine the changing face of childhood.

Gray, C. and MacBlain, S. (2015) *Learning Theories in Childhood* (Second Edition). London: Sage.

Chapter 7 (Bandura, Bronfenbrenner and social learning) explores the links between the theories.

Cairns, R.B., Elder, G.H. Jr and Costello, E.J. (eds) (1996) *Developmental Science*. Cambridge: Cambridge University Press.

Elder, G.H. Jr, Chapter 3 – Human lives in changing societies: life course and developmental insights – is an examination of the study of the life course as a means of studying human development. Elder offers an alternative but complementary theory to Bronfenbrenner's.

REFERENCES

Addison, J.T. (1992) Urie Bronfenbrenner. *Human Ecology, 20*(2), 16–20.

Bronfenbrenner, U. (1969) *Statement at Hearings before the Committee on Ways and Means,* House of Representatives. Washington DC: US Government Printing Office.

Bronfenbrenner, U. (1974 [1970]) *Two Worlds of Childhood: US and USSR*. London: Penguin.

Bronfenbrenner, U. (1977) Toward an experimental ecology of human development. *American Psychologist, 32*, 513–31.

Bronfenbrenner, U. (1979) *The Ecology of Human Development*. Cambridge, MA: Harvard University Press.

Bronfenbrenner, U. (1986) Ecology of the family as a context for human development: Research perspectives. *Developmental Psychology, 22*(6), 723–42.

Bronfenbrenner, U. (1989) Ecological Systems Theory. In: Vasta, R. (ed.) *Annals of Child Development, 6*, 187–249. Greenwich, CT: JAI Press.

Bronfenbrenner, U. (1993) The Ecology of Human Development: Research methods and fugitive findings. In: Wozniack R.H. and Fisher, K. (eds) *Scientific Environments*. Hillsdale, NJ: Lawrence Erlbaum. pp. 3–44.

Bronfenbrenner, U. (2007) *Making Human Beings Human*. Thousand Oaks, CA: Sage.

Bronfenbrenner, U. and Morris, P. (2007) The bioecological model of human development: Theoretical models of human development. *Handbook of Child Psychology, 1*, 14.

Bronfenbrenner, U., McClelland, P., Wethington, E., Mowen, P. and Ceci, S. (1996) *The State of Americans*. New York: Free Press.

Christensen, J. (2010) Proposed enhancement of Bronfenbrenner's development ecology model. *Education Inquiry, 1*(2), 101–10.

Damon, W. and Lerner, R.M. (2006) *Handbook of Child Psychology, Volume 1: Theoretical models of human development* (Sixth Edition). Chichester: Wiley.

Danner, F. (2009) *Bronfenbrenner, Urie 1917–2005 Biography*. Available from: www.education. com/reference/article/bronfenbrenner-urie-1917-2005 [accessed 10/03/18].

Department for Education (2017) *Statutory Framework for the Early Years Foundation Stage: Setting the standards for learning, development and care for children from birth to five years.* London: Department for Education.

Doherty, J. and Hughes, M. (2009) *Child Development: Theory and practice 0–11*. Harlow: Pearson.

Foley, P. and Leverett, S. (2008) *Connecting with Children: Developing working relationships*. Maidenhead: Open University Press.

Griffore, R.J and Phenice, L.A. (2016) Proximal processes and causality in human development. *European Journal of Educational and Developmental Psychology, 4*(1), 10–16.

Keating, D.P. and Hertzman, C. (eds) (1999) *Developmental Health and the Wealth of Nations: Social, biological and educational dynamics*. New York: Guilford.

Lang, S. (2014) Urie Bronfenbrenner, father of Head Start Program and pre-eminent 'human ecologist,' dies at age 88. *Cornell Chronicle*. Available from: www.news.cornell.edu/stories/2005/09/head-start-founder-urie-bronfenbrenner-dies-88 [accessed 10/03/18].

Lindon, J. (2007) *Understanding Child Development: Linking theory and practice*. Abingdon: Hodder Arnold.

MacBlain, S. (2014) *How Children Learn*. London: Sage.

Paquette, D. and Ryan, J. (2001) *Bronfenbrenner's Ecological Systems Theory*. Available from: http://pt3.nl.edu/paquetteryanwebquest.pdf [accessed 10/03/18].

Smith, P., Cowie, H. and Blades, M. (2011) *Understanding Children's Development* (Fifth Edition). Chichester: Wiley.

Tudge, J.R., Mokrova, I., Hatfield, B.E. and Karnick, R.B. (2009) Uses and misuses of Bronfenbrenner's bioecological theory of human development. *Journal of Family Theory and Review*, *1*, 198–210.

11
PAULO FREIRE

OPPRESSION, FREEDOM AND CRITICAL APPROACHES TO EDUCATION

LEARNING OUTCOMES

Having read this chapter you should be able to:

- appreciate the background and impact of Freire on critical approaches to education
- identify and understand his notions of dialogue, praxis, banking concept of education and problem-posing education
- apply the principles of problem-posing education in your practice
- critically evaluate his approach to education.

KEY WORDS

praxis; dialogue; conscientisation; banking concept of education; problem-posing education

INTRODUCTION

Paulo Freire (1921–97) was one of the most prominent thinkers and writers on education, specifically critical approaches to education. He was first recognised as an adult educator due to his radical and successful adult literacy programmes in his native Brazil. These programmes stemmed from Freire's deep conviction that education played a significant role in freeing people from oppression. His thoughts on critical education have since been applied, beyond the confines of adult literacy, to all sectors of informal and formal education. He possessed an unusual blend of Marxist ideology and a Christian ethos, which – together with a strong sense of social justice, clarity of intellectual thought and personal humility – made him one of the most important educational theorists of the twentieth and early twenty-first centuries. His concepts are still of significance today, particularly in a time of perceived international inequality in education (Apple et al., 2001).

Freire's earliest writing emerged from a radical viewpoint brought about by the frightening and helpless politically unstable situation in Brazil during the 1960s. Indeed, the military coup of 1964, as with a number of Brazilian activists and educators, led to Freire's imprisonment and exile. His writing and philosophy combines the extremes of the perils and futility of oppression with the delight and optimism in the possibilities that people and communities can achieve (Irwin, 2012). Apart from imprisonment and exile Freire had his work censored by a number of authoritarian governments of the time such as those of Chile, Argentina, Portugal and Spain, as well as apartheid South Africa (Schugurensky, 2014).

Although his earlier writings emerged from the political situation in Brazil, his work has had an impact throughout the world, influencing how education and, in particular, learning and teaching, is perceived. his major writing, *Pedagogy of the Oppressed* (first published in 1970, revised in 1996), has become a standard text for those studying education as a subject and for those undertaking teacher education programmes. It seeks to challenge the traditional processes and frameworks of education in order to enable those from disadvantaged groups in society to question the purpose of education. Even though his philosophy could be considered very radical in its approach, Freire managed to argue rationally and articulately, which in turn made it possible for him to communicate with others of contrasting ideologies. This ability to patiently listen and converse with others, despite holding very deep-seated radical convictions, allowed him to hold governmental roles in Brazil following his return from exile (Howlett, 2013).

Freire's educational theories were developed while working with underprivileged workers in north-eastern Brazil to develop their literacy. In doing this he created a method which drew from his own philosophy of education, which endeavoured to amalgamate teaching and learning with freedom. The features of his philosophy will be explored in greater depth further on in this chapter. These include: **praxis**, which is the practice of education informed by and based on values; the importance of

dialogue between students and teachers which is meaningful and based on mutual respect; and the significance of learners and teachers developing '**conscientisation**', which empowers both to change the world in the name of social justice. Finally, he criticised the traditional, oppressive and passive notion of education, which he termed the '**banking concept**', but promoted a more radical, reflective and active concept, which he called '**problem-posing**' education. To gain a true insight into factors that forged Freire's philosophy and his critical approach to education, we need to consider his upbringing and the political turmoil he struggled with in his career.

PAULO FREIRE, THE PERSON

From the start, Paulo Freire's own childhood in deprived and impoverished north-east Brazil made him aware of the reality of inequality and oppression. Although born into a relatively wealthy family, he and the rest of his family were to experience poverty when his father died when Freire was thirteen years old. This affected his own education, delaying the start of his secondary education until the age of sixteen. This unusual postponement in starting secondary education could have been, it is argued, the reason he regarded traditional and formal systems of education with a degree of suspicion (Irwin, 2012). The experience of living in poverty helped Freire to become acquainted with the language usage of the people he lived among. This also supported his future work as an adult literacy educator, moreover through the experience he witnessed the social inequalities of the poor. Freire's conversations with his father, a military police official, initiated his thoughts on social injustices and presented him with a political awareness at an early age (Schugurensky, 2014). It is suggested that what was mostly significant in forming his philosophy and perhaps contributed to his humble nature was his Catholic upbringing, nurtured by his mother's robust religious faith. Although he later confronted and condemned the more traditional Catholic Church when he felt it became an instrument of oppression, his ideal of Christianity was one of freedom and emancipation (Irwin, 2012). Freire started to study philosophy and sociology of language and then entered law school at the University of Pernambuco in 1943. After a short spell practising law he taught for six years at secondary school level before working as a welfare official. Then from 1947 until 1957 he was the director of Education and Culture of the Social Service of Industry (Schugurensky, 2014).

Freire's educational thinking emerged while developing adult literacy programmes with the workers and peasants in north-eastern Brazil, which became the focus of his doctoral thesis that he submitted to the University of Recife in 1959 (Spring, 1994). Following the success of these programmes the Brazilian Ministry of Education asked him to implement a national literacy scheme. This work was stopped during the 1964 military coup and he was arrested, imprisoned and then sent into exile to Chile. Nevertheless, he continued to develop his method of adult literacy in other parts of the world, in particular Latin America and Africa. During his time in exile he also advised UNESCO and the Department of Education of the World Council of Churches in Geneva. His work gained further influence in academia – he was offered a position at Harvard University and achieved acclaim and awards from numerous international universities who recognised his critical approach to education and his struggles against oppression (Apple et al., 2001).

Brazil declared an amnesty in 1979 and Freire and many other academics who were exiled were allowed to return. He first took up a lectureship at the Pontifical Catholic University of São Paulo and then at the University of Campinas. His long years in exile had not dampened his political activism and he joined the Workers' Party to advise them on matters of literacy and culture. When the Workers' Party were successful in the São Paulo municipal elections in 1989, Freire became Secretary of Education. During his tenure as Secretary he formulated and implemented many progressive educational policies, including revising and promoting adult and community education, restructuring of the curricula and making schools more democratic places of learning (Apple et al., 2001).

Following his time as Secretary of Education he gave lectures around the world and wrote numerous texts, all of which were well received. His thoughts remained very anti-oppression and political but increasingly personal and optimistic in nature. For example, *Pedagogy of Hope* (2004) revisits in a positive and encouraging manner the features of *Pedagogy of the Oppressed* and suggests a need for a continuation of the struggle to liberate, through education, the many who are still oppressed. Freire died in 1997, but his thoughts and philosophy remain. His main premise was that education is a political act. Furthermore, for many educators it is the clarity and the deep-seated ethos of social justice of his theories that continue to be influential.

FREIRE'S THEORIES

Before exploring the key features of Freire's theories we need to delve deeper into the origins of his educational practice and emerging philosophy, which developed from his work in adult literacy. For him literacy was more than merely imparting the physical and mental skills for reading and writing. It was a much more complex process, one that was liberating and lasted a lifetime:

> To be literate is not to have arrived at some pre-determined destination, but to utilise reading, writing and speaking skills so that our understanding of the world is progressively enlarged. Furthermore, literacy is not acquired neutrally, but in specific historical, social and cultural contexts. (Mackie, 1980: 1)

His idea was to popularise education and make literacy accessible, but in doing so to discard the traditional pedagogical methods used in schools. Freire and his teams of literacy practitioners set up what they called 'cultural circles' in the poor towns and villages around Recife. These cultural circles were purposely planned to be different from schools in both curricula and pedagogy. In place of teachers delivering information to passive learners, all were encouraged to exchange thoughts and take part in a dialogue of ideas that were considered by all to be of interest: 'topics for debates in the cultural circles included nationalism … illiteracy … [the] vote for illiterates, and democracy' (Bee, 1980: 39). These were topics which had a direct connection to the realities of their daily lives. Also, being involved in such topical themes and related problems allowed learners and teachers to be critically aware and seek the potential for action and transformation (Bee, 1980). From these origins in adult literacy Freire was convinced of the significance of dialogue, praxis and conscientisation in creating a critical and liberating problem-posing education, as opposed to the traditional 'banking' concept of education, which viewed the learner as a passive empty vessel to be filled with knowledge and information by a teacher.

Freire's concept of dialogue emerged from the cultural circles, where teachers and learners developed a mutually accepted vocabulary which enabled them to comprehend the social, economic and political influences that had created their level of existence. Such a dialogue is intended to increase the level of understanding between learner and teacher. To gain this understanding Freire felt it was important to observe the lives of the learners he and his teams worked with. The aim of these observations was to uncover the aspects of their lives which the learners considered important. The outcomes of these observations allowed teachers to begin a meaningful and critical educational dialogue. Furthermore, Freire stresses the importance of dialogue for teachers themselves, in that they learn more about the environment and culture they work in and how they themselves feel and think about the world (Spring, 1994). As such, dialogue is the start of a shared notion of learning. In Freire's words:

> The teacher is no longer merely the-one-who-teaches, but the one who is himself taught in dialogue with the students, who in turn while being taught also teach. (1996: 61)

Therefore, through dialogue, learning is based upon mutual respect between the learner and teacher with shared values and the need to act and transform the world. Such action was central to Freire's philosophy and he termed it praxis. Praxis, for Freire, was the need to act against oppression rather than simply criticise, 'which, in his terms, amounted to a passive legitimating of social inequality' (Howlett, 2013: 255). Action on its own was not a part of his notion of praxis. For Freire praxis required teachers not only to practise what they preached but also to underpin such action with reflection and theory, which in turn would give 'a dynamic example of teachers seeking practical wisdom' (hooks, 2003: x). Praxis is enabled by curious enquiry where knowledge is constructed and reconstructed, and allows learners to progress from a passive acceptance to a deeper understanding of the foundations of reality. This swing in awareness is affirmed by future involvement against oppression (Connolly, 1980).

Dialogue, praxis, and what Freire termed 'conscientisation', formed a foundation for constructing a pedagogical process which was embedded in the social, cultural and political realities of the learners and teachers. Conscientisation was the manner in which learners and teachers developed their consciousness, which would lead to decisions about pedagogy. Reading was central to the function of developing conscientisation. Freire argued that it was the process of learning to read which made it possible to better understand, and subsequently change, the world (Spring, 1994). Conscientisation was to be the catalyst which helped make decisions regarding pedagogy. In other words, what was to be learned, and in which way, was based upon dialogue, reflection and action, as well as theory. As such conscientisation 'allows for the building of programs *with* and *from* the communities rather than *for* them' (Torres, 2006: 543). These aspects of conscientisation were to bolster and give strength to Freire's critical problem-posing education in opposition to the traditional banking concept of education (Apple et al., 2001).

Freire felt that oppression was legitimised and sustained through the banking concept of education, a concept which is central to *Pedagogy of the Oppressed*. The underlying principle of banking education is the dominance of the oppressor over the oppressed, where learners are passive receivers of information delivered to them to memorise and regurgitate:

> In the banking concept of education, knowledge is a gift bestowed by those who consider themselves knowledgeable upon those they consider to know nothing. (Freire, 1996 [1970]: 53)

There are two interesting and topical aspects of Freire employing the banking metaphor here to describe this concept as an oppressive model of education. Firstly, he is using the vocabulary of conflict, one being the actor or the depositor (the teacher) and the other the passive receptacle (the learner). It becomes, therefore, apparent that he viewed the banking concept of education as unfair. Such inequity is also reflected in the world where access to knowledge and the educational choice of participation are determined by the oppressor (Howlett, 2013). Secondly, the vocabulary that links education and banking mirrors that used in an era of increasing austerity and the supremacy of market forces – that is, as we would deposit money in a bank, teachers deposit knowledge into their learners:

> Like banks, this share, is ultimately unequal with some (who are lacking). It is only those who are seen as being able to sufficiently repay the institutional investment (financially and intellectually) who will serve to gain from the system. Clearly a theory for the modern world! (Howlett, 2013: 257)

On a more practical level, the banking notion is typified by set curricula, such as the National Curriculum, and the content and pedagogy are prescribed and monitored by the government to ensure that teachers comply. The prescriptive and compliant nature of set curricula, Freire argued, stifles the natural curiosity, critical thinking skills and creativity of learners, which is abandoned in preference to an inflexible adherence to a socially established view of learning.

Freire offered problem-posing education as an alternative to the banking concept, which was steeped in his notions of dialogue, praxis and conscientisation. Problem-posing originated from the cultural circles for adult literacy and is connected to the needs and lives of the learners. The teachers' role is to pose problems to the learners regarding features of their lives. Both learners and teachers take part in a dialogue surrounding these problems and from that dialogue a range of recurrent words surface from the learners connected to their lives. The words that surface from the dialogue become the foundations of the learning and teaching of reading. Hence, there is a direct correlation between the process of learning to read and the manner in which the learner reads and thinks about the world (Spring, 1994).

A problem-posing teacher forms and re-forms their reflections through an ongoing dialogue with the learner:

> The students – no longer docile listeners – are now critical co-investigators in dialogue with the teacher ... Whereas banking education anaesthetizes and inhibits creative power, problem-posing education involves a constant unveiling of reality. The former attempts to maintain the *submersion* of consciousness; the latter strives for the *emergence* of consciousness. (Freire, 1996 [1970]: 62)

Therefore, problem-posing education is centred upon creativity, which encourages true reflection and action to transform the world. There is also an affirmation that education can be liberating – an ongoing and emergent activity where learners and teachers are in 'the process of *becoming* – as unfinished uncompleted beings in and with a likewise unfinished reality' (Freire, 1996 [1970]: 65). Problem-posing education was not only a notion which is in conflict with the banking concept but also one which, for Freire, offered hope for alleviating the situation for the oppressed of all social, cultural and racial backgrounds. He summed up the difference between banking education and problem-posing education: 'banking education treats students as objects of assistance; problem posing education makes them critical thinkers' (2007: 73). Such sentiments were shared by other educational thinkers, particularly humanists, social constructivists and those with radical or alternative viewpoints.

LINKS WITH OTHER THEORISTS

We have already noted how Freire was influenced by Christianity and by Marxism, both of which could be perceived as having contrasting ideologies, but he managed to incorporate facets of both philosophies into his work and life. Nevertheless, he was at odds with the more traditional aspects of the established Catholic Church. There are a number of other thinkers who are aligned with Freire or who were influenced by him. One with very similar ideas is Henry Giroux, a North American educational thinker and acclaimed founder of the notion of critical pedagogy. For Giroux it is important that learners understand the social structure of knowledge and that they are empowered to improve both the economic and social conditions of the world. At the centre of his critical pedagogy is the notion that learners should seek actions which promote social justice and break down the barriers of inequalities of power. Giroux has also supported the use of critical dialogue as part of teacher education programmes to help prepare student teachers for classroom practice (Spring, 1994).

There are also quite clear links between Freire and John Dewey, who both championed a democratic notion of teaching and learning and a child-centred and culturally-based approach to the curriculum. Moreover, Dewey, like Freire, was a critic of the traditional schooling system. Similarities with the social constructivist theories of Vygotsky, where learners are dynamically involved with teachers in developing knowledge, are also associated with Freire's notion of the learner as an activist. Freire's problem-posing education aligns closely with the socially situated learning theories of Lave and Wenger with their emphasis on culture, community and a shared vocabulary in the process of learning. Freire stressed that knowledge is historical and based upon the culture and language of the learner, which resonates fittingly with Bourdieu. Pierre Bourdieu's notion of cultural capital and social reproduction theory proposed that learners from disadvantaged and minority communities did not conform to the traditional 'norms' of society and, consequently, suffered oppression and social injustice. Freire's work with literacy and language is comparable with Basil Bernstein's theory of restricted and elaborate language codes. Bernstein argued that disadvantaged groups suffered if they did not communicate using the sophisticated elaborate language of the 'establishment' or that which was considered acceptable in the traditional school system.

Like A.S. Neil, the founder of the revolutionary Summerhill School, Freire maintained that children who grow up in an authoritarian home setting are prone later in their lives to accept dominance from authority and also have a tendency to dominate others (Spring, 1994). Another leading adult educator and humanist psychologist Carl Rogers agreed with Freire's thoughts concerning the need for the individual emancipation of learners from disfranchised social groups. Rogers' noteworthy books *On Becoming a Person* (1961) and *Freedom to Learn* (1969) have been standard texts used by teachers in adult education (Ecclestone, 2004). There are also links with prominent thinkers who focused on adult education. Malcolm Knowles' idea of andragogy and his emphasis on the importance of contextualising learning is similar to Freire's overall philosophy of adult education. Jack Mezirow argued that Freire's concept of conscientisation was closely aligned with his own radical notion of transformative learning. Finally, American feminist university educator bell hooks has employed much of the ethos of Freire's critical pedagogy in her own teaching. Interestingly, she is also one of his chief critics (Aubrey and Riley, 2017).

CRITIQUING FREIRE

Freire himself, true to his belief in the value of reflection, has critiqued his own work. *Pedagogy of Hope* (2004) revisited and revised his seminal *Pedagogy of the Oppressed* (1996 [1970]) to 'rethink', address and defend some of the criticism regarding the perceived politicisation of his writing. This willingness to be self-critical is exemplified and recognised by bell hooks: 'In so much of Paulo's work there is a generous spirit and quality of open-mindedness that I feel is often missing from intellectual and academic arenas' (hooks, 1994: 54). There has also been some comment about the relevance of his revolutionary stance and whether his notions on education can be transferred to other less chaotic regions of the world. For example, Moore argues that Freire's censure of the state educational system and his call for a more critical pedagogy are pointless as teachers are hindered by 'the rules, regulations and ideologies of the larger social system' (Moore, 2000: 154).

Freire has been criticised because of his sexist language. Indeed, the new revised 1996 edition of *Pedagogy of the Oppressed* (first published in 1970) was, according to its cover notes, 'modified to reflect the connection between liberation and inclusive language'. One of his main critics, among many feminist academics, was bell hooks. Freire and hooks formed a perplexing partnership because, although hooks abhorred his sexist language, she thought highly of his work and applied much of his philosophy in her own teaching. Furthermore, hooks accepted that Freire's notions on pedagogy and politics were closely connected with feminist thought (Irwin, 2012).

Apart from the sexist nature of Freire's language in his earlier work, there is also a view that the language was somewhat mystical and emotional in tone and style. However, his writing in later works, such as *Pedagogy of Hope* (2004) and *Teachers as Cultural Workers* (2005), was markedly more comprehensible (Smith, 2002). Freire tended to be quite one-sided in his arguments – his readers either supported the oppressed or were hostile to them. Although this might be seen as a clear and straightforward viewpoint, 'taken too literally it can make a rather simplistic (political) analysis' (Smith, 2002). There is the possible difficulty that because not all of his writing has been translated into English the wholeness of that writing cannot be fully analysed; there is also a risk that translation has obscured the meaning of his work (Schugurensky, 2014). Regardless of these criticisms, Freire's philosophy is one of emancipation and hope. In practice it is not suggested that teachers take a revolutionary stance to bring down what they may perceive to be an oppressive system, but should be aware of the signs of oppression so they are better able to challenge and manage the situation (Moore, 2000).

APPLYING FREIRE IN THE CLASSROOM

The 2005 book *Teachers as Cultural Workers* is a series of letters written conversationally in which Freire challenges teachers to critically reflect on their own meanings of learning and teaching. It explores and brings together the practical classroom implications of Freire's theories offered in *Pedagogy of the Oppressed* and in other works. He stresses that for teachers to become successful they need to be constantly dedicated to their own professional learning development and to reflect on their own classroom practice. His works have considerable commentary on features of classroom practice, such as the resistance to a banking concept of education, advice regarding problem-posing teaching, the role of the teacher and thoughts on the curriculum.

Freire considered that the purpose of education was to liberate and there should be mutual respect between the teachers and learners, who both have an equal role to play in the learning process. He argued that this was not to be achieved by adopting a banking concept of education. He set out the following attitudes and practices which exemplified banking education:

- The teacher teaches and the students are taught.
- The teacher knows everything and the students know nothing.
- The teacher thinks and the students are thought about.
- The teacher talks and the students listen – meekly.
- The teacher disciplines and the students are disciplined.
- The teacher chooses and enforces his choice, and the students comply.
- The teacher acts and the students have the illusion of acting through the action of the teacher.
- The teacher chooses the programme content, and the students (who are not consulted) adapt to it.
- The teacher confuses the authority of knowledge with his or her own professional authority, which he or she sets in opposition to the freedom of the students.
- The teacher is the Subject of the learning process, while the pupils are mere objects.

(Freire, 1996 [1970]: 54)

Teaching which embraces these practices and attitudes encourages learners to consent to a passive role enforced on them by the teacher, and hence gain only a 'fragmented view of reality deposited in them' (Freire, 1996 [1970]: 54).

Conversely, Freire argues for more dialogical problem-posing education. Learners are engaged with matters of their everyday lives to challenge and resolve issues that are important to them. They are actively involved in the process of deciding topics for discussion and the planning sessions. The teacher's role in this is to help learners create a critical aptitude and encourage the learners' historic and cultural backgrounds to help stimulate the content to be studied. Problem-posing education promotes the natural curiosity in learners. According to Freire, curiosity together with the use of critical readings are core to dialogic teaching. Without the use of curiosity and critical readings teachers are not truly dialogic, but 'instead [engaged] in a process of conversation without the ability to turn the shared experience and stories into knowledge' (Freire and Macedo, 1999: 51).

bell hooks has employed Freire's dialogical problem-posing pedagogy successfully in multicultural classrooms. She approaches each teaching session with the notion of building an active 'community' to generate an environment of openness and scholarly depth. In doing so she feels that this community creates a collective wish to learn from others and makes possible the 'magic that is always present when individuals are active learners' (hooks, 2003: 43). Her views are very inclusive and in keeping with Freire's notion of education being emancipating:

> One way to build a community in the classroom is to recognise the value of each individual voice. In my classes, students keep journals and often write paragraphs during class which we read to one another. This happens at least once irrespective of the class size. (hooks, 1994: 40)

This practical guidance is aligned with that of Freire, who also encouraged the notion of empowering learners by building knowledge through communities. This in turn can help learners to be transformed from a passive reliance on the teacher's knowledge. In fact the teacher, from Freire's experience with cultural circles, was 'no longer necessary because the community members have acquired their own expertise' (Freire, 2005: xix).

Freire was an opponent of the traditional standardised curriculum where the content of what was to be learned and the manner in which it was to be taught were prescribed by others. For him learning was most effective when learners were involved in the forming of their own educational aspirations by making curriculum choices. It is recognised that educators working within the restraints of standard curricula have little flexibility in allowing learners to make radical choices. However, one possible, if somewhat diluted, resolution is for the teacher to take time to know about the lives of the learners. As far as possible the curriculum should be pertinent and take into account the interests, culture and history of individual learners. Furthermore, the language used needs to be in tune with, and understandable by, the learners, so the language employed by the teacher 'demands an understanding of the structural conditions in which thought and language of the students are dialectally framed' (Connolly, 1980: 80).

Although Freire stresses the mutual relationship between teachers and learners, he does acknowledge that the teacher has a clear directional role to give clarity and to help learners become involved in the dialogical process. It is undeniable that Freire is a passionate student-centred teacher – he talks about the 'joy' and 'love' of teaching – but he also argues that 'teaching is not coddling' (Freire, 2005: 27). Neither does he shy away from the demands, and rewards, faced by teachers and learners alike in the process of study in 'which we encounter pain, pleasure, victory, defeat, doubt, and happiness' (Freire, 2005: 52). Before we close this section, let us reflect on the type of teacher he perceived himself to be:

> I am a teacher who stands up for what is right against what is indecent, who is in favour of freedom against authoritarianism ... I am the teacher who favours the permanent struggle against every form of bigotry and against the economic domination of individuals and social class ... I am the teacher full of spirit of hope, in spite of all the signs to the contrary. (Freire, 1998: 94)

It is acknowledged that some of his notions of education are quite idealistic and difficult to put into practice, particularly within the constraints of formally structured curricula. However, the struggle for social justice in our classrooms is a worthy cause. As already mentioned, there are some ways in which we can apply those theories in practice. As Moore (2000) has advised, even if we cannot apply these ideas in our own practice, we should be aware of the signs of oppression and hence be better able to challenge and manage the situation.

REFLECTIVE TASK

Freire argued that as educators we should not adopt a banking concept in our practice. In *Pedagogy of the Oppressed* (1996 [1970]: 54) he set out a list of ten attitudes and practices which typified banking education. Three are listed below:

- The teacher talks and the students listen – meekly.
- The teacher chooses and enforces his choice, and the students comply.
- The teacher is the Subject of the learning process, while the pupils are mere objects.

Reflecting upon your own practice and having an understanding of Freire's theories, what can you do and how can you counteract these three attitudes and practices?

SUMMARY

Freire's radical philosophy was, and still is, of great significance to educators throughout the world. Although his notions of critical pedagogy are applicable to all sectors of education, originally they were formed during his revolutionary and successful adult literacy programmes in Brazil. Freire held a strong belief that education was a significant factor in freeing people from oppression. This belief was firmly set within a political perspective based upon his own struggles and persecution in Brazil during a time of conflict and instability. The chief features of his educational philosophy were set out in his seminal *Pedagogy of the Oppressed* (1996 [1970]). His philosophy challenged the traditional banking concept of education, which he considered to be oppressive. Instead he called for a more critical libertarian problem-posing education which embedded dialogue, praxis and conscientisation.

Influenced by Christianity and Marxism, Freire's ideas can be associated with many other educational thinkers, particularly those concerned with social justice. One who is very similar in his ideas is Giroux, who established the concept of critical pedagogy with its emphasis on empowerment and the quest that education should be transformational. Dewey's criticism of traditional schooling and his emphasis on the importance of culture in the learning process strikes a chord with Freire's philosophy as well. There are also strong correlations with the socially situated learning concepts of Lave and Wenger, specifically with the significance of learning communities. Others with comparable ideas regarding the worth of culture and language are Bourdieu and Bernstein. Two others who epitomise Freire's views on authority and the need for mutual respect between learner and teacher are the radical educator A.S. Neill and the humanist Carl Rogers. There are also links between thinkers who have focused on adult education such as Knowles, Mezirow and bell hooks.

There has been a fair amount of criticism of Freire's ideas. This focuses on his sexist, mystical and emotional language, which was particularly evident in his early works. There has also been some negative evaluation that some of his writing is overly one-sided, simplistic and political in its nature. Furthermore, some of his ideas are quite difficult to put into practice in a time of standardised curricula and an environment of regulations and compliance. However, Freire's spirit of educational freedom against oppression and his democratic approach to teaching and learning deserve practical consideration – even if this is in the form of being aware of the indications of oppression.

GLOSSARY OF TERMS

Banking concept of education

The process of learners passively accumulating knowledge which is delivered by the teacher. The underpinning principle being the dominance of the oppressor over the oppressed; where learners accept as a gift, from professed educated teachers, information they are given to memorise and regurgitate.

Conscientisation

The way in which learners and teachers cultivate their consciousness, leading to the choices they both make regarding the adoption of methods of learning and teaching. Core to developing conscientisation is reading. The process of learning to read enables learners to understand and consequently transform their lives.

Dialogue

The fundamental basis of dialogue is the mutual respect between teachers and learners, a respect which is embedded in their cultural backgrounds. Learners and teachers foster a mutually agreed vocabulary so they can understand the social, economic and political drivers that have shaped their lives. Teachers need to understand the environment and the culture of the learners, and what they value, so they can begin a deep and critical learning experience. In doing this the teacher also becomes the one who is being taught through dialogue.

Praxis

The idea of a functional connection between theory and the world people live in, so they can be proactive in making changes and improvements in their lives. Being proactive also requires teachers to practise what they teach and support their actions with theory and reflection. Praxis is reinforced through a questioning approach to learning where knowledge is constructed and reconstructed; learners adopt a more active and critical way of understanding the world.

Problem-posing education

A concept in direct opposition to the established banking concept of education (see above). Evolving from the cultural aspects of adult literacy, it is closely associated with the lives of the learners where teachers pose problems to the learners relating to their social environments. Teachers and learners both engage in a dialogue about these problems. The words that emanate from the dialogue become the foundations of the learning and teaching of reading. Through this process learners become active, creative inquisitors in tandem with the teachers, and the teachers form and reform their reflections through the continuous dialogue process.

 ## FURTHER READING

Freire, P. (1985) *The Politics of Education: Culture, power, and liberation*. London: Bergin & Garvey.

An anthology of Freire's unpublished writing in English. The work affirms his political and activist stance of education being transformational.

Morrow, R. and Torres, C. (2002) *Reading Freire and Habermas: Critical pedagogy and transformative social change*. London: Teachers College Press.

This comprehensive text examines Freire's philosophy, particularly regarding issues of culture and power and the implications for practice.

REFERENCES

Apple, M., Gandin, L. and Hypolito, A. (2001) Paulo Freire, 1921–97. In: Palmer, J. (ed.) *Fifty Modern Thinkers on Education*. Abingdon: Routledge.

Aubrey, K. and Riley, A. (2017) *Understanding and Using Challenging Educational Theories*. London: Sage.

Bee, B. (1980) The Politics of Literacy. In: Mackie, R. (ed.) *Literacy and Revolution: The pedagogy of Paulo Freire*. London: Pluto.

Connolly, R. (1980) Freire, Praxis and Education. In: Mackie, R. (ed.) *Literacy and Revolution: The pedagogy of Paulo Freire*. London: Pluto.

Ecclestone, K. (2004) The Rise of Low Self-esteem and the Lowering of Educational Expectations. In: Hayes, D. (ed.) *The RoutledgeFalmer Guide to Key Debates in Education*. London: RoutledgeFalmer.

Freire, P. (1996 [1970]) *Pedagogy of the Oppressed*. London: Penguin.

Freire, P. (1998) *Pedagogy of Freedom: Ethics, democracy, and civic courage*. Lanham, MA: Rowman & Littlefield.

Freire, P. (2004) *Pedagogy of Hope*. London: Continuum.

Freire, P. (2005) *Teachers as Cultural Workers*. Cambridge, MA: Westview.

Freire, P. (2007) Banking v. Problem-solving Models of Education. In: Curran, R. (ed.) *Philosophy of Education: An Anthology*. Oxford: Blackwell.

Freire, P. and Macedo, D. (1999) Pedagogy, Culture, Language, and Race: A dialogue. In: Leach, J. and Moon, B. (eds) *Learners and Pedagogy*. London: Paul Chapman.

hooks, b. (1994) *Teaching to Transgress: Education as the practice of freedom*. New York: Routledge.

hooks, b. (2003) *Teaching Community: A pedagogy of hope*. New York: Routledge.

Howlett, J. (2013) *Progressive Education: A critical introduction*. London: Bloomsbury.

Irwin, J. (2012) *Paulo Freire's Philosophy of Education*. London: Continuum.

Mackie, R. (ed.) (1980) *Literacy and Revolution: The pedagogy of Paulo Freire*. London: Pluto.

Moore, A. (2000) *Teaching and Learning: Pedagogy, curriculum and culture*. London: RoutledgeFalmer.

Rogers, C.R. (1961) *On Becoming a Person*. New York: Houghton Mifflin.

Rogers, C.R. and Freiberg, H.J. (1969) *Freedom to Learn*. Columbus, OH: Merrill.

Schugurensky, D. (2014) *Paulo Freire*. London: Bloomsbury.

Smith, K. (2002) Paulo Freire and Informal Education. In: *The Encyclopaedia of Informal Education*. Available from: http://infed.org/mobi/paulo-freire-dialogue-praxis-and-education [accessed 10/03/18].

Spring, J. (1994) *Wheels in the Head: Education philosophies of authority, freedom, and culture from Socrates to Paulo Freire*. Maidenhead: McGraw-Hill.

Torres, C. (2006) Democracy, Education, and Multiculturalism: Dilemmas of Citizenship in a Global World. In: Lauder, H., Brown, P., Dillabough, J-A. and Halsey, A.H. (eds) *Education, Globalization and Social Change*. Oxford: Oxford University Press.

12
DONALD SCHÖN

REFLECTION AND LEARNING

LEARNING OUTCOMES

Having read this chapter you should be able to:

- understand Schön's theories of reflection-in-action and reflection-on-action
- understand the difference between espoused theory and theory-in-action
- recognise how his work can be applied in a practical situation
- critically evaluate his work.

KEY WORDS

reflection-in-action; reflection-on-action; learning society; double-loop learning; reflective practice; reflection; espoused theory; theory-in-use

INTRODUCTION

Donald Schön made a major contribution to developing our understanding of learning and its various processes through his introduction of the practices of **reflection-in-action** and **reflection-on-action**, alongside the notions of a **learning society** and **double-loop learning**. His work encouraged practitioners to critically reflect on their own work as a means of developing and improving their practice and, in so doing, 'touched numerous disciplines and professional practices' (Pakman, 2000: 5). Despite his early training as a philosopher, Schön made valuable contributions in a range of workplace settings, including a management consulting firm, a governmental agency, a non-profit centre for social development and a university department of urban planning, leading him to refer to himself as 'a displaced professional' (Waks, 2001: 37). It was through this vast experience that Schön began to postulate the notion that improvement comes about through reframing professional practice and identifying the importance of self-reflection as a vehicle for learning and improvement. At the same time, he also observed that this was often sadly lacking within organisations.

Influenced by John Dewey's 'theory of inquiry', Schön spent his early academic years examining learning and its cognitive tools (Pakman, 2000). He cautioned that Dewey's work should not be accepted uncritically (Waks, 2001) but instead sought to 'rethink and reconnect' Dewey (Schön, 1983: 357). Both Schön and Dewey saw reflective practice as an alternative to technical rationality, suggesting that the knowledge and experience of the practitioner, rather than science, should be the driving force behind **reflective practice**. However, while Dewey still saw a place for scientific enquiry as an intermediary stage in professional practice, Schön himself saw no place for science, suggesting that 'practice is a knowledge affair' (Waks, 2001: 40).

Schön emphasised the importance of recognising the knowledge of the professional as being key to the development of any organisation. He believed that the practitioner applied a tacit knowledge to any given situation, which he referred to as knowledge-in-action, and suggested that this formed the basis of any future reflections which in turn led to improvements in practice. His work, then, put the onus back on the professionals rather than the organisation's management, with Schön suggesting that any changes made should be a direct result of interactions and reflections within the workforce since those professionals have the best working practices of the organisation.

His work has had significant practical application in numerous organisations, including educational settings, which will form the basis for this chapter. Schön saw the school setting as an ideal platform for that work since he recognised that teachers had a significant amount of knowledge which was frequently constrained by the systems which controlled educational establishments. This will be elaborated on in subsequent sections.

DONALD SCHÖN, THE PERSON

Donald Schön was born in 1930 in Boston, in the United States, and was raised in Brookline and Worcester, Massachusetts. Schön studied philosophy at Yale University, graduating in 1951. He also studied the piano and clarinet at the Sorbonne, Paris, and the Conservatoire Nationale de Musique, and was awarded the Premier Prix. He was an accomplished musician and played in jazz and chamber groups. It was through this musical improvisation that he began to consider its application in a professional situation, through a practitioner's ability to 'think on their feet'. He also used his musical background as a metaphor for his observations on **reflection**.

Schön completed a BA in philosophy at Yale University, and on graduating he received the Woodrow Wilson Fellowship and went on to study for his Master's and Doctoral degrees in philosophy at Harvard University. It was during his doctoral studies that he became interested in the work of John Dewey, using Dewey's 'theory of inquiry' as a focus for his doctoral dissertation. It was this work which provided him with the pragmatic framework that can be seen as a constant through his subsequent work.

Schön spent a brief period working as an academic, teaching philosophy at the University of California, Los Angeles, followed by a period as Assistant Professor of Philosophy at the University of Kansas City; he also spent two years from 1955 in the US Army. On completion of his two years' Army service Schön took up a post as a senior staff member in a large industrial research and consulting firm, Arthur D. Little Inc., where he worked alongside his colleague Raymond Hainer, with whom he began to develop his early ideas on the structure and effectiveness of organisations. It was during this time that his first seminal work, entitled *Displacement of Concepts* (1963), was published. This was later republished as *The Invention and Evolution of Ideas* in 1967. Through this work he examined 'the ways in which categories are used to examine "things" but are not themselves examined as ways of thinking' (Parlett, 1991, in Pakman, 2000: 3).

This book was the first of many publications by Schön, who used his experience in a variety of organisations to examine the effectiveness of structural organisation. In his writing he encouraged organisations to look at things anew and he became fascinated by learning and its cognitive tools. He saw reflection as being an essential component in the learning process, but also identified that reflection was frequently lacking in organisations and questioned why this might be. In 1970 he was invited to deliver the Reith Lectures in London where he examined how learning occurs within organisations and societies which are in a permanent state of flux. This provided the catalyst for his groundbreaking book, *Beyond the Stable State* (1973), in which he argued that change was a fundamental part of modern life and, as such, it was imperative that organisations developed systems which were capable of learning and adapting to such changes.

In 1968 Schön became a visiting professor at the Massachusetts Institute of Technology (MIT) where he was later appointed Ford Professor of Urban Studies and

Education. He remained at MIT for the rest of his professional career until his death in 1997, serving as Chair of the Department of Urban Studies and Planning and later becoming Ford Professor Emeritus and Senior Lecturer in the School of Architecture and Planning.

It was during his time at MIT that Schön began his collaboration with Chris Argyris, a period that proved to be fruitful in terms of further writing and research, resulting in three key publications: *Theory in Practice: Increasing professional effectiveness* (Argyris and Schön, 1974), *Organizational Learning: A theory of action and perspective* (Argyris and Schön, 1978) and *Organizational Learning II: Theory, method and practice* (Argyris and Schön, 1996). These publications continued the themes which emerged in *Beyond the Stable State*, particularly around learning processes in organisations and the development of critical self-reflection as a means of operating in a more effective manner.

Schön's time at MIT also provided the catalyst for the work for which he is perhaps best known, that of processes and development of the reflective practitioner, leading him to 'develop an overall epistemology of professional practice, based on the concept of knowledge-in-action' (Pakman, 2000: 6). Evaluating the work of a range of practitioners in the field, Schön observed that such professionals demonstrated a capacity to reflect-in-action (that is, apply their knowledge to any given situation) and make any necessary adjustments to their practice in increasingly complex, uncertain and unique situations. He postulated that this was effective not just when acting in isolation but also when professionals had the opportunity to share their reflective practice, which would allow them to reconstruct theories of action and develop new strategies. These theories were expanded on in his book *The Reflective Practitioner: How professionals think in action* (1983), in which he continued to advocate the importance of a *reflective practicum*. It is this work that has perhaps had the most significant influence on professional development, particularly in the education sector, where the notion of reflective practice through training and development programmes has become firmly engrained.

SCHÖN'S THEORY OF REFLECTION AND LEARNING

We have already touched upon the notion that Schön's theories centre on his desire to support organisations in managing learning and change, particularly through the vehicle of self-reflection, and in this section we will consider further these theories of reflection and the important role of the individual within this. It should be noted that this captures only a small part of his theories, but due to the intended audience for this text it is the theories deemed the most relevant to the education profession which will be covered here.

When considering school effectiveness Schön identified a series of interrelated concepts which should be applied in assisting settings to become more reflective and therefore more effective. He recognised that within the school community there was a significant knowledge base which practitioners subconsciously applied to their everyday actions. This he referred to as tacit knowledge – the knowledge that an individual has which is both automatic and intuitive. He believed that this knowledge was reflected in the actions of the individual and coined the phrase *knowing-in-action* to explain this, suggesting that this is the knowledge that the practitioner holds within themselves to enable them to perform their daily activities effectively. However, Schön (1987) also observed that this tacit knowledge was often difficult to make verbally explicit, suggesting that while knowledge was clearly evident through actions, few practitioners were able to verbalise why certain actions had been taken, suggesting unconscious knowledge or in some cases unarticulated common sense revealed through action (Ghaye and Ghaye, 1998). In addition, he recognised that practitioners do not simply utilise someone else's theories but instead hold and develop their own theories – a particularly relevant skill when considering the importance of tailoring theories at an individual level.

It is important to consider at this stage a further theory which Schön advanced, that of technical rationality. Here he suggested a possible conflict between theory and practice, with the risk of the teacher becoming a mere technician, delivering content generated in higher educational establishments and research centres which may or may not be applicable to their particular setting and audience. He identified that teachers' practical, first-hand knowledge risks being devalued if they unquestioningly apply this theory to practice without considering the context of their own individual setting. Where they fail to question the values that underpin their practice and make them the teachers, this results in their being seen as technicians who simply deliver content (Ghaye and Ghaye, 1998).

Schön saw real problems with this approach to teaching, particularly given the varying contexts for which the theory might apply. He recognised that it was not possible to solve teaching problems by simply applying someone else's theory, and suggested that the application of theoretical knowledge may not be appropriate to the vast majority of problems experienced by teachers, cautioning against underestimating the first-hand knowledge and experience of the teaching profession. Ghaye and Ghaye explain that:

> Schön turns this technical–rational view around and talks about how reflection helps us to pose or 'frame' problems, how we should value and use this kind of knowledge that is embedded in our workplace, generated by our practice and shared among teachers themselves. (1998: 4)

Schön described *reflective practice* as 'a dialogue of thinking and doing through which I become more skilful' (1987: 31), suggesting a process by which thought is linked to action (Osterman, 1990). However, Argyris and Schön (1974) also identified that practitioners frequently needed support in framing their reflections, often being unaware of where theory was being applied to practice or how reflections could support the development of learning. They saw reflective practice as an integral part of a person's professional development, suggesting that reflection required concentration and careful consideration.

Schön identified two specific types of reflection undertaken by practitioners in the field, these being *reflection-in-action* and *reflection-on-action*. His distinction here is that a person who reflects on action is reflective and thoughtful, while one who reflects-in-action is reflexive (Thompson and Thompson, 2008). Reflecting-in-action first embodies the idea of 'thinking on one's feet', whereby the experienced practitioner consciously evaluates a situation and makes any necessary changes on the spot during the event. This relates specifically to uncertainty or unfamiliar situations, whereby an unanticipated circumstance is acknowledged and addressed with the minimum of fuss. As explained by Schön:

> The practitioner allows himself to experience surprise, puzzlement, or confusion in a situation which he finds unusual or unique. He reflects on the phenomenon before him, and on the prior understandings which have been implicit in his behaviour. He carries out an experiment which serves to generate both a new understanding of the phenomena and a change in the situation. (1983: 68)

It is the experienced practitioner with a wealth of knowledge and experience who Schön believed is able to deal with this type of situation most effectively. However, he also suggested that a person who has spent a long time doing the same job in the same way may be at risk of missing opportunities to think about what they are doing and may repeat the same errors over and over, suggesting that even when situations occur as expected a level of reflection should still be encouraged.

In addition to this process of reflection-in-action Schön suggested that thinking on one's feet should be later followed up with reflection-on-action, a process to be undertaken after the event. He argued that this may be done through recording an event, or discussing what happened with a colleague. The act of reflecting-on-action enables the practitioner to consider what happened and evaluate how effective the action was. This in turn supports the practitioner in their professional development, since reflections should form a bank of ideas which the practitioner may draw upon in their future practice. Schön also suggested that such reflections are best undertaken at a wider level in order that shared experiences might assist in whole-school improvement.

Argyris and Schön (1974) saw this shared reflection as being an important part of the developmental process for organisations, and they were interested in the contradictions they saw in workplace settings which might hinder effective reflective practice (Lindon, 2014). They identified two conflicting underpinning theories: that of **espoused theory**, the outlook and values on which people believe they base their behaviour; and **theory-in-use**, the outlook and values that are actually seen working in practice (Lindon, 2014). Argyris and Schön observed that there was frequently a gap between what people believed they did and what they actually did, which appeared to be a result of the conflict between the governing variables of the institution and those of the individual.

Since all situations require an action resulting in a consequence, Argyris and Schön (1974) suggested that reflections should be based around the processes of governing variables, action strategies and consequences. Here they coined the phrases *single loop learning* and *double-loop learning*, suggesting that in single loop learning reflection is centred around the action and consequence, whereby changes occur in response to the action taken when an unexpected situation occurs. In contrast, in double-loop learning the practitioner returns to the governing variables and examines whether changes need to be made at this level before considering alternative actions. Schön argued that, while this is the most desired model, it is not always possible if the organisation itself is not willing to examine and change its fundamental beliefs. This will be examined further when we explore how his theory might be applied to practice.

LINKS WITH OTHER THEORISTS

As we have seen previously, Schön built on Dewey's work in his doctoral thesis. As such, links between the two theories can be clearly seen. Dewey saw reflection as a rational and purposeful act, which was directly linked to thought. For him reflection was an active process in which prior belief and assumptions were examined and then used in future practice. However, Dewey applied a somewhat scientific approach to the reflection process in which various phases or aspects of thought should be viewed as part of the reflection process, including elaboration, hypothesis and action. Schön rejected this notion, believing there to be no place for science in the reflection process, suggesting instead that it should be a more natural and fluid process.

Perhaps the disparity here lies in the underlying beliefs regarding the purpose of reflective practice. For Dewey, reflection supports the practitioner in the development of democratic principles, whereas for Schön, reflection has a far more practical purpose, helping the practitioner to learn from and address complex problems experienced in the workplace. In this respect parallels can be seen with the work of David Kolb, who also sought a theory which was designed to offer solutions to everyday problems. In Kolb's model the process by which adults learn from their experience is elaborated on by way of a four-stage learning cycle, suggesting that learning is a cycle which perpetuates more learning. However, where Kolb suggested four phases of learning from experience – concrete experience, reflective observation, abstract conceptualisation and active experimentation – Schön identified only two processes – that of reflection-in-action and reflection-on-action – suggesting a much simpler and more practical approach.

In recent years Boud et al. (1985) have elaborated on the theories of Dewey and Schön, but they have also gone further and add another dimension to the reflection process which Schön largely ignored: the importance of emotion in the reflection process. Boud et al. have gone so far as to question the validity of a reflective process in which human emotion is ignored entirely and suggest that reflection is an activity in which people 'recapture their experience, think about it, mull it over and evaluate it' (Boud et al., 1985: 19). They have identified three key aspects to the reflection process: recalling or detailing salient events in a specific experience, attending to their feelings regarding the event and, finally, evaluating the experience in the light of existing knowledge whilst integrating new knowledge into an existing schema. We can see here parallels between Schön's work in terms of recalling and evaluating an event – reflection-on-action – but he made no reference to the feelings which came into play during the experience.

CRITIQUING SCHÖN

Schön's work was not without its critics and we have already seen that Boud et al. (1985) were critical of a model of reflective practice which did not account for the feelings and emotions of the practitioner at the time of the experience, since a person's emotional response to a situation will surely impact on their action. As each emotional response could potentially result in a different action, this must be taken into consideration when using reflection as part of the learning process.

A further criticism of his work relates to the distinction between reflection-in-action and reflection-on-action, with both Eraut (1994) and Usher et al. (1997) suggesting that he failed to make clear what is actually involved in the reflection process, resulting in work which lacked clarity and precision (Finlay, 2008). Thompson and Thompson (2008) acknowledge that Schön did draw a distinction between reflection-on-action (reflective) and reflection-in-action (reflexive). However, where Schön saw the reflective process as one which was thoughtful as opposed to reflexivity being self-aware and influencing the process, Thompson and Thompson (2008) believe the two should not be separated, suggesting that both encompass being thoughtful and self-aware. They state, 'in our view, reflective practice needs to be reflective in both senses of the word: thoughtful (analytical and well-informed) as well as self-aware or "reflexive"' (2008: 20), and propose that reflective practice is a dimension of reflexive practice.

Eraut (1994) suggests that Schön failed to take into consideration the time factor when developing his theories, arguing that good reflection is a time-consuming process and practitioners often have to make decisions in a hurried manner, leaving little time for effective reflection. Furthermore, Harris (1989) observes that Schön's reflection-in-action offered no place for technical or scientific knowledge in the reflections undertaken by teachers, and that while a starting place for reflection may well be through experiences, examples and observations, she cautions that there should still be a place for the explanatory theories which underpin practice.

There is some debate as to how far Schön's theories really impact on practice, with Richardson (1990: 14) suggesting that, as his theories are 'a descriptive concept, quite empty of content', there is no evidence to suggest that the reflections carried out by practitioners either in or on action have supported them directly in improving practice. This is further emphasised by the fact that Schön does not appear to have reflected on his own theories in order to ascertain the accuracy of his assumptions. Finally, Moon (2009) raises the question of the practicalities surrounding reflection-in-action and suggests that there is little difference between reflecting in and on action, since by stopping an activity in order to make adjustments the practitioner is then automatically reflecting-on-action. She also suggests that such adaptations are part and parcel of the practitioner's cognitive abilities and, as such, require no specific terminology to explain the process. This supports the earlier observation that it is not Schön's theories which are open to criticism, rather his ability to articulate and define meaning.

APPLYING SCHÖN IN THE CLASSROOM

Schön believed that skilled practitioners are reflective practitioners who use their experience as a basis for assessing existing theories and their observations to develop new theories (Osterman, 1990). He developed his theory by suggesting that it is the practitioner's ability to deal with unexpected or unexplained phenomena which truly reveals their ability to think on their feet and reflect-in-action, making any necessary adjustment to practice to counteract such events, and later reflecting on the effectiveness of this in order to build on and develop their skills as practitioners.

We can see, then, how Schön's theory should fit comfortably into an educational establishment, where teachers are frequently faced with an unpredictable audience alongside constant change through government agendas and changing school policy. It is not surprising, therefore, that his work was seen echoed in a growing focus on self-reflection in professional development programmes (Osterman, 1990). However, Osterman (1990) also observes that schools traditionally fall short of encouraging reflective practice, since reflection frequently results in critical thinking and innovation which is not necessarily valued in school settings.

In considering why this might be the case we need to return to the earlier discussion on technical rationality. Ghaye and Ghaye (1998) argue that schools have become guided by results-driven, standardised curricula which leave little room for teacher creativity and in which the necessity for teacher reflection is limited by the requirement to deliver a prescribed curriculum – in this scenario the teacher really does become the technician. Additionally, when considering the conflict between espoused theory and theory-in-action, there may well be a tension between the governing variables in an educational setting, which may well be in conflict with individuals' own guiding principles and perhaps in turn impact on the effectiveness of reflection.

However, setting aside these potential barriers, reflection is in fact a fundamental part of practice in schools. Limitations may well be observed at whole-school level as a vehicle for change, but individually, the most effective teachers undertake reflective practice as a matter of course in their everyday practice. Whether through a whole-school agenda or at an individual level there is a genuine desire to improve quality for the individual, and reflection-on-practice is a vehicle by which the quality of teaching and learning can be developed further. In practice, this may be as straightforward as evaluating the effectiveness of a session plan in terms of pupil outcome or undertaking an assessment at the end of a module to evaluate the effectiveness of a series of sessions. At each level the key to self-reflection is the practitioner's ability to consider the reasons why sessions were effective so the same might be repeated, but, more importantly, evaluating less successful sessions and asking themselves the more difficult question of 'What went wrong?' so as not to repeat mistakes. This self-reflection should not be seen as navel-gazing but a genuine attempt to build on good practice.

We have also seen that Schön did not believe reflection should be confined to happening after an event and perhaps of more importance to him was the notion of reflection-in-action – making necessary adjustments to actions during the event itself. Schön thought that this action celebrated the art of teaching, allowing for continual interpretation, investigation and internal conversation, and also allowing the teacher to apply existing knowledge to new situations (Sellars, 2013). Reflection-in-action involves a certain amount of self-confidence and experience since it requires the teacher, in some instances, to change a course of action midway through a teaching session or planned course of action. For example, if learners are not meeting the desired learning outcomes it may be necessary for the teacher to return to the basics before proceeding. Alternatively, if learners are finding that the work lacks challenge, then a course of action needs to be taken to ensure that they are able to proceed at a more appropriate level.

Such adaptations require a great deal of skill and mastery and Schön acknowledged the importance of the experience of the teacher as a source of knowledge for such action to be taken. Successful reflection-in-action requires a certain level of confidence and competence, but when carried out effectively provides the teacher with a degree of satisfaction and, if followed by reflection-on-action, a growing bank of ideas for future practice.

Of course, much of the reflection that occurs at an individual level is carried out subconsciously and, as previously discussed, Schön (1987) recognised that teachers frequently find it difficult to articulate what they did and why. For many it is a case of applying common sense. Osterman (1990) suggests that for reflective practice to be effective there needs to be a mindful consideration of one's actions, specifically those related to professional actions, but Schön observed that some professionals are resistant to thinking about what they did and why, suggesting that this may in fact paralyse action (Lindon, 2014).

In this respect there may be an argument for schools encouraging a more whole-school approach to reflection, since engaging in dialogue about practice may encourage practitioners to verbalise their actions and share good practice. Scott (2008) suggests that knowledge is frequently embedded as a result of previous experience, in which case discussing practice with others will allow the practitioner to rethink their actions and re-evaluate good practice. This in turn will support less experienced colleagues in developing their own practice. Osterman (1990) suggests that reflective practice fosters self-actualisation and engenders a sense of empowerment, which must be seen as a positive state in any educational setting or context.

This type of professional dialogue may also serve as an agent of change at a whole-school level. If we return to Argyris and Schön's notion of single- and double-loop learning, whole-school reflection may force schools to look at their underpinning values or governing variables. If practitioners feel constrained by the systems and values that govern their practice, then this may result in conflict, inhibiting effectiveness. Encouraging schools and other educational settings to confront assumptions may reveal that key values are outmoded and conflicting and require change. Bringing organisational values in line with those of practitioners should increase effectiveness. Schön saw this as true reflection, since practitioners are delving below the surface in order to address problems.

REFLECTIVE TASK

Argyris and Schön identified a potential gap between a person's espoused theories (the theoretical underpinnings they believed to govern their work) and theories-in-use (theories that were actually present in practice).

Make a list of the theories and values that you believe underpin your work in your own setting, then ask a colleague to observe you in practice. In your follow-up reflection discuss how far your espoused theory matched your theory-in-action and consider the reasons behind any discrepancies.

What could you do to ensure your vision becomes a reality?

SUMMARY

It is beyond doubt that Schön's work has impacted significantly on the work of practitioners, as well as influencing the work of other writers and theorists in the field of reflective practice (Moon, 2009). His work was a catalyst for encouraging practitioners to view their own practice more critically and, in so doing, enabled them to build on their own good practice and share experience. It could be said that this work empowered practitioners and supported a range of organisations in self-improvement.

In his writing with Chris Argyris on the dynamics of effective leadership, Schön introduced the concept of a learning society, encouraging organisations to view themselves as a learning society capable of undertaking self-improvement through the reflection process. He believed that all organisations should be able to manage and embrace the inevitable changes of an evolving society and look to change the processes and systems within establishments to manage such change.

Despite his early academic background in philosophy, Schön proved himself to be a versatile practitioner and had a long and illustrious career which saw him impacting on a range of workplace settings. He was a prolific writer and published a number of forward-thinking books which still influence practice today, leading the practitioner to become an expert in their field. His lasting legacies, in the field of education, are his theories of reflection-in-action and reflection-on-action, which have provided practitioners with a means to evaluate and celebrate their individual practices.

GLOSSARY OF TERMS

Double-loop learning

In double-loop learning a person will modify a goal based on their experience. The term derives from the fact that in the first loop goals or decision-making rules are used, and then in the second loop any modifications can be made – hence the double-loop.

Espoused theory

A person's beliefs in terms of personal values and attitudes, however what a person believes these values and attitudes to be may not always be seen in reality. For example, a person may perceive themselves to have the attributes of a team player yet other members of their team may see things differently (see theory-in-use).

Learning society

An educational philosophy which posits that learning should extend beyond that of formal learning into informal learning to build a knowledge economy. The learning society relates to the activity of learning rather than the place of learning and responds to a widening participation agenda in which lifelong learning is promoted.

Reflection

A process by which an individual explores their own actions, attributes, experiences and interactions in order to gain insight and move forward.

Reflection-in-action

Sometimes referred to as 'thinking on our feet', reflection-in-action involves drawing on experiences and feelings in order to make decisions as a situation unfolds.

Reflection-on-action

Retrospectively reflecting on practice presenting opportunities to explore actions taken and raise questions regarding why things happened the way they did with a view to informing future practice.

Reflective practice

A conscious process in which actions are reflected on to promote continuous learning.

Theory-in-use

The models which people actually use in practice which may differ from the models they believe they are using (see espoused theory). Theory-in-use is often a truer representation of the individual person.

FURTHER READING

Bassot, B. (2013) *The Reflective Journal*. Basingstoke: Palgrave Macmillan.

A practical student guide to reflective practice which supports beginning practitioners in deep and critical reflection.

Bolton, G. with Delderfield, R. (2018) *Reflective Practice: Writing and professional development* (Fifth Edition). London: Sage.

A critical presentation of theoretical models of reflective practice illustrated with case studies. Chapters 1 and 3 look specifically at Schön's work.

Newman, S. (1990) *Philosophy and Teacher Education: A reinterpretation of Donald A. Schön's epistemology of reflective practice*. London: Avebury.

A new interpretation of Schön's work which encourages practitioners to interpret reflection-in-action in a way which encourages development in practice.

Schön, D.A. (1973) *Beyond the Stable State: Public and private learning in a changing society*. Harmondsworth: Penguin.

A follow-up to Schön's 1970 Reith Lectures encouraging the development of social systems which can adapt to the inevitable changes in society.

Schön, D.A. (ed.) (1991) *The Reflective Turn: Case studies in and on educational practice*. New York: Teachers College Press.

A series of case studies on reflective practice in education, raising questions for the reader in terms of methodical approaches and points of view.

REFERENCES

Argyris, C. and Schön, D. (1974) *Theory in Practice: Increasing professional effectiveness*. San Francisco, CA: Jossey-Bass.

Argyris, C. and Schön, D. (1978) *Organizational Learning: A theory of action and perspective*. San Francisco, CA: Jossey-Bass.

Argyris, C. and Schön, D. (1996) *Organizational Learning II: Theory, method and practice*. Malden, MA: Blackwell.

Boud, D., Keogh, R. and Walker, D. (eds) (1985) *Reflection: Turning experience into learning*. London: Kogan Page.

Eraut, M. (1994) *Developing Professional Knowledge and Competence*. London: Falmer.

Finlay, L. (2008) Reflecting on Reflective Practice. PBPL Paper 52. Open University.

Ghaye, A. and Ghaye, K. (1998) *Teaching and Learning through Critical Reflective Practice.* London: David Fulton.

Harris, I.B. (1989) A critique of Schon's views on teacher education: contribution and issues. *Journal of Curriculum and Supervision, 5*(1): 13–18.

Lindon, J. (2014) *Reflective Practice and Early Years Professionalism: Linking theory and practice.* London: Hodder Education.

Moon, J.A. (2009) *Reflection in Learning and Professional Development: Theory and practice.* London: Kogan Page.

Osterman, K.F. (1990) Reflective practice: a new agenda for education. *Education and Urban Society, 22*(2), 133–52.

Pakman, M. (2000) Thematic foreword: reflective practices: the legacy of Donald Schön. *Cybernetics and Human Knowing, 7*(2–3), 5–8.

Richardson, V. (1990) The Evolution of Reflective Teaching and Teacher Education. In: Clift, T.T., Houston, W.R. and Pugach, M.C. (eds) *Encouraging Reflective Practice in Education: An analysis of issues and programs.* New York: Teachers College Press.

Schön, D.A. (1963) *Displacement of Concepts.* London: Tavistock.

Schön, D.A. (1967) *The Invention and Evolution of Ideas.* New York: Taylor & Francis.

Schön, D.A. (1973) *Beyond the Stable State: Public and private learning in a changing society.* Harmondsworth: Penguin.

Schön, D. (1983) *The Reflective Practitioner: How professionals think in action.* New York: Basic Books.

Schön, D. (1987) *Educating the Reflective Practitioner: Towards a new design for teaching in the professions.* San Francisco, CA: Jossey-Bass.

Scott, D. (2008) *Critical Essays on Major Curriculum Theorists.* Abingdon: Routledge.

Sellars, M. (2013) *Reflective Practice for Teachers.* London: Sage.

Thompson, S. and Thompson, N. (2008) *The Critically Reflective Practitioner.* Basingstoke: Palgrave Macmillan.

Usher, R., Bryant, I. and Johnston, R. (1997) *Adult Education and the Postmodern Challenge: Learning beyond the limits.* London: Routledge.

Waks, L.J. (2001) Donald Schön's philosophy of design and design education. *International Journal of Technology and Design Education*, 11, 37-51.

13
DAVID KOLB

EXPERIENTIAL LEARNING THEORY

LEARNING OUTCOMES

Having read this chapter you should be able to:

- understand Kolb's Experiential Learning Theory and his notion of learning styles
- recognise and appreciate each of the four stages of his Experiential Learning Theory
- use and develop his notions of learning through experience in your practice
- critically evaluate his theories.

KEY WORDS

experiential learning; concrete experience; abstract conceptualisation; reflective observation; active experimentation; diverger; converger; accommodator; assimilator

INTRODUCTION

American psychologist and educational theorist, David Kolb, is probably best known for his research on **experiential learning** and learning styles. Building on the theories of Dewey, Lewin and Piaget and influenced by Carl Jung and Carl Rogers, Kolb looked to ways in which learning in informal situations could be optimised and identified those mechanisms by which experience could be transformed into knowledge, skills and attitudes (Dennick, 2008).

While Kolb's work is underpinned by theories of cognitive development, his links to adult learning are clearly identifiable and the application of his theory sits most comfortably in the professional working environment – the learner either shadowing a more experienced colleague or being engaged in some form of educational programme whilst in work. Kolb saw learning as 'the process whereby knowledge is created through the transformation of experience' (Kolb, 1984: 38), and in this respect he saw learning as proceeding through **concrete experiences** which were then transformed into **abstract conceptualisation** through the processes of **reflective observation** and **active experimentation** (Dennick, 2008).

Kolb is most renowned for his learning cycle, which Elkjaer describes as being, 'one of the most cited in educational research' (2009: 84). This may in part be due to its holistic, integrative perspective on learning which combines experience, perception, cognition and behaviour (Kolb, 1984), rather than one which focuses on either behaviourist or cognitive theories of learning. Within his learning cycle there are two key aspects: firstly, the concrete or immediate experiences which are used to create meaning from a learning experience, and secondly, this is followed by feedback from these experiences which forms the basis for goal-directed actions and subsequent evaluations.

Kolb's experiential learning cycle also formed the basis for his identification of four different learning styles which he saw as being fundamental to the grasping and transforming of experiences, as typified in his learning cycle. Each of his learning styles was characterised by particular strengths in two of the four major steps in the learning cycle. Kolb postulated that the learning experience could be maximised if both learner and facilitator made a conscious effort to play to an individual's unique learning style. However even at this early stage of the chapter a word of caution is required regarding his experiential theory and, in particular, his learning styles. These concepts have attracted considerable criticism for being, amongst other reasons, too simplistic, problematic and even misleading; these criticisms are explored in greater depth further on in the chapter (Huddleston and Unwin, 2002: McLay et al., 2010). Nevertheless, it is the application of such theories, predominantly in higher and further education institutions, which may explain why Kolb's model has influenced many of the discussions around the practice of adult education.

DAVID KOLB, THE PERSON

David Kolb was born in 1939 and he currently holds the position of Professor of Organisational Behaviour in the Weatherhead School of Management at Case Western Reserve University, Cleveland, Ohio. Kolb has had a long and illustrious academic career. He gained an undergraduate degree in psychology from Knox College in 1961, which was followed by a PhD in social psychology from Harvard University in 1967.

Kolb's work has predominantly centred on his Experiential Learning Theory, which he first began to develop in the 1970s. This was later expanded to incorporate his Learning Style Inventory. Kolb undertook extensive research into experiential learning, culminating in his 1984 book, *Experiential Learning: Experience as the source of learning and development*. Here he set out the model for his Experiential Learning Theory (ELT) and introduced his Learning Style Inventory (LSI). Through the LSI he explained how learning can be categorised into four individual learning styles: diverging, assimilating, converging and accommodating. He expressed the notion that each individual had an orientation towards one of these learning styles, and by identifying a particular learning style it was possible to tailor learning to meet the needs of each individual.

Unlike many of his contemporaries Kolb's career has been situated in academia where he has held a number of high-profile positions, including Assistant Professor of Organisational Psychology and Management at the Massachusetts Institute of Technology (1965–70), Senior Associate, Development Research Associates (1966–80) and Visiting Professor at the London Graduate School of Business Studies in 1971. He joined the faculty of Case Western Reserve University as Professor of Organisational Behaviour in 1976, where he remains today, serving as Professor and Chair, and as de Windt Professor in Leadership and Enterprise Development. Alongside his current role, Kolb is also the founder of Experience Based Learning Systems Inc. (EBLS), a company which continues to develop research into experiential learning with a focus on self-directed change and learning, achievement motivation, professional development and leadership and management development.

His work has received much recognition through the awarding of four honorary degrees between the years 1984 and 1996, alongside numerous awards and citations, the most recent being the Distinguished Paper Award of the Decision Sciences Institute in 2011. He was also the recipient of the Educational Pioneers of the Year Award from the National Society for Experiential Education (with Alice Kolb). His list of publications, including books and monographs, journal articles, interviews and tests and educational materials, is vast, and spans from the 1960s to the present day. This is a testament to his passion for his subject and dedication to the field of adult learning.

Kolb continues to research in the field of experiential learning and is dedicated to the concept of learning through experience, which he sees as being one of the most important processes by which learning occurs. His current work examines some of the different aspects of experiential learning, specifically those related to cultural determinants of learning styles, learning flexibility and experiential learning in conversation.

His most recent works (with Simy and Kolb) reflect these aspects of experiential learning and include 'Are there cultural differences in learning styles?' (2008), 'Learning styles and learning spaces: Enhancing experiential learning in higher education' (2005) and 'The learning way: Meta-cognitive aspects of experiential learning' (2008).

Kolb co-founded EBLS Inc. in 1981, the website he now uses to disseminate much of his recent research into experiential learning. The company goal as stated on the website is to 'provide ongoing quality research and practice on experiential learning' (http://learningfromexperience.com) and its mission reflects a desire to share good practice and provide a forum by which research can be disseminated and advanced. In the Foreword of Kolb's book *Experiential Learning*, Bennis writes:

> Kolb's achievement is providing the missing link between theory and practice, between the abstract generalization and the concrete instance, between the affective and cognitive domains. By this BIG achievement he demonstrates conclusively – and is the first to do so – that learning is a social process based on carefully cultivated experience which challenges every precept and concept of what nowadays passes as teaching. (1984: ix)

It is perhaps this practical application of Kolb's theory which makes his work so accessible to the field of higher and further education today.

KOLB'S EXPERIENTIAL LEARNING THEORY AND LEARNING STYLE INVENTORY

Kolb's theory of experiential learning determines that people learn best when they are engaged in first-hand experiences, which can later be reflected on through thinking about the details of the experience alongside the feelings and perceptions which emerged during the experience (Harkin et al., 2001). Working alongside his colleague Roger Fry, Kolb theorised that learning occurred by way of progression through a four-stage cycle, which he referred to as the Lewinian experiential model, a name derived from his use of Lewin's work on group dynamics, action research and organisational behaviour. Dennick (2008) points out that the terms used by Kolb to describe the phases of the learning cycle are indeed taken directly from Lewin's work on action research.

Kolb's learning cycle is then constructed through the following four stages or learning modes: concrete experience (CE), reflective observation (RO), abstract conceptualisation (AC) and active experimentation (AE) (see Figure 13.1). Each stage defines a particular mode of learning which was favoured by the learner when engaged in a learning experience. These stages in the first instance can be seen at opposite ends of two intersecting continua (Terry, 2001) and these relate to the learner's personal preference while engaged in a learning experience. Kolb argues that each learner will have a propensity to either feeling versus thinking (CE versus AC) or watching versus doing (RO versus AE). In Kolb's cycle it is not possible to engage in activities which are at opposite ends of the continuum – that is, it is not possible to watch and do or think and feel at the same time, which therefore categorises the learner into one domain over the other.

Within Kolb's model, learning is seen as an integrated process in which each stage is 'mutually supportive of and feeding into the next' (Harkin et al., 2001: 40). Kolb suggests that it is possible to begin the cycle at any stage, although for effective learning to proceed it is necessary to follow the cycle through its natural progression with no stage of the cycle being sufficient on its own. The learner, then, needs to be involved in the experience (concrete experience) but must follow this with some form of reflection, for example as an observer analysing the experience and creating their own concepts based on their observations (AC). In addition the individual must also have the capacity to move between the interpretation of data collected from their experience (RO) and the testing of theories and subsequent adaptations made as a result of reflections (AE). It is only through this process that the learner might gain new experiences, perspectives, understanding and knowledge (Harkin et al., 2001). Kolb and Fry see the process as a continuous spiral, since on completion of one cycle the learner will then move on to the next stage of the process, being informed by the preceding stage, and so learning develops.

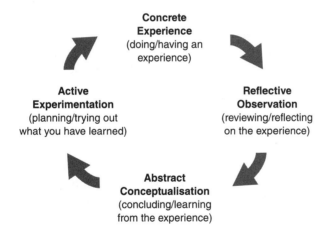

Figure 13.1 Kolb's learning cycle

Source: Kolb, D.A. (©1984) *Experiential Learning: Experience as the source of learning and development* (First Edition). Printed and electronically reproduced by permission of Pearson Education Inc., New York, NY.

In acknowledging that no one individual can possess all four learning abilities as seen in their model, Kolb and Fry (1975) identified four distinct learning styles which were typified by a combination of preferred styles based on the four-stage learning cycle.

These learning styles are then defined as:

- **diverger** – combining CE and RO
- **assimilator** – combining AC and RO
- **converger** – combining AC and AE
- **accommodator** – combining CE and AE.

Kolb identified particular qualities of learners who fit into each of his learning styles and suggested that by recognising a learning type it was possible to tailor learning in order to play to an individual's strengths. In the 'Applying Kolb in the classroom' section of this chapter we will explore further how the defining qualities of each learning style might impact on how a learner engages in study or how the teacher might help to facilitate learning.

Kolb's theory suggests that people will naturally form preferences for a particular learning style, largely because these have proved successful in past experiences. As a result, a particular approach to learning will naturally be adopted. However, Kolb and Fry also saw benefits to a learner in being able to identify their own learning style, which led to the development of the Learning Style Inventory (LSI). Kolb (1976) referred to this as a self-descriptive inventory which measures different learning styles along the process continuum. The original LSI has been adapted and developed by Kolb and Fry and has also been used as a basis for work by Honey and Mumford (1992) in order for individuals to gain self-knowledge about their individual learning style, as well as a means by which facilitators and educators might design curriculum content and programmes to better meet the needs of their learners. This will be developed further on in the chapter as we link theory to practice.

⟳ LINKS WITH OTHER THEORISTS

As we have already noted, Kolb's work on ELT evolved from the ideas of Dewey, Lewin and Piaget, indeed he called his model the experiential learning cycle to stress the links with these three, and to highlight the importance experience played in the learning process (Jarvis et al., 2003). He was further inspired by Carl Jung and Carl Rogers. Dewey felt that true learning was a democratic and dynamic process which was based upon experiences. He argued that learners should not be inactive observers but fully involved in the 'process of active engagement [which] allows a learner to become immersed in experience, an undertaking that can form the basis of reflection' (Harkin, et al., 2001: 39). Similar to Dewey, Lewin also believed in the importance of experience in successful learning, in particular the remodelling of experiences based on the feelings and reflections that transpired from experiences. Indeed, as we have seen, Kolb's learning cycle was based upon Lewin's ideas. These ideas were developed from his research on group work where learners not only encountered differences of opinion but also formed a collaborative and problem-solving consensus with others. These ideas form the basis of the small groups teaching activities now used in schools, colleges and universities (Dennick, 2008).

Piaget also had an impact on Kolb's theories, especially ELT. Piaget argued that knowledge is constructed through interaction with others and with the environment. His cognitive theory, which is comparable to Kolb's concepts, entails learners gaining new information which then allows them to develop and reshape their current knowledge in order that it can be re-formed and applied to new situations – an ongoing process of cognitive development. Even though Piaget's work is mostly concerned with the stages of children's cognitive development, his ideas are also of significance for adults since his theory states that adults have reached an established stage in their intellectual development (Armitage et al., 1999).

Many of Kolb's ideas have emerged from his work with groups, which include their dynamics and organisation. This can be closely aligned with Lave and Wenger's notion of situated learning which concerns learners as active participants within a community of practice. There is a direct connection with Kolb's ELT, although Lave and Wenger's ideas are even more uncompromising, as Armitage offers:

> Here is experiential learning in its most direct form, or rather learning-*as*-experience since Lave and Wenger would quarrel with the notion of learning as a discrete activity occurring independently of other activities. (2003: 37)

Teaching methods employed in education generally now involve interaction and the use of learners' experience advocated by Kolb. These ideas are also very evident in the thinking of two eminent adult education thinkers: Malcolm Knowles and Paulo Freire. Knowles promoted the notion that teachers should start the learning process from the basis of the adult's existing experience and knowledge. Freire argued against the traditional view of teaching, which he termed the 'banking concept' where education is considered as a means of 'depositing' knowledge on a passive learner. As such, Freire, like Kolb, called for a more interactive and 'problem-posing' process of teaching based on the needs and experiences of the learners.

Reflection as an instrument of cognitive and professional development is a key aspect of Kolb's theory of experiential learning and also a valuable part of Schön's reflection-in-action and reflection-on-action. Gibbs also emphasises reflection following group work and problem-solving activities. In addition, Carl Rogers highlights the significance of learners being able to construct meaning from their learning through their feelings and reflection from experience.

Kolb's LSI, which emerged from his notion of a learning cycle, has a number of links with others who promote the idea of separate and preferred learning styles. Kolb was influenced by Carl Jung's psychotherapeutic work that found individuals had inherent ways of behaving and learning: some preferred to be active (extrovert) and others more thoughtful and reflective (introvert). This in turn was further developed and used in the Myers-Briggs psychometric test. A closer connection with Kolb's LSI is Howard Gardner's concept of multiple intelligences (MI). Although these differ from Kolb's, Gardner contested that successful teaching should involve all the intelligences identified and not just the learner's preferred intelligence (Williams, 2004). As we have discovered, Kolb's LSI directly informed the Honey and Mumford (1992) learning styles. The main difference between the two ideas of learning styles is that Honey and Mumford saw the learning style as an objective product of what individuals do, while for Kolb it was an 'holistic interpretation, which also counts subjective elements of thoughts, feelings and perceptions of experience' (Harkin et al., 2001: 42). These differences will be evident later when considering the application of Kolb's LSI.

CRITIQUING KOLB

Gould writes that 'Kolb's model of experiential learning has been the subject of considerable criticism' (2009: 103). Most of these criticisms appear to be levelled at the LSI, which Kolb himself acknowledges has its limitations, predominantly due to the fact that results are based solely on the learner's view of themselves with some of the terminology being open to interpretation (Kelly, 1997). In accord with this, Tennant (1997) also questions the validity of the four learning styles. He suggests that the close ties between the learning styles and the experiential learning cycle require all situations to be applicable to the experiential learning model, and he posits that this is not always the case, arguing that there are alternatives, such as information assimilation and memorisation, which Kolb has failed to acknowledge.

A report by Coffield et al. (2004) questions whether learning styles should be used at all, and while this related to a wider critique of learning style theory we cannot discount Kolb's model in this criticism which questions the reliability and validity of the LSI. Coffield et al. (2004) also suggest that the notion of a learning cycle is seriously flawed, with no tangible evidence of its pedagogical impact being found. This is supported by Jarvis (1987) and Tennant (1997) who suggest that the initial research base into the application of the model was too small to form generalisations. There is also a danger of assuming that a learning style is a fixed entity which remains with the learner, and then the learner becomes 'labelled' as such for the rest of their studies. This has the further potential to adversely affect an individual's learning development, as the method used to identify their particular learning style 'may be specific to culture, gender or age and can lead to the incorrect assessment of learners from different backgrounds' (McLay et al., 2010: 96). Furthermore, Sharp and Murphy provide a thought-provoking observation regarding the juxtaposition between the impact of learning style and performance:

> The difficulty of establishing whether an individual's preferred learning style affects performance or an individual's performance affects learning style should not be overlooked. (Sharp and Murphy, 2006: 44)

A further criticism of Kolb's experiential learning cycle relates to the scant regard for cultural experiences and conditions, which in today's multicultural society must be seen as a limitation. The inventory has been used with a limited range of cultures and could therefore be seen to be underpinned by Western assumptions. Tennant (1997), citing Anderson (1988), suggests this could be an oversight, since cognitive and communication styles are often culturally based. Jarvis et al. argue that the experiential learning cycle 'is fundamentally weak in that it is over-simple, it also implies that experience is cognitive and omits both the physical and the emotional' (2003: 58).

Jarvis (1987) suggests that Kolb fails to fully explore the nature of knowledge in any depth, and given that the experiential learning cycle seeks to explore the relationships between learning and knowledge, then this could prove to be problematic. Jarvis (1987) also criticises Kolb's failure to connect with debates around the acquisition of knowledge and suggests that Kolb fails to grasp the different ways of knowing. Interestingly, Jarvis sees Kolb's emphasis as on the production of knowledge, with a focus on the individual mind, rather than through situated learning (Lave and Wenger, 1991). In this respect Kolb's vision of experiential learning should be viewed with caution. Moreover, it is argued that there is further research needed for ELT and in particular learning styles. As such, and in light of the previous criticisms, it is advocated that educators and educational establishments are judicious in the over-dependance of these models in practice (McLay et al., 2010).

Nevertheless, despite such criticisms we should not discount the practical application of Kolb's work since, as Tennant points out:

> … the model provides an excellent framework for planning teaching and learning activities and it can be usefully employed as a guide for understanding learning difficulties, vocational counselling, academic advising and so on. (1997: 92)

APPLYING KOLB IN THE CLASSROOM

So, it is with caution that we suggest that the experiential learning cycle and learning styles can be employed by teachers to appraise the types of learning and teaching undertaken by students so that they can then enhance the quality of provision in the future. This is achieved in the first place by teachers knowing their group of learners and understanding their learning preferences. This understanding can then be used to offer opportunities for learning where the students feel at ease and have a sense of achievement in a way that fits their learning preference. The next step is to discover their less preferred ways of learning and give them opportunities to strengthen these through each stage in the experiential learning cycle. Finally, and most importantly, teachers should consider the influence their own preferred learning style has on their own students and from that start to reflect on ways that will further improve the quality of the students' learning. This in turn should result in the teacher creating and using classroom activities and resources which take into account all stages of the experiential learning cycle and avoid teaching which concentrates on one particular learning style over others. This can be achieved by the teacher promoting reflection after activities and by encouraging and supporting students to try new experiences – through each stage of the learning cycle (Harkin et al., 2001).

The general idea of experiential learning is not new, but Kolb's theory has allowed teachers to create learning experiences for their students which are sequential, progressively developmental and give opportunities for reflection on their experience. Using the experiential learning cycle does not require a radical change in learning and teaching methods. However, because teachers are encouraging students to try new activities and then to reflect and honestly acknowledge their errors, the teaching does require a thoughtful and receptive approach. What makes the application of ELT even more interesting is that teachers themselves, through attempting new methods (some of which may result in emotional outcomes) and reflecting on these experiences, are also developing their own learning and professional practice (Petty, 1998).

To explore specific examples of how Kolb's ideas can be put into practice it is fitting that we follow the sequence of each stage of the learning cycle, then consider how learners learn best in relation to Kolb's LSI. In the first stage, CE, the activity should where possible be a real-life experience, such as carrying out an experiment or workshop task. Although they are of less value, other non-real-life activities could be used, such as case studies, role play, projects, simulation and demonstration. It is a period for trying and testing out new ideas. The experiences should be challenging in their nature and the use of social interaction and discussion encouraged. Activities could be cognitive, but they could also involve the development of practical skills. Preferably, the actual concrete experience used should be as a result of the active experimentation stage of the previous learning cycle (Petty, 1998).

The RO stage is where students undertake an objective and honest appraisal of their CE. This can also include their feelings during their experience. At first, this will need to be done with the help of the teacher, but the aim is that the student will eventually be able to complete this on their own. This in turn will hopefully lead to honest attempts at self-assessment, rather than always relying on the teacher's evaluation of their efforts. The goal at this stage is to trust the students to self-appraise their experiences. This in effect will help create reflective practitioners who will have the confidence to learn, and continue to learn, from their experiences. The promotion of self-assessment can take a number of forms. Asking open questions following activities allows the students to take ownership of their own feelings. Encouraging them to construct a self-assessment checklist before activities begin is a way of stimulating reflection and ensuring they remain on task. Using diaries to record their reflections directly following experiences is particularly helpful in reflecting on emotional events and experiences. The recording of reflections is an important aspect of the RO stage where portfolios could also be used. What is considered paramount at this stage is the need for a trusting relationship between the students and teacher, as the students will need to have the confidence to be open about what they think they did well, and what did not go so well, during the experience. Therefore, it is argued that this stage should be free from any assessment processes with the students (Petty, 1998; Dennick, 2008).

The purpose of the AC stage is for the students to link their concrete experience with the theory. It is at this stage where, after reflection, students endeavour to connect their own experiences to the experiences of others. This can involve talking over their experiences and their resultant reflections (what went well and not so well) with teachers, other students or referring to textbooks and other associated literature. This stage offers the students a chance to test their ever-increasing skills, knowledge and feelings with others. This in turn may convince them to alter the way they think about what they have experienced. Equally, this stage may just validate their ideas about the theory. This then leads to the fourth and final stage of the learning cycle: AE. Students have reflected on their CE and tried to correlate this with theory. From this they now need to make sense of the process and ask themselves how they will improve next time they begin the learning cycle at the CE stage. This can be helped by feedback and discussions with teachers, but students should take ownership of this stage by again using written documents, such as action plans, portfolios, targets and goals for future development (Petty, 1998; Dennick, 2008).

There are four distinct learning styles relating to the stages of the learning cycle. Although it is imperative that students experience all four learning styles for a deep and meaningful learning experience, highlighted below are suggestions on how students with particular learning preferences/styles may learn best:

Accommodator – learns best by doing things; from short here-and-now tasks; in carrying out plans/experiments; through trial and error/taking risks; with other people.

Diverger – learns best when standing back, listening and observing; from collecting information and thinking it through, through different perspectives and grasping the bigger picture; by sharing and discussing ideas with others; through searching for meaning; with others.

Assimilator – learns best when reviewing things in terms of systems, concepts, models, theories; when absorbing ideas and providing integrated explanations/theories; solving problems; by data collection; planning and organising work; through critical evaluation; working alone.

Converger – learns best when integrating theory and practice; in the workshop or laboratory using skills/learning and testing theories and applying common sense; with clear goals and rewards; with things rather than people.

(Adapted from Harkin et al., 2001: 42)

Despite the criticism of Kolb's work, particularly in relation to his LSI, there are many aspects of his theories which can be applied in certain learning situations. This is especially the case for the further and higher education sectors and in adult learning. Key to the successful application of ELT is building a trusting relationship between student and teacher, promoting reflection, valuing students' previous experiences, and giving them the opportunity of experiencing 'real-life' learning.

REFLECTIVE TASK

Thinking about your own learning in relation to ELT, identify specific actions or tasks you could do in each of the four stages of the experiential learning cycle listed below to improve your future professional practice. Also consider the barriers that may hinder you in implementing these actions or tasks and then give examples of how you could overcome these barriers.

1. CE
2. RO
3. AC
4. AE

SUMMARY

David Kolb has had a significant influence on the thinking behind educational practices over the last half century. His ideas on experiential learning and individual learning styles have evolved from theories from the eminent educationalists and psychologists Dewey, Lewin, Piaget, Jung and Rogers. Furthermore, his ideas have been influential in developing the concepts of more contemporary thinkers, such as Knowles, Lave and Wenger. The main driver of his work has been his enthusiasm for adult learning and his experiential learning cycle has had an important role to play in the way teaching and learning are approached in the further and higher education sectors.

Central to Kolb's standpoint on experiential learning is that students learn best when they are actually engaged in first-hand experiences, which they then reflect upon, along with the feelings and emotions which came with this experience (Harkin et al., 2001). From this premise he, along with Fry, created the four-stage sequential learning cycle, encompassing CE, RO, AC and AE. What was important for Kolb was that it did not matter at which stage the student started on this learning cycle as long as the cycle was completed. He identified that each of these stages related to a particular preferred way (style) of learning by individual students as they engaged in the learning experience. These learning styles embodied in his LSI are Diverger, Assimilator, Converger and Accommodator.

Kolb's concepts have generated a considerable amount of criticism, especially his ideas on learning styles. Negative comments regarding his LSI focus on the narrowness of his research sample alongside criticism that there is little evidence of the learning cycle having an impact on teaching and learning practices (Jarvis, 1987; Tennant, 1997; Coffield et al., 2004). Furthermore, ELT has attracted criticism because as a concept it is too simple, as well as suggesting that experience is cognitive while ignoring emotional and physical aspects (Jarvis et al., 2003). Nevertheless, his work provides a positive structure which is embedded by reflection and the opportunity for both students and teachers to continually develop their knowledge, skills and attitudes.

GLOSSARY OF TERMS

Abstract conceptualisation

The third part of Kolb's four-stage learning cycle. Having concrete experience and the opportunity for reflective observation the learner then refines these experiences, reflections and observations in the light of their understanding of associated theory producing new ideas and plans.

Accommodator

One of four learning styles proposed by Kolb. Learners develop best by working with others in doing things, by carrying out plans and learning from their mistakes.

Active experimentation

The final part of Kolb's four-stage learning cycle following abstract conceptualisation which creates new experiences which are once again reflected upon, and the learning cycle is repeated over and over.

Assimilator

One of four learning styles proposed by Kolb. Learners develop best when working on their own by reviewing things in terms of systems, concepts, models and theories. They absorb ideas and provide their own concepts/theories. They also solve problems through data collection, planning and organising work, and critical evaluation.

Concrete experience

The first part of Kolb's four-stage learning cycle. The learner needs to be actively involved in the learning experience.

Converger

One of four learning styles proposed by Kolb. Learning develops best when working with things rather than people, and by integrating theory and practice in a workshop or laboratory environment. Using skills/learning, testing theories and applying common sense as well as working to clear goals.

Diverger

One of four learning styles proposed by Kolb. Learning develops best through working and sharing ideas and solutions with others by listening and observing to understand the bigger picture.

Experiential learning

The concept of learning through practical experience rather than being taught by the teacher with a stress on the significance of practice over theory. This process is reinforced by learners reflecting on their practice and the feelings and insights they developed as part of the experience.

Reflective observation

The second part of Kolb's four-stage learning cycle. Once a learner has been involved in a concrete experience it gives them the foundation for reflective observations of their experience.

FURTHER READING

Moon, J. (1999) *Reflection in Learning and Professional Development*. London: Kogan Page.

This is a comprehensive and useful book with detailed links between reflection and professional practice. Chapter 3 – Reflection in experiential learning – explores the wider application of Kolb's ELT, including action research.

Schön, D. (1983) *The Reflective Practitioner: How professionals think in practice*. New York: Basic Books.

This is an important and practical text which emphasises the significance of reflection in developing professional practice, and introduces the reader to Schön's concepts of reflection-on-action and reflection-in-action.

REFERENCES

Armitage, A. (2003) In Defence of Vocationalism. In: Lea, J., Hayes, D., Armitage, A., Lomas, L. and Markless, S. (eds) *Working in Post-Compulsory Education*. Maidenhead: Open University Press.

Armitage, A., Bryant, R., Dunhill, R., Hammersley, M., Hayes, D., Hudson, A. and Lawes, S. (1999) *Teaching and Training in Post-Compulsory Education*. Buckingham: Open University Press.

Bennis, W. (1984) Foreword. In D.A. Kolb (ed.) *Experiential Learning: Experience as the source of learning and development*. Englewood Cliffs, NJ: Prentice Hall.

Coffield, F., Moseley, D., Hall, E. and Ecclestone, K. (2004) *Should We Be Using Learning Styles? What research says about the practice*. London: Learning Skills and Research Centre. Available from: www.itslifejimbutnotasweknowit.org.uk/files/LSRC_LearningStyles.pdf [accessed 10/03/18].

Dennick, R. (2008) Theories of Learning: Constructive experience. In: Matheson, D. (ed.) *An Introduction to the Study of Education*. Abingdon: Routledge.

Elkjaer, B. (2009) Pragmatism: A learning theory for the future. In: Illeris, K. (ed.) *Contemporary Theories of Learning: Learning theorists … in their own words*. Abingdon: Routledge.

Gould, J. (2009) *Learning Theory and Classroom Practice in the Lifelong Learning Sector*. Exeter: Learning Matters.

Harkin, J., Turner, G. and Dawn, T. (2001) *Teaching Young Adults*. Abingdon: Routledge.

Honey, P. and Mumford, A. (1992) *The Manual of Learning Styles*. Maidenhead: Peter Honey.

Huddleston, P. and Unwin, L. (2002) *Teaching and Learning in Further Education* (Second Edition). London: RoutledgeFalmer.

Jarvis, P. (1987) *Adult Learning in the Social Context*. London: Croom Helm.

Jarvis, P., Holford, J. and Griffin, C. (2003) *The Theory and Practice of Learning* (Second Edition). London: Routledge.

Kelly, C. (1997) David Kolb: The theory of experiential learning and ESL. The Internet *TESL Journal*, *3*, 9. Available from: http://iteslj.org/Articles/Kelly-Experiential [accessed 08/03/18].

Kolb, D.A. (1976) *The Learning Style Inventory: Technical manual*. Boston, MA: McBer & Co.

Kolb, D.A. (1984) *Experiential Learning: Experience as the source of learning and development*. Englewood Cliffs, NJ: Prentice Hall.

Kolb, D.A. and Fry, R.E. (1975) Toward an Applied Theory of Experiential Learning. In: Cooper, C. (ed.) *Theories of Group Processes*. New York: Wiley.

Kolb, A. and Kolb, D.A. (2005) Learning styles and learning spaces: Enhancing experiential learning in higher education. *Academy of Management Learning and Education*, *4*(2), 193–212.

Kolb, A. and Kolb, D.A. (2008) The learning way: Meta-cognitive aspects of experiential learning. *Simulation and Gaming*. Available from: http://sag.sagepub.com [accessed 08/03/18].

Lave, J. and Wenger,E. (1991) *Situated Learning: Legitimate peripheral participation*. Cambridge: Cambridge University Press.

McLay, M., Mycroft, L., Noel, P., Orr, K., Thompson, R., Tummons, J. and Weatherby, J. (2010) Learning and Learners. In: Avis, J., Fisher, R. and Thompson, R. (eds) *Teaching in Lifelong Learning*. Maidenhead: Open University Press.

Petty, G. (1998) *Teaching Today* (Second Edition). Cheltenham: Nelson Thornes.

Sharp, J. and Murphy, B. (2006) The Mystery of Learning. In: Sharp, J., Ward, S. and Hankin, L. (eds) *Education Studies: An issues-based approach*. Exeter: Learning Matters.

Simy, J.A. and Kolb, D.A. (2008) Are there cultural differences in learning styles? *International Journal of Cultural Relations*, *33*(1), 69–85.

Tennant, M. (1997) *Psychology and Adult Learning*. London: Routledge.

Terry, M. (2001) Translating learning style theory into university teaching practices: An article based on Kolb's experiential learning model. *Journal of College Reading and Learning*, *32*(1), 68–85.

Williams, J. (2004) Great Minds: Education's most influential philosophers. A *Times Education Supplement Essential Guide*.

14
JEAN LAVE AND ETIENNE WENGER

SOCIALLY SITUATED LEARNING AND COMMUNITIES OF PRACTICE

LEARNING OUTCOMES

Having read this chapter you should be able to:

- understand the impact of both Lave and Wenger on social learning
- recognise the aspects of both situated learning and communities of practice
- apply these notions of social learning to your practice, setting and professional development
- appraise the facets of social learning in a variety of formal and informal educational settings.

KEY WORDS

situated learning; communities of practice; apprenticeship; legitimate peripheral participation; situatedness

INTRODUCTION

Jean Lave and Etienne Wenger's concept of socially **situated learning** offered a notion of learning which was at odds with conventional thinking regarding teaching and learning. For them, learning was about individuals being involved in the processes of social activity rather than being passive receivers of knowledge. Huddleston and Unwin give an outline of the main premise of Lave and Wenger's concept of socially situated learning:

> What is important here is that knowledge and skills are seen as not belonging solely to an individual but things which are to be shared and developed collectively. In addition, it is the social, political, economic and cultural dimensions of any community of practice and the nature of the interactions between members that determine how much learning occurs. (2002: 97)

Lave and Wenger's ideas were first published in their co-authored book, *Situated Learning: Legitimate peripheral participation* (1991), and later enhanced by Wenger's *Communities of Practice: Learning, meaning and identity* (1998), which considered further the development of **communities of practice** in organisations. These works are of significant relevance in offering a different perspective on how we learn and how that learning can be further developed. Although these notions of socially situated learning are of particular importance for work-based learning, they could also be applied in school classrooms and workshops.

The motivation behind *Situated Learning: Legitimate peripheral participation* was a desire to explore how people learned new knowledge and skills without being part of a formal training process. Data came from empirical research from different geographical locations and work contexts (Lave and Wenger, 1991). From the outcomes of these studies, Lave and Wenger believed that looking at '**apprenticeship** simply in terms of "learning by doing" provided an unsatisfactory account of the ordered way in which apprentices learned their craft' (Fuller et al., 2005). They felt that the true nature of such situated learning involved a multifaceted process including relationships and culture.

This notion of learning as being a situated and social pursuit of knowledge and skill is core to the procedure they termed **legitimate peripheral participation**, where learners involve themselves in communities with other practitioners to develop their practice. Learners become increasingly adept in their mastery of skills and knowledge which they gain from the more experienced practitioners, eventually developing into fully fledged members of that community. As such, legitimate peripheral participation describes the 'relationships between newcomers and old-timers, and about activities, identities, artefacts' (Lave and Wenger, 1991: 29) and how learners become part of a community of practice. Lave and Wenger argue that such communities of practice are widespread and learners are involved in a variety of them. These can include formal settings such as organisations, schools and universities or more informal situations such as hobby and interest groups. Furthermore, as individuals we may be on the periphery or indeed a central figure of these communities of practice, but what is of importance is that all members have a common interest and share practice (Lave and Wenger, 1991). The conceptual details of situated learning and communities of practice will be explored later in this chapter.

JEAN LAVE AND ETIENNE WENGER, THE PEOPLE

Both Jean Lave and Etienne Wenger are academics from the United States and although they come from different scholarly fields they share a fascination for the social aspects of learning. Jean Lave gained her PhD at Harvard in 1968 and is an anthropologist by profession with a research interest in social theory. As Professor of Education at the University of California, Berkeley, she concerned herself with the way learners interact socially between themselves and with their educational institutions. Her (1988) *Cognition in Practice: Mind, mathematics, and culture in everyday life* was a fresh and radical exploration of human cognition and problem solving. It was radical because previous ways of studying human cognition involved laboratory research, but Lave employed ideas of social history and culture to discover how everyday arithmetic problems were solved in different social settings. Two of her other major works which sought to understand social cognition in everyday settings are *Understanding Practice: Perspectives on activity and context* (co-edited with Seth Chaiklin, 1993) and *Apprenticeships in Critical Ethnography* (2011).

Etienne Wenger is an independent researcher and author. He also acts as a consultant helping organisations to develop communities of practice. Prior to this he was a teacher, and after completing his PhD at the University of California, Irvine, in artificial intelligence, he became a Senior Research Scientist at the Institute for Research, Menlo Park. His (1987) book *Artificial Intelligence and Tutoring Systems: Computational and cognitive approaches to the communication of knowledge* considers, in a scientific manner, the nature of cognition and knowledge and how they are communicated to the learner. His ideas from the book challenged the traditional and didactic approach to learning and teaching evident in schools and universities (Lave and Wenger, 1991; Wenger, 1998).

LAVE AND WENGER'S CONCEPT OF SITUATED LEARNING AND COMMUNITIES OF PRACTICE

Situated learning and communities of practice are clearly located within social learning, but before we proceed any further it is fitting that we briefly consider social learning as a notion and why Lave and Wenger's ideas are different and advanced in their concept. Although in the past the study of learning has been examined through a psychological rather than a sociological lens, it has become increasingly obvious that learning is a social activity, a notion supported by the works of Vygotsky and Bruner (see Chapters 4 and 8). Both of these educational philosophers argued that knowledge was socially constructed. These social constructivist approaches stress that knowledge allows learners to have a 'holistic understanding … an integrated view of learning rather than a disciplinary-based one' (Jarvis et al., 2003: 43). Yet it is argued that, unlike social constructivist learning, socially situated learning emphasises the culture of the social participation, the nurturing of relationships and, in particular, the shared specific purpose of the activity. Therefore situated learning 'should be viewed as sociocult[...] Gredler, 2005: 8). It is with this unde[...] e theories are distinct from the more [...] we can now seek to analyse and chart t[...]

Lave and [...] e concept of situated learning was to lo[...] e concept of apprenticeship. The idea that [...] one of legitimate peripheral practice initial[...] mentioned craft apprentices who were: Lib[...] kets, Mayan midwives, US Navy quarterma[...] were members of Alcoholics Anonymous (AA[...] ered to be craft apprentices, but the findings a[...] re surprisingly parallel with the craft apprentic[...] ered some interesting data which differed from [...] iceships – that learning was more complex and i[...] ot just a routine and mechanistic matter of the [...] he old-timer or master, for example. Although the types [...] en their geographical locations were varied, all – apart from the butchers – were found to offer effective learning opportunities.

It is important to briefly compare and contrast each of these apprenticeships in order to understand the nature of Lave and Wenger's analysis and their concept of situated learning and communities of practice. The midwives were mostly the daughters of experienced midwives themselves and used herbal remedies and ritual practices; their practice was very much part of their daily life. The tailors and quartermasters both used technology. The tailors used basic forms of technology, such as sewing machines, scissors and needles, and master tailors worked individually but were assisted by their apprentices. The quartermasters used higher forms of technological instruments and worked collaboratively with others, including their trainers, to become qualified. Butchers received formal learning at trade schools as well as situated learning in supermarkets. Both quartermasters and butchers gained formal certification. The non-drinking alcoholics were members of AA and saw themselves as a part of that community. Their apprenticeship was 'sanctified by an explicit commitment … through well-defined "steps" of membership' (Lave and Wenger, 1991: 67).

There are a number of associations which come to the fore when considering these different apprenticeships. In particular, all are concerned in the development of an ever-increasing level of participation and knowledge accumulation which have differing degrees of difficulty to be overcome (Lave and Wenger, 1991). For the midwives, it was how learning progresses without a formally organised curriculum. For the tailors, it was about access to a curriculum within the restrictions of the day-to-day practice in busy workshops. For the non-drinking alcoholics, talk was a significant aspect in their transformation. The quartermasters underwent formal training in groups under the watchful eyes of their trainers in a realistic and purposeful environment mostly undertaken on board ships, moving steadily from peripheral to vital collaborative tasks such as plotting the position of their ship. The findings from the apprentice butchers are particularly interesting. It was found their training could hinder rather than help learning, mainly for two reasons. Firstly, because of the type of teaching employed, where trainers saw 'apprentices as novices who "should be instructed" rather than as peripheral participants in a community engaged in its own reproduction' (Lave and Wenger, 1991: 76). Secondly, apprentices felt that assignments in the trade school were not relevant to their practice in supermarkets. However, the studies did reveal that learning from everyday practice, the importance of motivation and the need for learners to develop an identity through a notion of legitimate peripheral practice were central to the concept of situated learning.

The links between the traditional view of apprenticeship and the theory of situated learning were strengthened by the analysis of these studies, through which a more thorough idea of the varied methods of what Lave and Wenger termed '**situatedness**' emerged (Lave and Wenger, 1991: 32). The more effective approaches to situatedness occurred when legitimate peripheral participation was embraced by the whole community. We have already seen that legitimate peripheral practice enables practitioners to learn from their more experienced peers, gradually becoming fully fledged members of their community. It is a truly interactive and dynamic practice where skills and knowledge are achieved:

> The individual learner is not gaining a discrete body of abstract knowledge which (s)he will then transport and reapply in later contexts. Instead, (s)he acquires the skill to perform by actually engaging in the process. (Lave and Wenger, 1991: 14)

This engagement (or participation) is centred upon socially situated interpretations of knowledge, which in turn entail a shared view of experience and comprehension between novice and experienced participants. Legitimate peripheral participation, then, does not involve a prescribed process between teaching, learning and the learner carrying out an activity; it is a more encompassing notion where 'persons, actions, and the world are implicated in all thought, speech, knowing, and learning' (Lave and Wenger, 1991: 52). Legitimate peripheral participation is a transformational process and is inspired by the increasing worth of belonging and the novices' wishes to become full and experienced members of a community of practice.

Participants in communities of practices learn how to fit in, how to contribute and how to change their community. As we have seen, the new participant moves from novice to experienced and full member of their community. Wenger (1998) argues that communities of practice have the following three essential characteristics: mutual engagement (as participants work and support each other); joint enterprise (a mediated and collective understanding of their activities and purpose); and a shared repertoire (members employ a range of related manners, tools, artefacts, ways of behaving and communicating). Communities of practice require members to have shared ways of 'doing and approaching things' (Smith, 2003). It involves a participation that not only 'shapes what we do, but also who we are and how we interpret what we do (Wenger, 1998: 4). Wenger considered that participation alone was not enough to build meaningful communities of practice, what was needed was structure to support and complement participation. This structure is what Wenger terms 'reification' – the mission statements of values and norms, the protocols for getting things down; and at the same time genuine opportunities for 'participation' – acting, interacting mutually. Structures with too little participation are bureaucratic shells; participation without structure may be experienced as chaos. Both structure and participation are needed in balance (Collins et al., 2002: 135).

Wenger (1998) put forward the theory of socially situated learning comprised of four peripheral components, all of which were required to exemplify social engagement as a manner of knowing and learning. Each of these components emphasises the importance of 'ways of talking'. This was particularly important for the non-drinking alcoholics, who considered that telling their own stories of how they became alcoholics and their efforts in not drinking was a significant medium for exhibiting their membership of their community of practice. The components for socially situated learning were as follows:

1. *Meaning*: a way of talking about our (changing) ability – individually and collectively – to experience our life and the world as meaningful.
2. *Practice*: a way of talking about the shared historical and social resources, frameworks, and perspectives that can sustain mutual engagement in action.
3. *Community*: a way of talking about the social configurations in which enterprises are defined as worth pursuing and our participation is recognisable as competence.
4. *Identity*: a way of talking about how learning changes who we are and creates personal histories of becoming in the context of our communities.

(Wenger, 1998: 5)

Many of Lave and Wenger's notions of learning being a social and active process and a central aspect of our everyday lives and experiences are not entirely original. Indeed, their ideas have similarities with those of a range of theorists, particularly those who promoted the importance of social and cultural attributes in learning.

LINKS WITH OTHER THEORISTS

Although we have argued at the start of the previous section that Lave and Wenger's ideas are socially situated rather than socially constructed, there are many similarities between their work and that of Vygotsky and Bruner. Lave and Wenger's work became a part of a growing interest in the 1990s which 'centred around socio-cultural activity theory which builds on the work of Russian psychologist Lev Vygotsky' (Huddleston and Unwin, 2002: 98). Vygotsky's notion of the zone of proximal development (ZPD) was based on a child's learning being enhanced through problem solving in partnership with others, mainly in the classroom. Lave and Wenger have broadened Vygotsky's concept to include adults learning in work as well as in other informal settings (Huddleston and Unwin, 2002). Furthermore, Bruner's application of scaffolding, an important and common practice in contemporary classrooms, is strongly associated with Lave and Wenger's concept of apprenticeships; an association however which is sometimes unrecognised (Olson, 2007). Additionally, Vygotsky's and Bruner's theories are also evident in the emerging ideas of socially situated learning where matters of culture, environment and active participant learning are all significant factors. Lave and Wenger's ideas expanded social constructivism further. This is particularly the case for adults where socially situated learning, supported by reflection and within a community of practice, formed the basis of continuous professional development (Dennick, 2008).

Lave and Wenger's notions are also comparable with those of Bourdieu who contested that people discover how to learn by what is around them; in this way they become a part of the learning community by adopting culturally accepted feelings and behaviours. As such learning is perceived as being socially situated within a culture which:

> Shapes individual disposition and physical behaviour in relation to their situation ... Thus a person gets a feel for a situation which may look like the rational consideration, yet it is not, but upon an unstated, usually unnoticed incorporation of culture, which is simultaneously shaped through individual participation. (Avis et al., 2010: 53)

An interesting association with children's learning is the work of Bandura who argued that for children to reach their full potential they needed to acquire a 'mastery' of skills by watching other children achieving. Although children were central to Bandura's work, it is appealing to consider that it has many similarities with Lave and Wenger's notion of socially situated learning, which was originally focused on adult learning. For example, Bandura emphasised the importance of experience and observation in gaining 'mastery', as well as children hearing supporting comments from others and appreciating the emotions involved by learning with their peers (MacBlain, 2014). There are also close links with Guy Claxton's notion of epistemic apprenticeship with situated learning, and communities of practice (Claxton, 2012). Finally, parallel to Lave and Wenger's views that learning was a more complex process than just experience and the observation of others, Kolb argued that experience must be transformative and include both action and practice for true learning to take place. Moreover, according to Kolb (1984), learning is an ongoing process and involves reflection; it is a culturally grounded experience where the process is more important than the product.

At the end of this section it is fitting to comment on how other scholars have adapted the concept of communities of practice, using the overarching meaning of the concept to develop their own ideas. Coffield and Williamson's book *From Exam Factories to Communities of Discovery* (2011), which took an interesting and radical view of the function of schools with their increased emphasis on exams rather than learning, is an example of such an adaptation. They use the term 'communities of discoveries' as an 'extension' to the concept of communities of practice, 'to describe the creative engagement of citizen-learners at all stages of their lives in tackling the collective problems we face in new ways' (Coffield and Williamson, 2011: 12).

CRITIQUING LAVE AND WENGER

Both Lave and Wenger have experienced a fair degree of criticism of their works. This is mainly due to the perceived simplicity of their theory of socially situated learning and their concept of communities of practice, as well as a romanticised notion of apprenticeship (Grubb and Lazerson, 2006). In particular, the relevance of their ideas in modern and complex settings, matters of consensus and power and the relationships between novices and old-timers have all been areas of dispute. There is a level of uncertainty as to whether or not the findings from the five craft apprenticeships they analysed are an appropriate base to apply in the very pressurised, sophisticated and highly technological settings of most modern industries (Fuller et al., 2005). However, Wenger did try to address this in *Communities of Practice: Learning, meaning and identity* (1998) when he used the outcomes of an ethnographic study in a large medical insurance claims processing centre in the United States.

Some critics contest the idea that workplaces, and educational settings, are not always places where colleagues share their practices willingly. In many larger settings, there may be a number of communities of practice created in specific departments which are at odds with other departments. Where this conflict does happen it is likely to cause tension and disharmony rather than lead to shared knowledge and consensus (Entwistle, 2009). It is argued that the major reason for communities of practice not working could be the result of excessive power interactions which hinder admission and participation. For example, in educational settings, methods of learning and teaching, possibly because of individual deep-seated philosophical preference, are often the areas of dispute (Trowler, 2009). However, it is because communities of practice have hierarchical structures (novices and old-timers) that power can be used to either enable or disable legitimate peripheral participation. Such differences between novices and old-timers can cause discord, but perhaps this is pragmatically necessary to enhance the authentic nature of the learning experience. There is an understandable degree of threat that novices present to old-timers, and indeed that threat could be posed by old-timers to novices:

> Each threatens the fulfilment of the other's destiny, just as it is essential to it. Conflict is experienced and worked out through a shared everyday practice in which differing viewpoints and common stakes are in interplay. (Lave and Wenger, 1991: 116)

It is the perceived imbalance of the importance of the learning process between novices and old-timers that is also an area for concern. Lave and Wenger's work emphasises the significance of learning as a developmental process where the novice moves through increasing levels of participation. This focus on the novice mainly overlooks the learning of the more experienced old-timers; furthermore, it disregards the impact on the community of practice when old-timers are brought in from other communities (Fuller et al., 2005). The nurturing of true communities of practice, it is argued, is a problematic undertaking because it requires creating a structure and involves activities which need the shared agreement of those in the community (Collins et al., 2002). Furthermore, Olson contests that by using specific community-structured activities 'students often fail to grasp "the longer purpose" behind the local tasks' (Olson, 2007: 46). In fairness to both Lave and Wenger, they were aware that their socially situated learning theory did not include all the aspects and complexities involved in learning. Wenger later reflected that he 'did not make any sweeping claim that the assumptions that underlie my approach are incompatible with [those] other theories' (Wenger, 2009: 216). Despite the criticisms aimed at socially situated learning, there are many examples where Lave and Wenger's notions can be applied to enhance the learning experience.

APPLYING LAVE AND WENGER IN THE CLASSROOM

The case for the use of a 'community' philosophy in learning and teaching is progressive and convincing. In her (2003) work *Teaching Community: A pedagogy of hope*, bell hooks appeals for a shared and social approach to learning which does not bolster the forces of the market, racism, sexism and elite educational systems. She contests that one of the hazards we face in our current educational systems is the demise of an attachment to the community. This is more than just being close to our colleagues and the learners we work with. It has wider implications in that we are in danger of a 'loss of a feeling of connection and closeness with the world beyond the academy' (hooks, 2003: xv). Applying socially situated learning in education systems which value target setting, accreditations and the advancement of individual achievement could be perceived as a problematic and challenging aspiration for teachers. This is particularly so for teachers in formal educational settings.

However, having developed an understanding of learning in communities of practice and the nature of legitimate peripheral participation gives teachers the opportunity to think about pedagogy in other ways and foster the use of group work, collaborative projects and social media.

Previously, situated learning and communities of practice have been employed in a research context when exploring workplace learning. However, they could also be applied in classrooms where teachers can explore the social environments in which their pupils learn. Furthermore, teachers can also use Lave and Wenger's ideas to reflect on their own practice within specific faculty teams or within the whole school or college to evaluate these communities of practice – whether they help or hinder their continuous professional development (Huddleston and Unwin, 2002). New staff members in schools learn through a form of joint enterprise with other more experienced staff through talking through matters and sharing ideas and resources. This talking could include: the best ways of dealing with behaviour issues; how to access IT systems; the meaning of, and compliance with, school policies; and, possibly, socially accepted practices in the staffroom. This joint enterprise would also involve the more experienced staff sharing learning and teaching resources and sharing their ideas about planning and assessment with new staff members.

New staff members start their time in new schools in a peripheral position, and through time and by gaining increasing self-assurance and competence ultimately become fully fledged members of that community of practice within that particular school (Avis et al., 2010). Equally, if the new member is completing a temporary placement in the school as a trainee teacher, it is argued that that trainee will only ever be in a peripheral position within that school. The trainee is only a transient member of the community, as they will move on to other placements or on to a job as a newly qualified teacher. For this trainee when they move to another school 'the process of learning will have to begin again to some extent as no community of practice is the same' (Avis et al., 2010: 55).

Although socially situated learning has mainly been the domain of the researcher and applied to work-based learning, creating communities of practice in classrooms involving teachers, teaching assistants and pupils is possible. Even though there is an acknowledged difference between learning in work and learning in the formally taught environment of the classroom, the potential for communities of practice in classrooms is an exciting prospect. For example, Wenger's three characteristics could be applied as follows: a mutual agreement by employing group work and shared projects; joint enterprise which negotiates what learning is to take place; and finally, a shared repertoire in a recognised manner of speaking and the use of agreed and authentic resources (Wenger, 1998). It is suggested that fostering such communities within classrooms can be achieved in three particular ways – namely learning and teaching methods, assessment and IT.

Similar to the manner in which craft apprentices informally learn, teaching can comprise activities which are socially considered and planned, which in turn allow pupils to gain a mastery of skills and knowledge. In this way pupils can be supported to learn through working in groups where the pupils and the teachers and teaching assistants all work together to resolve tasks and problems, create a shared understanding of situations and communicate their findings and difficulties to the others in their community (Gredler, 2005). However, for these learning and teaching methods to function as part of a community of practice, activities need to be planned and agreed with the pupils and be of interest to them. It is also an opportunity for teaching staff to learn themselves by being a part of the planning and by being immersed in the learning and teaching process. Such immersion and involvement, it is suggested, possibly reveals that 'learning does not belong to individual persons, but to various conversations of which they are a part' (Smith, 2003).

These conversations can take place through e-learning in the form of blogs where pupils write reflections on their learning to share with others in their group. Pupils can communicate difficulties that they have encountered. Realising that other pupils are finding difficulties in understanding topics can also facilitate learning. Furthermore, blogs offer an informal method of writing and give a writer the option to air an individual commentary (Rai, 2008: 96).

One possible obstacle to creating communities of practice in classrooms is the matter of assessment. Schools are involved in delivering an accredited curriculum which includes formally measuring the learning of an individual pupil. Assessment in this formal and individually focused sense is at odds with the notion of socially situated learning where assessment 'is situationally contingent, rooted in local cultures and reliable and robust only in terms of assumptions, attitudes and values which are, in part at least, localised' (Trowler, 2009: 95). Nevertheless, it is argued that it is feasible – if somewhat problematic – for assessment to be adapted to be used in a socially situated manner in classrooms. What is suggested here is a pragmatic solution of a blend of a socially situated notion of assessment which would then lead to a more formal and summative method. The socially situated notion of assessment would involve a series of group activities where legitimate peripheral participation is evidenced through increasing levels of engagement and competence with the more experienced others. This then becomes an acknowledged level of achievement by the community of pupils. Therefore, in this communal notion of assessment pupils see and value assessment as part of their learning and not as a final outcome (Avis et al., 2010). However, as previously recognised, formal methods of assessment are necessary in classrooms because they work in accredited, qualifications-based curricula. To conclude this section Smith (2003) offers some overarching advice for educators on how they can enhance communities of practice in their settings. Firstly, educators should investigate, with learners, parents and other educators how they can all fully participate. Secondly, educators should endeavour to extend the community with other regional schools and institutions.

REFLECTIVE TASK

Reflect on the ways you learn in different communities of practice. Applying the notion of legitimate peripheral participation give examples of what helps you become (or hinders you from becoming) a valued member of those communities.

SUMMARY

Lave and Wenger's work challenged the traditional notion of learning and teaching. For them, learning was a shared social experience rather than the process of individuals passively gaining knowledge. Their socially situated learning theory offered an alternative view in which interaction, culture and politics were significant elements for learning in communities of practice. The stimulus for their seminal work, *Situated Learning: Legitimate peripheral participation* (1991), was a desire to discover how craft apprentices learned new knowledge and skills without necessarily being part of a formal training process. Their text drew from research into the learning of four types of craft apprenticeships and also from non-drinking alcoholics from AA. They argued that the learning in these circumstances was considerably more complex than 'learning by doing'. Socially situated learning was through a process of legitimate peripheral participation, where learners gradually become more competent in their mastery of skills and knowledge. This increase in competence is gained from learning from more experienced members of the community of practice.

Although there is a strong argument for linking Lave and Wenger's socially situated learning with the works of other educational thinkers such as Vygotsky and Bruner, there are subtle differences. Vygotsky and Bruner's ideas were from a social constructivist standpoint where the purpose of learning was to gain non-specific knowledge and skills. Conversely, Lave and Wenger's notion was that communities of practice engage in particular shared activities with an exclusive purpose. It is this shared purpose in becoming a more adept member of a particular community of practice which Wenger's *Communities of Practice: Learning, meaning and identity* (1998) explored in greater depth. In this work he suggested there were three essential characteristics in true communities of practice, which were mutual agreement, joint enterprise and a shared repertoire. Moreover, the components of successful socially situated learning were meaning, practice community and identity (Wenger, 1998).

Lave and Wenger's ideas have received a fair amount of criticism. These criticisms have been with regard to their relevance in modern complex organisations, concerns over aspects of power and consensus and the relationships between novices and old-timers. Nevertheless, socially situated learning and communities of practice have practical applications, particularly in work-based learning but also in classroom learning. In work-based learning there is a naturally shared identity and belonging to a specific professional or skill role. It is acknowledged that applying Lave and Wenger's ideas in a classroom environment might be a more challenging prospect. However, the use of shared group and project work, socially reflective blogs and a sensitive approach to assessment can enable socially situated learning to prosper in classrooms.

GLOSSARY OF TERMS

Apprenticeship

A different notion to the traditional assumptions regarding the meaning of apprenticeships. This concept involves social interaction where the process of learning becomes increasingly complex. This is not just a routine and mechanistic process where the learner copies the actions of a master, rather learning through apprenticeship is one of legitimate peripheral participation (see below).

Communities of practice

A concept which contends that interactive social commitment is crucial in how people learn and form their distinctiveness. Participants learn how to fit in and how they can influence the changing nature of their community, they progress from a novice to a full member of the community. Communities of practice can be present in formal or informal groups, and they have three essential characteristics: mutual engagement, joint enterprise, and a shared repertoire.

Legitimate peripheral participation

Where learners involve themselves in communities with other more experienced practitioners to develop their skills and knowledge. In doing so learners progressively become more proficient in advancing their mastery, until ultimately they become fully fledged members of their community of practice.

Situated learning

The process of being involved in a community of practice (see above). The notion that learning takes place within the framework of a community's shared experience during day-to-day living; the social, economic, political and cultural experience of the community of practice are key. Knowledge and skills are seen as being a shared acquisition, and an emphasis on the fostering of relationships and a focus on a shared purpose are seen as crucial.

Situatedness

A term which describes the link between the traditional notion of apprenticeship and the theory of situated learning. Situatedness is enhanced when legitimate peripheral participation is accepted and welcomed by the whole community.

FURTHER READING

Carr, D. (2003) *Making Sense of Education*. London: RoutledgeFalmer.

Chapter 12 – Community, identity and cultural inheritance – offers an exploration of the philosophical complexities and problems involved with educational communitarianism.

Lave, J. (2009) The practice of learning. In: Illeris, K. (ed.) *Contemporary Theories of Learning: Learning theorists … in their own words*. Abingdon: Routledge.

This is a replication of the introductory chapter of the 1993 book Lave co-wrote with Seth Chaiklin, *Understanding Practice: Perspectives on activity and context*, which further highlights her ideas of social cognition in everyday situations.

Rogoff, B. (1990) *Apprenticeship in Thinking: Cognitive development in social context*. Oxford: Oxford University Press.

An exploration of how children develop their thinking as they interact with adults and other children.

REFERENCES

Avis, J., Orr, K. and Tummons, J. (2010) Theorizing the Work-based Learning of Teachers. In: Avis, J., Fisher, R. and Thompson, R. (eds) *Teaching in Lifelong Learning*. Maidenhead: Open University Press.

Chaiklin, S. and Lave, J. (1993) *Understanding Practice: Perspectives on activity and context*. New York: Cambridge University Press.

Claxton, G. (2012) 'School as an epistemic apprenticeship: the case for building learning power', Education section of the British Psychological Society's 32nd Vernon-Wall Lecture.

Coffield, F. and Williamson, B. (2011) *From Exam Factories to Communities of Discovery: The democratic route*. London: Institute of Education, University of London.

Collins, J., Harkin, J. and Nind, M. (2002) *Manifesto for Learning*. London: Continuum.

Dennick, R. (2008) Theories of Learning: Constructive experience. In: Matheson, D. (ed.) *An Introduction to the Study of Education* (Third Edition). London: David Fulton.

Entwistle, N. (2009) *Teaching for Understanding at University: Deep approaches and distinctive ways of thinking*. Basingstoke: Palgrave Macmillan.

Fuller, A., Hodkinson, H., Hodkinson, P. and Unwin, L. (2005) Learning as peripheral participation in communities of practice: a reassessment of key concepts in workplace learning. *British Educational Research Journal, 31*, 49–68.

Gredler, M. (2005) *Learning and Instruction: Theory into practice* (Fifth Edition). Upper Saddle River, NJ: Prentice Hall.

Grubb, W. and Lazerson, M. (2006) The Globalization of Rhetoric and Practice: The education gospel and vocationalism. In: Lauder, H., Brown, P., Dillabough, J-A. and Hasley, A. (eds) *Education, Gobalization and Social Change*. Oxford: Oxford University Press.

hooks, b. (2003) *Teaching Community: A pedagogy of hope*. Abingdon: Routledge.

Huddleston, P. and Unwin, L. (2002) *Teaching and Learning in Further Education* (Second Edition). London: RoutledgeFalmer.

Jarvis, P., Holford, J. and Griffin, C. (2003) *The Theory and Practice of Learning* (Second Edition). London: RoutledgeFalmer.

Kolb, D. (1984) *Experiential Learning: Experience as a source of learning and development.* Upper Saddle River, NJ: Prentice Hall.

Lave, J. (1988) *Cognition in Practice: Mind, mathematics and culture in everyday life.* New York: Cambridge University Press.

Lave, J. (2011) *Apprenticeships in Critical Ethnographic Practice.* Chicago, IL: University of Chicago Press.

Lave, J. and Wenger, E. (1991) *Situated Learning: Legitimate peripheral participation.* Cambridge: Cambridge University Press.

MacBlain, S. (2014) *How Children Learn.* London: Sage.

Olson, D. (2007) *Jerome Bruner.* London: Bloomsbury.

Rai, H. (2008) e-Learning. In: Matheson, D. (ed.) *An Introduction to the Study of Education* (Third Edition). London: David Fulton.

Smith, K. (2003) Jean Lave, Etienne Wenger and communities of practice. *The Encyclopaedia of Informal Education.* Available from: www.infed.org/biblio/communities_of_practice.htm [accessed 11/03/18].

Trowler, P. (2009) *Culture and Change in Higher Education.* Basingstoke: Palgrave Macmillan.

Wenger, E. (1987) *Artificial Intelligence and Tutoring Systems: Computational and cognitive approaches to the communication of knowledge.* San Francisco, CA: Morgan Kaufmann.

Wenger, E. (1998) *Communities of Practice: Learning, meaning and identity.* Cambridge: Cambridge University Press.

Wenger, E. (2009) A Social Theory of Learning. In: Illeris, K. (ed.) *Contemporary Theories of Learning: Learning theorists … in their own words.* Abingdon: Routledge.

15
GUY CLAXTON

LEARNING POWER

LEARNING OUTCOMES

Having read this chapter you should be able to:

- appreciate Claxton's notions of learning to learn
- identify and understand his ideas on epistemological apprenticeship and building learning power
- apply the principles of building learning power and soft creativity in your practice
- critically appraise his theories.

KEY WORDS

Building Learning Power; lifelong learning; epistemic apprenticeship; dispositions; soft creativity

INTRODUCTION

Guy Claxton is a major contemporary thinker in education who argues that the traditional concept of education, which is still the focus of government policy for schools, is unfit for preparing students for the challenges and complexities of the twenty-first century. Claxton's theories have had a practical impact in many schools which have engaged with his **Building Learning Power** (BLP) programme, a programme which will be explored in detail later in this chapter. As a starting point, Claxton makes a case for paying less attention to the curriculum content and the emphasis on summative assessment and more to the building of students' confidence and character. Building confidence and character, he reasons, is crucial to developing students' 'ability to learn: they need, for example, to be curious, independent and reflective … but to foster them [teachers] need to change pupils' attitudes and values' (Williams, 2004: 32).

There are two central aspects of Claxton's ideas. One is the need for educational change and the other is the positive notion that most students have the capacity to become better learners. Firstly, the world is a changing environment where students will have to cope with uncertainties, the complexities of developing technology and complicated infrastructures. For Claxton, education must also change to meet these challenges, but, he cautions:

> … this will not happen if they remain founded on a narrow conceptualisation of learning; one which focuses on content over process, comprehension over competence, 'ability' over engagement, teaching over self-discovery. (2002c: 121)

Secondly, he states that cognitive science suggests that most students have the faculty to become better learners if the conditions for learning are appropriately supportive and encouraging. He believes science now offers a broader means of perceiving what learning is all about. This perception 'includes feeling and imagination, intuition and experience, external tools and the cultural milieu, as well as the effort to understand' (Claxton, 2002c: 121). If this fresher notion of learning and teaching is adopted, instead of the more traditional approaches, then students will be better prepared to confront the challenges they face throughout their lives. Being aware of the influence of culture is paramount in this new fresher notion of learning and teaching, as 'it impacts on pupils' interpretation of task performance and their views of themselves as learners' (Pollard, 2005: 158).

Interestingly, Claxton does not shy away from the effort students need to exercise in building a capacity to learn and is quite forthright in questioning levels of student persistence:

> Learning is finding out something that you did not know and struggling with it. It's almost as if, if [today's students] do not know something immediately they feel as though they are failing. (2012: 7)

What hampers such lack of persistence and the realisation that learning is a struggle could be the students' possible deficiency in suitable habits, skills and attitudes, which Claxton states are needed for what he termed 'learning power'. If they acquire this learning power and if the teacher creates and structures appropriate lessons, they can work at noticeably greater levels of learning and achievement (Griffith and Burns, 2013).

This notion of learning power is the driving force behind Claxton's Building Learning Power, a practical school and classroom learning and teaching improvement programme. BLP is an evidence-based programme which followed on from the findings of his (2001) book *Wise Up: The challenge of **lifelong learning***, in which he researched the different worldwide methodologies of applying ways of 'learning to learn' in classrooms. BLP has evolved from the motivation of teachers to improve the quality of what Claxton termed the '**epistemic apprenticeship**' that students were offered in classrooms (Claxton, 2012). Before this chapter explores the facets of epistemic apprenticeship and the theory and application of BLP, it is necessary to consider his background to gain a deeper understanding of the foundations of his theoretical perspectives.

GUY CLAXTON, THE PERSON

Guy Claxton is a prolific researcher and writer, and an eminent and renowned thinker regarding learning. He is a cognitive scientist and has degrees from Cambridge (a double first in Natural Science) and Oxford universities (a PhD in Cognitive Psychology) and is a Fellow of the British Psychological Society. He has held, and still holds, many notable positions in his field, which include an Academician of the Academy of the Social Sciences, Assistant Director for Learning at the Specialist Schools and Academy Trust, Co-Director of the Centre for Real-World Learning (CRL) at the University of Winchester, and Director of Development of the research initiative on the Culture and Learning Organisation (CLIO) at the University of Bristol. His research interests include learning to learn, dispositional teaching, unconscious mental processes, emotions, neuroscience and learning.

He has written a number of important and thought-provoking books and numerous papers, which have practical application and challenge the more traditional educational viewpoints of education and learning. His books include *Becoming a Teacher: A positive approach to change and stress* (1989), *Hare Brain, Tortoise Mind: Why intelligence increases when you think less* (1998), *Wise Up: The challenge of lifelong learning* (2001), *Building Learning Power* (2002a) and *What's the Point of School? Rediscovering the heart of education* (2008). In addition, a text which probably encapsulates his thinking and offers practical solutions is the British Psychological Society's 32nd Vernon-Wall Lecture, 'Schools as an epistemic apprenticeship: The case of building learning power' (2012).

Many of Claxton's ideas have been developed from his collaborative studies as part of the Centre for Real-World Learning at Winchester and also his work with numerous schools and teachers. He has additionally worked with a small company, TLO (The Learning Organisation) Ltd, based in Bristol. Both of these connections have enabled him to seek ways of applying his theories in very practical terms, mainly in the form of the BLP programme.

CLAXTON'S THEORIES

Claxton's theories are derived from his concern that current schooling does not prepare students for a life of learning in an increasingly complex and challenging world. The term 'lifelong learning' was first coined to mean that education was an 'essential part of life and an ongoing pursuit' for personal development' (Wallace, 2008: 165). Schools, Claxton argues, despite the rhetoric of lifelong learning are more concerned with examination results and league tables, which hamper the development of students' ability to learn for themselves and to enjoy learning. Furthermore, he feels that otherwise success-ful students may 'become brittle and insecure when confronted with real problems they can't immediately solve' (Claxton, 2008: 20). Even if they do become 'successful learners' this probably means no more than achieving in terms of examination results rather than having the competence to learn in the real world away from school (Claxton, 2007). Claxton's theories come from his cognitive science background and a deep-seated inter-est in learning. These include: aspects of the brain and notions of intelligence; the importance of apprenticeship; culture; encouraging **dispositions** and creativity for learning; and the foundations of learning power behind his BLP programme.

Neuroscience has demonstrated that learning to learn is achievable and it is also possible for students to cast off old habits and develop more productive ways of learn-ing. Unlike most other animals, we are born into the world in a very undeveloped and vulnerable state which means that our process of maturing is over a longer term and is a more complicated process. However, this slow maturation process 'allows children to tune themselves much more precisely into the particular world in which they live. This tuning in is what we call learning' (Claxton, 2008: 94). During this learning pro-cess there are a number of things that can go awry or not as predicted and further tuning is needed. The brain learns through continually checking how accurately its predictions have worked out and adjusts by developing new attitudes and habits of thinking to resolve complex problems which occur in life.

These relatively new understandings of the workings of the brain, derived from research over the past twenty to thirty years, have led us into thinking about intelli-gence in a more flexible and developmental manner. Previously, intelligence was perceived to be a fixed phenomenon where 'people's "ability" was a stable feature of their minds that did not change and "being dim" stayed with you in the same way that your eye colour or blood group stayed with you' (Claxton, 2008: 59) – a view of educational thinking that Claxton argues still exists today. Intelligence, according to him, is not a single fixed commodity but a combination of habits of thinking which can be refined to deal with the challenges of real-life learning.

An important part of this notion is emotional intelligence, which begins at an early age. Young children, who are uncertain how to react to people or experiences not previously encountered, respond by reciprocating the behaviour of those they know and trust, such as family members and carers. The actions of these significant others, whether deemed to be positive or negative, can have a profound effect on the emotional intelligence and development of children. If children have positive and reasoned experiences which are modelled by these significant others they are more likely to have the emotional intelligence to enable them to work under pressure. They are also better equipped to relate to others in thoughtful and meaningful ways. In so doing, young children undergo an apprenticeship of their emotions (Association of Teachers and Lecturers, 2005).

Apprenticeship is a theme that recurs in much of Claxton's work. He offers the viewpoint that, over the period of their schooling, students will have undergone a lengthy and somewhat intensive apprenticeship in what they learn and how to think. It is the varying outcomes of the learning offered by schools which he explores and criticises in the search for a more effective model of apprenticeship where students can become better equipped for lifelong learning. This model he terms an '"epistemic apprenticeship" – "epistemic" in that it is to do, centrally, with the activities of thinking, learning and knowing' (Claxton, 2012: 3). Currently, he argues, schools concentrate on two dimensions – that of what is to be taught (the content) and that of how this is assessed. An epistemic apprenticeship consists of a third dimension which involves 'the skills and attitudes towards learning students are cultivating by the way they are taught and addressed' (Claxton, 2012: 4). These skills and attitudes comprise what he calls 'dispositions', such as creativity, perseverance, resilience, empathy and imagination; epistemic qualities which are crucial to living a rewarding life in an ever-changing world (Claxton, 2012).

Unlike gaining a skill, such as structuring a sentence or solving mathematical equations, students who develop dispositions such as those mentioned are enabled to respond in difficult circumstances and in times of conflict. The starting point in developing such dispositions is in early childhood and is closely aligned to the learning culture that individual children have experienced. This early stage is where an encouraging and supportive culture leads to children gaining self-belief, being brave enough to take risks and make mistakes and develop their learner identity. This identity is passed on through the culture of the setting children inhabit. This early starting point is a crucial stage in developing dispositions:

The habits and rituals of culture enable certain kinds of learning and disable others ... Experience in childhood, at home and at school, is particularly important because these early belief systems, whether functional or dysfunctional, can be carried through into people's lives as adults. (Claxton, 2002c: 122)

Creativity is one of the learning dispositions that Claxton argues is significant. However, there are a number of conventional meanings for the term 'creativity', all of which are quite complex involving innovation and uniqueness, so expecting students to achieve creativity at this level of originality would therefore be problematic. For example, Shaheen states that creativity can fall into the following groups:

a. production of something original;
b. production of something original and of value;
c. production of something new, of value and imaginative;
d. production of something original, of value and which is accepted by the group.

(2012: 58)

However, Claxton offers another definition which he calls '**soft creativity**' – a more accessible form of creativity but which nevertheless allows the learner to give 'a satisfying scratch to the creative itch' (Claxton, 2006: 353). Soft creativity gives learners the opportunity to explore and nurture facets of creativity over a period of time, which can be achieved by involving them in interesting problem-solving projects and activities (Claxton, 2006). Such activities, which develop dispositions, are the mainstay of his BLP programme which endeavours to encourage students to be '"ready", "willing" and "able" to engage profitably with learning' (Claxton and Carr, 2010: 87).

Learning power is about developing the whole student. It is more than just learning skills, it is about enjoying the learning experience, about having a learner identity and seeking out opportunities for learning. Building learning power involves developing four aspects of student learning: 'the four Rs', which are helping students to become more resilient, resourceful, reflective and reciprocal. These four aspects are further explained below:

Resilience	*– being ready, willing and able to lock on to learning*
Absorption	– flow; the pleasure of being rapt in learning
Managing distractions	– recognising and reducing interruptions
Noticing	– really sensing what's out there
Perseverance	– stickability, tolerating the feelings of learning
Resourcefulness	*– being ready, willing and able to learn in different ways*
Questioning	– getting below the surface; playing with situations
Making links	– seeking coherence, relevance and meaning
Imagining	– using the mind's eye as a learning theatre
Reasoning	– thinking rigorously and methodically

Capitalising	– making good use of resources
Reflectiveness	*– being ready, willing and able to become more strategic about learning*
Planning	– working learning out in advance
Revising	– monitoring and adapting along the way
Distilling	– drawing out the lessons from experience
Meta-learning	– understanding learning, and yourself as a learner
Reciprocity	*– being ready, willing and able to learn alone and with others*
Interdependence	– balancing self-reliance and sociability
Collaboration	– the skills of learning with others
Empathy and listening	– getting inside others' minds
Imitation	– picking up others' habits and values

(Claxton, 2002a: 17)

The 'four Rs of BLP' will be further explored in the application section of this chapter.

LINKS WITH OTHER THEORISTS

Much of Claxton's notions offer attractive solutions to developing learning and, as we shall discover, have practical implications for the classroom. Also, many of his ideas can be associated with other educational theorists. These come under the following headings: social and cultural constructivism, socially situated learning and ways of locating intelligence. Dewey's emphasis on the importance of reflection and the use of active learning methods which relate to real life, as well as his opposition to the traditional school subject-focused curriculum, are akin to Claxton's ideas. There are also close similarities with Vygotsky's emphasis on the significance of 'thinking-in-action' as being central to lifelong learning, as well as the notion of the zone of proximal development (ZPD). However, for Claxton, the ZPD is arguably more than just a conceptual framework, it should be used to build meaningful, supportive and encouraging relationships between students and teachers to form a 'creative collaboration' (Mahn and John-Steiner, 2002). Additionally, Claxton's approach implies an active coaching and prompting model of 'scaffolding' – a concept created at first by Vygotsky but given a more practical application by Bruner.

The theme of apprenticeship, which is very evident in Claxton's work, has a close association with situated learning (Lave and Wenger, 1991) and with communities of practice (Wenger, 1998). Claxton's epistemic apprenticeship draws from communities of practice:

> In which an interwoven set of attitudes and skills are passed on from 'old timers' to 'newcomers' over time, through a whole host of methods and media. These may include modelling, casual feedback and correction, and the telling of pointed jokes and stories, as well as direct instruction and the design of explicit activities. (2012: 8)

The value of students being infused with, and learning from, the culture of the epistemic apprenticeship is parallel with Bourdieu's cultural capital and social reproduction theories where culture has an impact on the learning potential for life.

Claxton's thinking behind dispositions for learning is similar to that of two other educational theorists with alternative views on intelligence. Firstly, there is Howard Gardner's multiple intelligences – a model 'which regards intelligence as multiperspectival, rather than logical–deductive' (Bianchi, 2013: 201). Comparable to Claxton's less fixed idea of intelligence, Gardner's model includes visual, spatial, musical, kinaesthetic, interpersonal and spiritual intelligences, although it also retains the more traditional mathematical and linguistic intelligences. Secondly, perhaps even closer linked with Claxton's dispositions for learning is Daniel Goleman's theory of emotional intelligence, although Claxton was somewhat critical of the overly simplistic nature of Goleman's work (Association of Teachers and Lecturers, 2005). According to Goleman, what is important in developing emotional intelligence is the capacity to control emotional impulses and use reasoning to overcome stressful situations and resolve problems. Acquiring emotional intelligence enables students to cope with the complexities and challenges of real-life learning. For Goleman, which is similar to Claxton in many ways, educational achievement is 'as much to do with socio-emotional and self-regulatory capacities as academic skills and knowledge' (Rose et al., 2013: 180).

Claxton's BLP – which endorsed the four Rs of resilience, resourcefulness, reflectiveness and reciprocity in developing learning – is closely linked to Albert Bandura's concept of self-efficacy. For Bandura self-efficacy is 'children's belief in their abilities to do well and, through their capacity to exercise control over their own acctions, achieve success' (MacBlain, 2014: 172). In fact Claxton also used the phrase self-efficacy for a similar reason as Bandura to demonstrate that 'some beliefs determine how much we generally see the world as potentially comprehensible and controllabe' (Claxton, 2002c: 122). Finally, there are strong associations between Claxton's ideas and those of Carol Dweck who advocates the notion of resilience as being vital for successful learning. Dweck, like Claxton, contests that intelligence is not a fixed entity.

CRITIQUING CLAXTON

It may appear quite a hard task to be critical of Claxton's ideas, because they seem sensible and rational, and perhaps more importantly they offer, especially BLP, a very applicable and inclusive concept for the classroom. Yet it is the very straightforward-ness of his concepts which merits some critical review. In *Building Learning Power* (2002a) particularly, he becomes heavily reliant on lists and guidelines which could be construed as a prescriptive and overly simplistic model to use in developing learn-ing in the complexity of the twenty-first century. Also Pollard gives warning about the use of words such as 'intelligence' and 'ability' as being 'imprecise, insecure and unreliable – but … often put to rhetorical use' (Pollard, 2005: 158). Furthermore, although it is acknowledged that BLP and other similar models such as 'Philosophy 4 Children' are successful in what they do and are widely used programmes in schools, Robins cautions that 'there is a need to ensure that these do not become ends in themselves but a means of producing learning tools' (Robins, 2012: 133).

Claxton himself acknowledges the problems his work creates, especially around the matters of monitoring and evaluating in what are subjective topics such as culture, creativity and intelligence. Although he has tried to formulate ways to measure these subjective topics, he recognises the problems that arise in attempting to show how students increase their learning power and how teachers change their habits when engaging in epistemic apprenticeships. However, in relation to evaluation, Claxton also clearly affirms that the BLP programme is not about the improvement of test scores. Rather, the aim of BLP is:

> To improve the transferable learning dispositions of students – to develop their broad epistemic mentality and identity – *without jeopardising their performance on more con-ventional measures of school success.* (Claxton, 2012: 16)

While learning power is a popular programme it is still a relatively new concept and, although Claxton has been involved and has collaborated with others in numerous action research projects, it is suggested that perhaps further empirical research is needed. Nevertheless, these comments do not in any way mask the acclaim that Guy Claxton's work deserves. He has created truly applicable and inclusive processes which develop students' learning power and create learning cultures in schools and other learning settings.

APPLYING CLAXTON IN THE CLASSROOM

Claxton is very clear in explaining the application of his ideas for classroom practice and in developing epistemic apprenticeships in learning settings. He also firmly rein-forces the need for an interactive and collaborative learning and teaching practice: 'we might remind ourselves that qualities such as resilience, imagination or empathy can-not be developed merely by students being taught *about* them' (Claxton, 2012: 7). Much of the practical advice stresses that the habits and attitudes required for building learning power need to be nurtured through an encouraging and supportive culture. Before we explore and offer practical examples of applying Claxton's work, it is appropriate to briefly explore how learning power can be developed. This will come about not through the complete redesign of educational programmes or indeed by implementing radically new ways of teaching, but what is needed, Claxton argues, is:

> An attention to the implicit values and assumptions of the culture, and to making sure that its objects, its tasks, its non-verbal signals and so on are consonant with the dispositions that the culture wishes to develop. (2002b: 32)

Many of the practical ideas for classroom practice come from *Building Learning Power* (2002a) and associated resources. As such, he focuses on how teachers can develop 'the four Rs' of BLP – resilience, resourcefulness, reflectiveness and reciprocity – in their students. Teachers encourage learning power through what they themselves value, how they talk with their students about learning and attainment and how they themselves model learning. This, Claxton argues, is achieved by teachers explaining, commenting, orchestrating and modelling from the perspective of the particular subject. These four aspects are major factors in developing learning power. Some elements of these will be explored further, but a synopsis of them, with some practical ideas, is given below.

Explaining: telling students directly and explicitly about learning power

Informing: making clear the overall purpose to the classroom

Reminding: offering ongoing reminders and prompts about learning power

Discussing: inviting students' own ideas and opinions about learning

Training: giving direct information and practice in learning: tips and techniques

Commenting – conveying messages about learning power through informal talk, and formal and informal evaluation

Nudging: drawing individual students' attention towards their own learning

Replying: responding to students' comments and questions in ways that encourage learning to learn

Evaluating: commenting on difficulties and achievements in learning-positive ways

Tracking: recording the development of students' learning power

Orchestrating – selecting activities and arranging the environment

Selecting: choosing activities that develop the four Rs

Framing: clarifying the learning intentions behind specific activities

Target-setting: helping students to set and monitor their own learning power targets

Arranging: making use of displays and physical arrangements to encourage independence

Modelling – showing what it means to be an effective learner

Reacting: responding to unforeseen events, questions, etc., in ways that model good learning

Learning aloud: externalising the thinking, feeling and decision-making of a learner-in-action

Demonstrating: having learning projects that are visible in the classroom

Sharing: talking about their own learning careers and histories

(Claxton, 2002a: 9)

These offer succinct, yet, in their own way, comprehensive guidelines for teachers. While they should be used by teachers to develop learning power, Claxton reinforces that they are not to be employed at the expense of gaining subject-specific knowledge and the completion of tasks. This, he states, requires teachers using what he terms 'split-screen thinking', wherein they need to retain 'a dual focus on the content of the lesson and the learning dispositions that are currently being expanded' (Claxton, 2007: 127). Furthermore, he warns that the opposites of the four Rs should not be undervalued. For example, although single-minded perseverance could be seen as a positive learning disposition, 'judicious giving up' is also a quality, as 'an effective learner knows when it is smart to abandon a project and move on, just as much as when and how to persist' (Claxton, 2007: 13).

Many students 'often underachieve not because they don't know what to do, but because they don't do what they know' (Claxton, 2002a: 103). He suggests that teachers encourage students to think about and comprehend the process of learning – this being the first stage in learning to learn. This is a long process and is further developed by teachers continually prompting and reminding and 'scaffolding' learning, which in the first stages should be done often and overtly. As the process develops the prompts should 'fade' and become less frequent so that students develop the practice of doing it on their own: 'They are developing the voice of the guiding, prompting coach inside their own head, so they cease to need external direction' (Claxton, 2002a: 103).

Claxton suggests three ways in which soft creativity can be developed. Firstly, that students should not discard any rough notes or 'working outs' they have made. These can be included in a separate section of their exercise books and used to talk about their early thoughts and plans with others. Secondly, students should be persuaded to keep a 'commonplace book' in which they keep records of their thoughts during learning, a log of what has been discussed with teachers and fellow students, drawings and quotes. Thirdly, that teachers should create displays in corridors and classrooms that not only depict finished work but also develop plans and drafts the students have made to show the creative process that is involved. This, he suggests, would give authenticity and significance to the creative process (Claxton, 2006: 353).

Schools and teachers need to change themselves to embrace and sustain the culture of epistemic apprenticeship. The type of teaching required for forming new learning habits is a lengthy process and one which differs from the type of teaching used to pass on information to reproduce facts for examinations; it requires teachers to think and act differently. This involves thinking about creating a learning-friendly and supportive classroom environment which gives students the self-belief to take risks and experiment knowing that true real-life learning involves uncertainty, confusion and challenge. It also requires teachers to notice and nurture the learning habits of their students and give encouragement when needed. This could include changing the way they create activities and structure lessons. This willingness by teachers to embrace a change of culture involves the same difficult process of habit change as their students experience, and as such teachers also need 'the same kinds of understanding, patience, determination and support' (Claxton, 2012: 15). However, on a more positive note, Claxton also offers some comfort for those teachers who perhaps feel they need to be an 'all-knowing' oracle for students to have respect for them. During his work in schools he found that students 'like their teachers to be fallible and inquisitive and not Know Alls' (Claxton, 2007: 128–9).

To end this section, it is fitting to reflect on what being a powerful learner means to teachers and students, and these are listed in eight broad 'qualities or dispositions' which Claxton calls 'The Magnificent Eight'. Powerful learners are curious; have courage; are good at exploring and investigation; are good experimenters; have imagination; are creative; are sociable; and are reflective (Claxton, 2008: 122).

REFLECTIVE TASK

Consider the four Rs of the BLP programme – resilience, resourcefulness, reflectiveness and reciprocity – from the viewpoint of your practice. Under each of these four Rs list what you currently do to address them, then what you could do in the future to further strengthen learning power with your students.

SUMMARY

Guy Claxton continues to make a crucial contribution to helping students have the self-belief to learn in a changing world by encouraging their acquisition of the values, attitudes and habits they need to be successful lifelong learners. His theories have clear practical applications that teachers can transfer to schools and classrooms. Claxton's argument is that not enough effort and time is currently given to developing how students learn to learn. His ideas for improving students' learning power are set out in *Building Learning Power* (2002a), which is an informative and practical text and the basis for his BLP programme, which is used in numerous schools. Apart from BLP, Claxton's main themes and interests, which have become the foundations for his many writings, are the concepts of intelligence, the importance of culture in learning and the building of epistemic apprenticeships, dispositions for learning and soft creativity. All of these themes have a very functional application for educational practice.

There are similarities between Claxton's ideas and those of others. For example, there are close links with the social constructivists Vygotsky and Bruner (ZPD and scaffolding) which are evident in Claxton's practical classroom practice in the BLP programme of explaining, commenting, orchestrating and modelling. There are also possibly even closer links with the socially situated thinkers Lave and Wenger and the significance placed on the concept of apprenticeships and the value of culture and learning from others. There are connections, even though critical at times, with Gardner's multiple intelligences and Goleman's emotional intelligence. Furthermore, there are similarities with Albert Bandura's notion of self-efficacy, and Carol Dweck's theory which argues that intelligence is not a fixed entity. Critiquing Claxton's works can be challenging as they appear sensible, inclusive, practical and positive in their nature, but perhaps a main criticism is the problem of evaluating and moderating the effectiveness of some of the more subjective areas, such as creativity and concepts of intelligence. Regardless of this, there is no doubt that Guy Claxton's ideas are popular in classrooms. His argument for encouraging personal learning power to prepare students for lifelong learning is a positive notion and a refreshing change from the traditional focus on curriculum content and assessment.

GLOSSARY OF TERMS

Building Learning Power

A practical and useful school and classroom learning and teaching improvement programme, which comprises of developing 'the four Rs' of student learning to become more resilient, resourceful, reflective and reciprocal.

Dispositions

The skills and attitudes needed by students towards meaningful learning which include creativity, perseverance, resilience, empathy and imagination; all of which are key to living a worthwhile life in uncertain and difficult times. These dispositions need to start in early childhood within a supportive culture which leads to children not being afraid of making mistakes, developing their own identities, and being confident in their own self-belief.

Epistemic apprenticeship

A concept of learning where students become better equipped for lifelong learning where activities of thinking, learning and knowing are key. In contrast schools currently concentrate on just two aspects: what is being taught and how it will be assessed. The third aspect of epistemic apprenticeship is needed to develop the skills and attitudes – what Caxton terms dispositions (see above) – required for meaningful longstanding learning.

Lifelong learning

A concept that education is an enduring, encompassing and unending process which enables people to thrive in life as a whole. Therefore, it is much more than the idea that learning finishes when students complete their school, college and university education.

Soft creativity

An idea of a more reachable form of creativity which gives learners an opportunity to sample being creative. The goal in the long term is that they develop their creative attributes through being involved in projects and problem-solving activities. These activities are fundamental in cultivating dispositions (see above).

 FURTHER READING

Claxton, G. and Lucas, B. (2004) *Being Creative: Essential steps to revitalize your work and life.* London: BBC Books.

This is an informative, practical self-help guide to unlocking the reader's creativity. Not specifically related to education.

Gilbert, I. (2002) *Essential Motivation in the Classroom.* London: RoutledgeFalmer.

Although not directly linked to Claxton's BLP, this concise and very practical book seeks to help teachers motivate their pupils and change the culture of their classrooms, which is very much in line with Claxton's ideas.

Hattie, J. (2012) *Visible Learning for Teachers: Maximizing impact on learning.* Abingdon: Routledge.

Following on from Hattie's research-based (2008) *Visible Learning*, this text is aligned with Claxton's notions of school improvement.

Lucas, B., Claxton, G. and Spencer, E. (2012) Progression in creativity: developing new forms of assessment. Background paper for the OECD conference: 'Educating for Innovative Societies'. Available from: http://oecd.org/edu/ceri/50153675.pdf [accessed 09/03/18].

This paper attempts to address the vexed question of assessing creativity.

REFERENCES

Association of Teachers and Lecturers (2005) *An Intelligent Look at Emotional Intelligence*. London: Association of Teachers and Lecturers.

Bianchi, J. (2013) Culture, Creativity and Learning: Arts education for a changing world. In: Ward, S. (ed.) *Education Studies* (Third Edition). Abingdon: Routledge.

Claxton, G. (1989) *Becoming a Teacher: A positive approach to change and stress*. London: Cassell.

Claxton, G. (1998) *Hare Brain, Tortoise Mind: Why intelligence increases when you think less*. London: Fourth Estate.

Claxton, G. (2001) *Wise Up: The challenge of lifelong learning*. Stafford: Network Educational Press.

Claxton, G. (2002a) *Building Learning Power*. Bristol: TLO.

Claxton, G. (2002b) Education for the Learning Age: A sociological approach to learning to learn. In: Wells, G. and Claxton, G. (eds) *Learning for Life in the 21st Century: Sociocultural perspectives on the future of education*. Oxford: Blackwell.

Claxton, G. (2002c) Learning and the Development of 'Resilience'. In: Pollard, A. (ed.) *Readings for Reflective Teaching*. London: Continuum.

Claxton, G. (2006) Thinking at the edge: developing soft creativity. *Cambridge Journal of Education, 36*(3), 351–62.

Claxton, G. (2007) Expanding young people's capacity to learn. *British Journal of Educational Studies, 55*(2), 115–34.

Claxton, G. (2008) *What's the Point of School? Rediscovering the heart of education*. Oxford: Oneworld.

Claxton, G. (2012) 'Schools as an epistemic apprenticeship: the case of building learning power', Education Section of the British Psychological Society's 32nd Vernon-Wall Lecture.

Claxton, G. and Carr, M. (2010) A framework for teaching learning: the dynamics of disposition. *Early Years: An International Research Journal, 24*(1), 87–97.

Griffith, A. and Burns, M. (2013) *Engaging Learners*. Carmarthen: Crown House.

Lave, J. and Wenger, E. (1991) *Situated Learning: Legitimate peripheral participation*. Cambridge: Cambridge University Press.

MacBlain, S. (2014) *How Children Learn*. London: Sage.

Mahn, H. and John-Steiner, V. (2002) The Gift of Confidence: A Vygotskian view of emotions. In: Wells, G. and Claxton, G. (eds) *Learning for Life in the 21st Century: Sociocultural perspectives on the future of education*. Oxford: Blackwell.

Pollard, A. (ed.) (2005) *Reflective Teaching* (Second Edition). London: Continuum.

Robins, G. (2012) *Praise, Motivation and the Child*. Abingdon: Routledge.

Rose, J., Gilbert, L. and Smith, H. (2013) Affective Teaching and the Affective Dimensions of Learning. In: Ward, S. (ed.) *Education Studies* (Third Edition). Abingdon: Routledge.

Shaheen, R. (2012) Creativity. In: Arthur, J. and Peterson, A. (eds) *The Routledge Companion to Education*. Abingdon: Routledge.

Wallace, S. (2008) *Oxford Dictionary of Education*. Oxford: Oxford University Press.

Wenger, E. (1998) *Communities of Practice: Learning, meaning, and identity*. Cambridge: Cambridge University Press.

Williams, J. (2004) *Great Minds: Education's most influential philosophers. A Times Education Supplement Essential Guide*.

16
DYLAN WILIAM

ASSESSMENT FOR LEARNING

LEARNING OUTCOMES

Having read this chapter you should be able to:

- Appreciate Dylan Wiliam's work on assessment for learning and understand how this can be applied in the classroom
- Understand the difference between assessment for learning and assessment of learning, and recognise the implications for pupils
- Critically appraise his work.

KEY WORDS

assessment for learning; Black Box; formative assessment; Teacher Learning Communities; summative assessment; assessment of learning

INTRODUCTION

Dylan Wiliam is perhaps most well-known for his pioneering work on **assessment for learning**, work undertaken with his colleague Paul Black, which culminated in the best-selling publication *Inside the **Black Box*** (Black and Wiliam, 1998). Currently Emeritus Professor of Educational Assessment at University College, London, Wiliam's career began as a secondary school teacher, initially as a tutor of mathematics and physics at a private school in Worcestershire, followed by teaching positions in schools in inner city London. His career in academia began in 1984 when he took a two-year research fellow post at Chelsea College working on a scheme called Graded Assessment in Mathematics – a precursor to **formative assessment**.

Wiliam's academic career has seen him combine his early experience as a classroom teacher with research work into education systems, initially in assessment practices and latterly in looking at the professional development of teachers. His current work centres around the development of **Teacher Learning Communities** (TLCs), his vision for which he presents as a support group for teachers in which teachers choose an area of practice which they wish to change, and colleagues within the group support individuals in making these changes. He explains:

> What you as a teacher are trying to learn comes from your own needs – so it's a bit like Alcoholics Anonymous or Weightwatchers – the support group aren't there to tell you what to do, but to help you achieve what you want to do. (Wiliam, cited in Goodwin, 2008: 4)

Wiliam's TLCs have been particularly successful in Southern Australia, Singapore and Sweden and he currently divides his time between these countries and the UK.

McInerney (2015) suggests that Wiliams is 'dangerously close to being a public intellectual', and observes that he is 'one of the few modern educationalists to become a familiar staffroom name'. This may be in part down to his appearance on the 2010 BBC documentary 'The Classroom Experiment', in which he introduced his teaching methods to a group of Hertfordshire teachers. In this documentary he attempted to demonstrate how subtle changes to teaching methods could reap rewards, and advised that such methods were more effective than spending vast sums of money on school buildings and reducing class sizes, arguing that instead investment should be on raising teachers' skill levels.

Wiliams' work has shown a commitment to improving aspects of the education system in the best interests of both children and practitioners, and while some of his ideas have proved controversial, it cannot be denied that he has made a significant impact on teaching practices, especially in the area of whole-school assessment and feedback.

☌ DYLAN WILIAM, THE PERSON

Dylan Ap Rhys Wiliam was born in North Wales, the son of an Oxford-educated professor. Wiliam was brought up as a Welsh speaker, and did not really speak any

English until he went to grammar school in Cardiff and Manchester (Wilby, 2011). He admits to being a poor student, stating 'I was very badly co-ordinated and couldn't write legibly. I still print, basically' (McInerney, 2015). He has also reflected on being badly behaved, uncoordinated and having a stammer, always being the last to be picked for teams in physical education (Wilby, 2011). Fortunately for Wiliam he found that he had a talent for mathematics in his late teens, and was awarded a school maths prize for the best A-level results. In addition, he also began weight training at the age of 14, and after training for an hour every day for three years he explained that he was transformed from 'being completely useless at sports to being a kind of jock' (McInerney, 2015), making captain of the rugby team and house captain in athletics.

Wiliam's average education performance continued throughout university, and after failing to get an interview for both Oxford and Cambridge he accepted a place at Durham studying mathematics and physics. Of his time at Durham he explains 'I don't know if I was depressed at university or not, but there are large areas where there is a sort of haze about what actually happened' (McInerney, 2015). Wiliam eventually graduated with a third-class honours degree. While at university he became heavily involved with music, and this distraction may well further explain his poor academic performance. He played in a 'jazz-folk' band called Lynx, and wholly intended to pursue a musical career on graduation. However, McInerney (2015) states that his plans to pursue a career in music were impeded after his father took a job at the University of Connecticut and informed Wiliam that he would not be able to remain in the family home.

Wiliam decided to apply for teaching as a means of supporting himself while he continued to play in his band, however after failing to get a place on a PGCE course at Goldsmiths, he went to an employment agency specialising in recruiting teachers to private schools where he was offered a job working at a private school in Worcestershire. It was at this time that he realised his musical ambitions would be unfulfilled since occasional gigs in pubs had proved insufficient to make a living. He reflected that 'I hadn't realised how hard it is to make any kind of a living as a musician. If you get enough money to cover your petrol, you're lucky' (Wilby, 2011). Fortunately for Wiliam this realisation came around the same time that he determined that he actually enjoyed teaching, and thus he decided to dedicate himself to this profession. In addition, he decided to move out of the private and into the state sector, working in secondary schools in West London while at the same time gaining further degrees in mathematics and mathematics education through the Open University and the Polytechnic of the South Bank.

Wiliam taught in London secondary schools for seven years and quickly gained promotions, in part because he was teaching a 'shortage subject'. However, after eight years of teaching, and following a disagreement with his headteacher over a promotion opportunity, he joined Chelsea College to work on a research project involving Graded Assessment in Mathematics. He has reflected that at the time everyone thought he was being somewhat rash, leaving a secure job for a two-year fixed contract, however he has responded to this by saying that he jumped at the chance to work on something that interested him in greater depth (Goodwin, 2008). While Wiliam suggests that research was not something he wanted to do, his time at Chelsea College, later to become a part of King's College in London, led to further roles at King's as a lecturer in mathematics, dean of the school of education and then assistant principal. It was during this period that he studied for his doctorate which he gained in 1993 from the University of London.

It was during his time at King's College that Wiliam first worked with Paul Black, a relationship which he describes as 'intellectually the most productive of my career' (Goodwin, 2008). Wiliam believes that the success of their working relationship is due to the fact that they work very differently, and having different areas of expertise (Black is a physicist), they have been forced to think about things, and make connections, that they would not have done had they worked independently. It was his work on formative assessment with Paul Black that led to his most well-known work, *Inside the Black Box*, and while Wiliam jokes that this made them what appeared to be an overnight success, the work actually took over twenty years to come to fruition.

It is possibly due to his early career as a teacher that Wiliam has dedicated his academic career to improving classroom practice and supporting classroom teachers. He believes that one of the reasons for the success of *Inside the Black Box* is due to the embedding of formative assessment into practice rather than just through policy (Goodwin, 2008). He has spoken out against a results-driven agenda, and has sought ways of supporting high-quality teaching through methods which will be further explored in the application section of this chapter. Despite not having a traditional teaching degree he appears to have gained a 'guru-like' status amongst the teaching profession, however he remains humble, and reflecting on his academic career he says 'certainly for a long time in my career I had this imposter syndrome thing of "they will find out there has been a mistake and I will have to go back to teaching in Shepherd's Bush"' (McInerney, 2015). However, he also shows the courage of his convictions, refusing to do something just because others expect him to. This can be seen reflected in his work with teachers, which frequently shows him throwing out the rulebook as we will see later in the chapter.

THE BLACK BOX

As we have seen earlier in the chapter, Wiliam's most influential work was a result of studies into the impact of assessment on pupils, culminating in the publication *Inside the Black Box* (Black and Wiliam, 1998). For Black and Wiliam, the Black Box referred to the classroom in which outside inputs from policy makers are fed in with the hope that this will result in desirable outputs. For example, policy related to testing and assessment should result in better outcomes for pupils and teachers. However, Black and Wiliam raised the question 'how can anyone be sure that a particular set of new inputs will produce better outputs if we don't at least study what happens inside?' (1998:1). Black and Wiliam went on to suggest that the impetus was on teachers to make the inside work better, however they saw this as an unfair system, especially in areas as important as standards raising. They suggested that policy makers should take on more responsibility for providing direct help, setting out their recommendations in the aforementioned publication.

Black and Wiliam had a specific interest in assessment practices, defining assessment as 'all those activities undertaken by teachers, and by their students in assessing themselves, which provide information to be used as feedback to modify the teaching and learning activities in which they are engaged' (Black and Wiliam, 1998: 2). For them, it was not just the end result which was important, but also the learning process; key to the success of assessment was the ongoing changes which were made as a result of the observations made. Black and Wiliam called this process formative assessment in which 'the evidence is actually used to adapt the teaching work to meet the needs' (1998: 2). In forming their conclusions they conducted a longitudinal project, reviewing research in books and journal articles over a nine-year period. Their results were first published in the journal *Assessment in Education*, in which they drew the conclusion that formative assessment did indeed raise standards, however there was room for improvement, especially in relation to formative assessment practices.

Formative assessment is a complex process, far more so than **summative assessment** which Black and Wiliam suggested formed the basis of public and political attention. At the time of the Black Box publication assessment had been very much concentrated around the tests conducted at the end of each key stage, with a focus on the overall levels and grades. Black and Wiliam acknowledged that teachers did make some contribution to these, but also suggested that little attention was paid to this. Summative assessment then would be interpreted as an **assessment of learning**, referring to an assessment type which yields a final result – for example, numerical data to be published in league tables, or certificates given to students such as GCSEs which give employers or education providers an indication of a pupil's performance. While valid in terms of providing a reliable indication of pupil performance, comparable across the country, this type of assessment forms no useful purpose in promoting pupil learning or in informing teachers of how they might move that learning forward. Summative assessment normally takes place at the end of a learning unit or module, by which time it is often too late to address any difficulties pupils may have experienced.

Formative assessment on the other hand is far more effective as a diagnostic tool, allowing for difficulties to be seen and addressed prior to summative assessments being carried out. Following on from *Inside the Black Box*, the Assessment Reform Group (ARG) (1999), of which Dylan Wiliam was a part, set out five elements for assessment to improve learning in the follow-up publication *Assessment for Learning: Beyond the Black Box,* these being:

1. The provision of effective feedback to students.
2. The active involvement of students in their own learning.
3. The adjustment of teaching to take into account the results of assessment.
4. The recognition of the profound influence assessment has on the motivation and self-esteem of students, both of which are critical influences on learning.
5. The need for students to assess themselves and understand how to improve.

At this point the term 'formative assessment' was rejected in favour of *assessment for learning*, since it was considered that formative assessment was open to interpretation and simply suggested that assessment was carried out and planned at the same time as teaching, negating the notion that it should be used to inform planning. Nevertheless, the fundamental principles behind formative assessment remained, and the five elements as set out by the ARG will now be considered in more detail.

Black and Wiliam (1998) observed that teacher feedback to pupils frequently served a social and managerial function with little attention paid to the learning function it should play. Wiliam suggested that 'much of the feedback that students get has little or no effect on their learning, and some kinds of feedback are actually counterproductive' (2011: 107). The traditional methods of providing feedback to students came through the marking of work, normally after the event, and a major criticism of this was that this type of marking rarely offered advice as to how the work could be improved (Black et al., 2003). A further criticism of this type of marking was that it often reinforced underachievement, and frequently gave pupils little time to address any shortcomings or misconceptions. For Black and Wiliam quality feedback 'should be about the particular qualities of his or her work, with advice on what he or she can do to improve, and should avoid comparisons with other pupils' (1998: 9). Ideally feedback would take place during the event, and time should be given for pupils to read and address the feedback given, since as Wiliam observes 'the only important thing about feedback is what students do with it' (2016: 10).

Moving on to the second element, involving pupils in their own learning, Black and Wiliam (1998) advised that pupils should be involved in the choice of tasks, in as much as prior learning is considered at the planning process. Additionally, the sharing of learning aims is encouraged, with pupils having the opportunity to 'communicate their evolving understanding' (1998: 10). Black and Wiliam (1998) suggested that time should be set aside for this, also encouraging pupil–teacher dialogue, which might allow teachers to respond to and re-orientate pupils' thinking without inhibiting future learning. Black and Wiliam recommended that 'the dialogue between pupils and a teacher should be thoughtful, reflective, focused to evoke and explore understanding, and conducted so that all pupils have an opportunity to think and to express their ideas' (1998: 12).

Black and Wiliam (1998) did not reject the notion of summative assessment, however for them the end result of the assessment – the result – was less important than what a teacher could learn from the result, hence the third element which promotes the adjustment of teaching to take account of the result of the assessment. In this instance, summative assessment is used in a formative way. In *Inside the Black Box* (1998) they outlined that a good test should be a learning as well as a testing opportunity. The ARG (1999) advised that high stakes testing, such as end of key stage tests, had resulted in teachers adopting practice testing rather than focusing on assessment for learning, which was resulting in pupil anxiety, particularly amongst lower achievers. This reflects the fourth element relating to the influence of self-esteem and motivation of pupils. Black et al. (2003) observed that the overemphasis on such testing can lead to comparisons between students, which lead to the emergence of a competitive element to classroom practice as opposed to the self-improvement which should be advocated.

In the final element the ARG outlined the importance of pupils being involved in self-assessment and understanding how they can use this to improve their own learning. Wiliam (2011) expressed this as students being owners of their own learning, reinforcing the notion that it is the learners and not the teachers who should create the learning experience. However Wiliam also reflected that the school culture appeared to 'be based on the opposite principle – that if they try really hard enough teachers can do the learning for the learners' (2011: 145). In this scenario the pupils become passive recipients of their own learning. From the research which informed *Inside the Black Box*, Wiliam made the point that, if allowed, pupils are more than capable of developing sufficient insights into their own learning to make the necessary improvements, and furthermore evidence suggests that such involvement can also improve pupils' motivation. Black and Wiliam (1998) advised that pupils should be trained in self-assessment, thereby giving them ownership of their own learning and recognising for themselves what they need to do to achieve. Black and Wiliam (1998) also suggested that pupils were very much capable of assessing their own work and tended to be both honest and reliable in their assessments of their own performance and that of their peers – in fact they were frequently much harder on themselves than their teachers. However, Black and Wiliam (1998) also proposed that self-assessment could only happen if the pupils were aware of what they were trying to achieve, hence the importance of sharing targets and learning outcomes with pupils. There was no misapprehension of the challenges of this aspect of formative assessment, since a tradition of passive receptivity had been ingrained in the education system, however Black and Wiliam observed that self-assessment by pupils 'far from being a luxury, is in fact an essential component of formative assessment' (1998: 10) and well worth the effort of teaching pupils how to carry this out effectively.

It should be noted that the application of formative assessment to a school system which had come to rely on more traditional methods was always going to be a challenge, however Black and Wiliam (1998) determined that there was a need for an increased focus on the inside of the Black Box which could best be achieved through a change to policy. Additionally, practical advice for classroom practitioners became a key focus for Wiliam, advice which will be covered later in the chapter as we see how this work can be applied to practice.

LINKS WITH OTHER RESEARCHERS

In formulating the original *Inside the Black Box* material Black and Wiliam (1998) conducted an extended literature review of research into assessment, commencing with 580 articles or chapters of which 250 sources were eventually chosen to examine in more detail. In view of this it can be seen that their work was influenced by a significant number of researchers in the field, some of whom will be explored in this section.

Wiliam (2014) proposed that Michael Scriven was the first to use the term 'formative assessment' as early as 1967, but as a means of on-going improvement of the curriculum as opposed to the assessment of individual pupils. This was further developed by Benjamin Bloom (1969), predominantly in the higher education context, where formal assessments or tests were used to inform future teaching or curriculum management. However, Wiliam (2014) suggests that Sadler (1989) was the most influential in terms of seeing 'formative assessment as being intrinsic to, and integrated with, effective instruction' (2014: 2). Sadler defines formative assessment as being concerned with how judgements about the quality of students' responses (performances, pieces of work) can be used to shape or improve their competence by short circuiting the randomness and inefficiency or trial and error learning (1989: 120). Black and Wiliam (1998) used Sadler's observations on the role of the student in their own learning to develop their ideas on peer and self-assessment. Sadler (1989) argued that students could only achieve a learning goal if they could understand that goal and recognise how to achieve it – a concept which is inherent in the Assessment for Learning (AfL) guidance produced by the Department for Children, Schools and Families in response to Black and Wiliam's work, which sees teachers sharing learning goals with pupils, and offering guidance as to what a successful outcome might look like.

Ruth Butler's (1988) work on feedback to pupils influenced Black and Wiliam's work on closing the gap feedback. Butler (1988) observed that pupils tended to ignore feedback when marks were given, resulting in their being mark driven and not seeking to find ways of improving that work through engagement with the written feedback. Black and Wiliam further developed these observations, and through working with pupils and teachers they proposed that feedback and marks should not be used together, and that if marks were to be given this should happen after pupils had had sufficient time to read and address the feedback given.

Finally, Black and Wiliam (1998) were influenced by Rowe's (1974) work on the use of questioning in the classroom. Rowe identified that teachers did not give pupils sufficient time to respond to teachers' questions (usually approximately 0.9 seconds). Conducting her own research, Rowe (1974) found that increasing the 'waiting time' had positive effects on pupil engagement, including longer and more confident responses, a decrease in a failure to respond and an increased chance of pupils challenging or improving on their own answers. Black and Wiliam's own research led to further suggestions around the use of questioning to include the increasing of wait time, but also in the framing of questions to allow pupils opportunities to explore their own understanding of a concept (Black et al., 2003).

CRITIQUING WILIAM

Wiliam is one of the first to admit that the response of the government to the *Inside the Black Box* research left a lot to be desired (Goodwin, 2008), and suggests that the challenge of encouraging people to change an already entrenched way of thinking was one of the reasons why he and Paul Black were not as successful in promoting their ideas as they might have been. Likewise, Wiliam acknowledges that the exposure he received as a result of the BBC2 documentary could have come across as gimmicky, agreeing that the 'programme failed to convey a coherent message' (Wilby, 2011). These views are supported by education blogger Joe Kirby (2013) who suggests that formative assessment is a distorted educational concept, backed by a range of gimmicks, unhelpful acronyms and government-led policy which confused AfL with national levels. Kirby also posits that school leadership teams who stuck rigidly to the 'letter of the AfL law' (2013) failed to embrace the flexibility of formative assessment, and in so doing allowed the spirit of what Black and Wiliam (1998) were trying to achieve to be lost. Indeed, the very fact that Ofsted began to focus part of their observations on establishing how far pupils understood what levels they were at, suggests a system which was far removed from what Black and Wiliam originally intended.

Wiliam refers to this as *policy diffraction* (Menzies, 2010) and uses this to explain how what appears to be a positive message from policy publications becomes bastardised once it reaches the classroom. This he suggests is a result of the government being in a rush, or looking for a quick fix. Christodoulou (2016) supports this, observing that the government support for the policy was counter-productive and suggesting that the government were too concerned with high-stakes monitoring and tracking rather than low-stakes diagnostics. She advises that the government interpretation of assessment for learning meant it changed from being formative to summative, and in so doing lost the key messages which Black and Wiliam were trying to promote.

Kirby (2013) suggests, however, that Wiliam failed to articulate his ideas clearly, and despite the early criticism of some of his ideas, particularly around some of the aforementioned classroom strategies, has continued to promote these ideas in his later works. Didau (2014) agrees with Kirby and concludes that the 'big idea of AfL is all wrong', and although he concurs that some of Wiliam's ideas such as the traffic light system will not do any harm to the pupils, he also argues that he doubts they will have much impact on their metacognition. Wiliam (2011) himself notes that even where teachers have followed his advice, particularly in the case of replacing grades with comments, such comments have not proved to be helpful or formative, with teachers frequently focusing on what is deficient about a piece of work rather than providing helpful comments which would help pupils improve. It could be argued that this was down to a failure to express just what would constitute formative feedback, however Christodoulou (2016) suggests that the issue may be down to a lack of clear understanding regarding the outcome of a piece of work. She suggests that assessment for learning should be more about how a skill is acquired, with a focus on the method and process of acquiring a skill rather than the end product. She also advises that while the final outcome may well be summatively assessed it is important that pupils are supported formatively along the way. For her the processes of formative and summative assessment may well co-exist but should also be kept apart where necessary, something which Wiliam failed to acknowledge as he attempted to integrate the two (Wiliam, 2016, cited in Christodoulou, 2016).

Didau (2014) proposes that a major flaw of AfL is the idea that learning can be assessed during the learning process in order to adapt future teaching, however he argues that this is an impossible task for teachers, suggesting that there is no meaningful way of assessing learning during the process. Didau (2014) believes that Wiliam's assertion that learning is being assessed is actually the assessment of performance, and this is problematic since performance is influenced by cues and stimuli from the teacher, and does not give an accurate assessment of the retention or transfer of the knowledge and skills taught.

Both Didau (2014) and Kirby (2013) acknowledge that Wiliam's ideas have worth, and as we have seen here it may well be the government's attempts to formalise the process which have proved to be its biggest downfall, since as Christodoulou (2016: 18) observes 'the assessment in AfL went from being formative to being summative: no longer assessment for learning but assessment of learning'. Nevertheless, there is still value in applying some of the methods proposed in the *Inside the Black Box* (1998) guidance, which will be discussed in the next section of this chapter.

⚙ APPLYING FORMATIVE ASSESSMENT IN THE CLASSROOM

As we have seen previously, both *Inside the Black Box* (1998) and *Beyond the Black Box* (ARG, 1999) advocated a holistic approach to classroom assessment which was built on formative assessment. The government response to the proposals set out by the ARG was the launch of the Assessment for Learning strategy in 2008, followed by the publication of a set of assessment for learning (AfL) materials and guidance for schools in 2009; these materials were based around the five key elements discussed earlier offering guidance to schools as to how formative assessment could be implemented in the classroom. The AfL materials offered teachers practical guidance much of which can be seen echoed in Wiliam's own work, and which can still be seen embedded into practice today.

The assessment for learning strategy outlined five main processes which were key to the successful implementation of a formative assessment programme. These areas will now be discussed:

1. *Questioning*

Questioning serves the purpose of finding out where a learner is at with their learn-ing, however as previously noted research from Black and Wiliam (1998) revealed that the 'wait time' between asking the question and waiting for an answer was around 0.9 seconds, which is not sufficient for a young learner to think about the question and formulate an answer (Black et al., 2003). Rowe (1974) recommends that a more appropriate wait time would be 3 seconds which she suggests would improve the quality of answers. In the assessment for learning guidance one way of increasing this wait time is the use of mini whiteboards on which pupils will write their answers. Not only does this give pupils time to formulate their answers, it also affords teachers the opportunity to assess which students have understood a concept as answers are revealed. A further strategy adopted by some practitioners is the use of 'talk partners' in which pupils share their responses to questions with their partner, thereby giving them the reassurance of the potential accuracy of a response which in turn can help to build confidence. This is especially effective if talk partners are of a different abil-ity level, allowing discrete opportunities for peer support.

Wiliam (2016) suggests that by requiring all pupils to respond to questions also increases inclusivity in the classroom. In the traditional method of pupils putting up their hands to answer questions he advises that some pupils become invisible, with the same pupils always answering the questions. In order to involve all pupils, he warns that participation must be compulsory, with no pupils being given the option of being able to opt out of responding. A method which he employs to encourage participation is the use of lollipop sticks on which he writes the names of all the pupils in the class; the sticks are then selected at random to ensure a non-biased approach to selecting pupils to answer questions. In this way they remain alert because they never know when their name will be selected, and all pupils have an equal opportunity to answer questions. It should be noted however that this method comes with a health warning: especially where pupils give the wrong answers, a positive teacher response is paramount here to avoid pupils becoming disheartened and fearful of the process.

A further benefit of questioning is the development of dialogic teaching, in which on-going talk between teacher and learner is encouraged, largely through the use of open questions. Open questions normally elicit a longer response from a pupil, in which they are able to expand on an answer and reveal much about their thought processes. Further probing by the teacher can reveal the levels of understanding of pupils but more importantly highlight any misconceptions which can then be addressed.

2. *Feedback to students*

Formative feedback allows both teachers and learners to come together to assess where the learner is at, where they want to be and how they are going to get there. Traditionally feedback comes through teachers marking pupils' work, however in a 2002 interview Wiliam observed that in marking work teachers spend too long in correcting pupil errors, especially in cases where the school marking policy sets out that all spelling and grammatical errors must be corrected (Marshall, 2002). Wiliam advises that a learner who sees a page full of corrections will undoubtedly feel demoralised, but more importantly there is nowhere for him or her to go with this. Instead Wiliam advocates that pupils should be directed towards the error and then given the opportunity to correct this. For example, rather than correcting errors he suggests that the teacher points out how many errors have appeared on the page and gives the student time to find these. This in itself has implications for traditional classroom practice in which pupils are rarely given the opportunity to amend mistakes. Wiliam (2002) advocates that students should spend twice as much time addressing feedback as a teacher spends giving it, but suggests in reality the opposite is often true. The AfL guidance recommends that marking should be comment-only guidance, avoiding giving any grades or marks. Comments should avoid generalisations such as 'good' or 'well done', and instead teachers should be providing comments which tell pupils what they have done well and the next steps for improvement. More importantly time should be set aside for reading and addressing comments, and planning should allow opportunities for pupils to take the next steps needed.

3. *Self-assessment*

Self-assessment requires that a pupil evaluates their own learning against the learning intentions, and then sets their own goals in terms of what they need to improve and how this might be achieved. However, it should be noted that self-assessment does not come easily to pupils and is something which must be taught. Black et al. observe that 'it is very difficult for students to achieve a learning goal unless they understand a goal and can assess what they need to do to reach it' (2003: 49). The role of the teacher then is imperative in supporting this understanding and strategies for achieving this involve sharing the learning intentions with the learners, and then modelling what a successful outcome might look like. In the classroom this might be seen by displaying learning outcomes on walls or whiteboards, and producing classroom displays with exemplars – sometimes referred to as learning or working walls.

A simple approach to self-assessment proposed by Black et al. (2003) was through the application of a traffic light system, with pupils indicating with red, amber or green labels as to how far a concept had been understood. In the 2010 BBC2 documentary, 'The Classroom Experiment', Wiliam demonstrated this technique using plastic cups, in which pupils placed the appropriate coloured cup on their desks as they completed their work, thereby giving the teacher instant feedback as to how far they had understood a concept. Or as Wiliam (2010) reflects, allowing teachers to recognise when pupils simply don't get their brilliant lesson. Black et al. (2003) suggest that peer support can also be used here – for example, pupils who indicate a green traffic light might support those with an amber indication, while the teacher concentrates on the red traffic lights.

Guidance from Cambridge International Examinations (CIE) (undated) advises that teachers should ask pupils a series of questions about their work to scaffold an approach to self-assessment, and these might include asking them what they understood of the work and what they didn't, how it fits with their existing knowledge and what they might do to improve. This encourages pupils not only to reflect on their work, but also to begin thinking about next steps. Such ownership of their own work can be a powerful motivating force in helping pupils control and direct their own learning.

4. *Peer assessment*

Peer assessment is a means by which pupils evaluate one another's work and can be used as complementary to, or even as a prior requirement for, self-assessment (Black et al., 2003). Peer assessment was found to be a motivating force for pupils, with pupils applying more care to their work knowing that their peers would be assessing it. One of the benefits of peer assessment is that pupils are often able to use language that is better understood by one another, so explanations can be voiced in a more accessible way. Black et al. (2003) also found that pupils were more accepting of critique from peers than from teachers.

As with the renewed attention to marking and feedback it is necessary to provide time in a lesson for peer assessment to proceed, and as with self-assessment it is important to teach pupils to focus on the learning intentions in order that feedback is objective. Nevertheless, if managed appropriately, utilising peer assessment can support pupils in their social skills, and also support their own critical and analytical thinking. At the same time, if pupils are involved in peer assessment then the teacher is able to observe and reflect on what is happening in the classroom to inform future intentions (Black et al., 2003).

Black et al. observe that both peer and self-assessment 'can make unique contributions to the development of students' learning' (2003), however they also caution that the process does not always come naturally to pupils and reinforce the notion that pupils need to be taught skills in collaboration, listening and turn taking to achieve success. However, if managed correctly both peer and self-assessment can strengthen student voice and improve communication between pupils and their teachers (Black et al., 2003).

5. *The formative use of summative assessment*

As we have previously noted Black and Wiliam (1998) did not disregard the importance of summative assessment, especially since this is the method most widely used to assess where students are with their learning. Indeed, at the time of publishing *Inside the Black Box* it could be argued that high stakes testing was more prevalent than ever before as a result of the political commitment to external tests and published league tables. However, Black et al. (2003) advocate that summative testing should work alongside formative assessment, rather than the two being seen as entirely separate processes. Assessment for learning guidance advises returning test papers to pupils so they are able to see where mistakes have been made. For teachers, the analysis of test papers is essential, with a focus on identifying which questions have been answered incorrectly by a majority of pupils and addressing this through future planning.

Black et al. (2003) suggest that for older pupils a reflective review of test papers might help them plan their revision more effectively, so practice or end of module assessments can reveal areas of potential weakness and the development of personal revision targets. This can be done through the application of the traffic light system previously discussed, revealing how aspects of formative assessment can be seen working holistically.

It can be stated then that summative assessment should be viewed as a key part of the learning process – not something to be feared, but as a means of charting the process and identifying weaknesses so these can be addressed. Pupils should be the 'beneficiaries rather than the victims of testing, because testing can help to improve learning' (Black et al., 2003: 56).

REFLECTIVE TASK

Consider the five processes for the implementation of formative assessment in the classroom:

1. Questioning.
2. Feedback.
3. Self-assessment.
4. Peer assessment.
5. Formative use of summative assessment.

Under each make a list of practices that you have observed in the classroom, or experienced firsthand, which reflect how this work might have been embedded in the classroom.

SUMMARY

As we have seen Black and Wiliam's work on assessment for learning made a significant impact on practices in educational settings, and it could be argued that it was Wiliam's passion for publicly promoting these ideas which led to the success of the Black Box materials. Wiliam has never been afraid of speaking his mind when discussing how improvements to education can be made, and openly expresses that success in schools is not a result of investment in school buildings or decreasing class sizes (Wilby, 2011), but instead promotes the idea of teacher development as being the key to successful learning. His current work focuses on the development of Teacher Learning Communities (TLCs) as a means by which to change teacher behaviour (Goodwin, 2008) through self-supporting self-improvement groups.

It is noteworthy that Wiliam's own relationship with education was not always harmonious, admitting that he was not the best student, and only finding an affinity with education once he had discovered a talent in mathematics. Likewise, his journey into teaching and later academia appeared to be through chance rather than deliberate career moves, starting with a teaching career which began to fund a fledgling music career, and then a research career as a seemingly churlish response to not getting a promotion. Nevertheless, despite the route into these careers Wiliam has made a success of all he has done, resulting in a significant number of publications and accolades – testament to his hard work and tenacity.

Wiliam currently works as a freelance academic giving talks and presentations to a range of institutions and dividing his time between the United States, Australia, the United Kingdom and the Far East. He has continued his work on supporting schools in developing their assessment and teaching practices and is also working alongside his wife, Siobhan, on developing their aforementioned vision for building TLCs.

GLOSSARY OF TERMS

Assessment for learning

The process of using assessment as means of informing learning, usually carried out during the learning process.

Assessment of learning

The process of assessing learning at the end of a unit or module, usually conducted through testing.

Black Box

Name derived by Black and Wiliam to describe the classroom in which inputs from the outside are fed in with the intention that a set of desirable outputs will follow.

Formative assessment

A means by which student learning is monitored, providing ongoing feedback which can be used constructively by both students and teachers.

Summative assessment

A formal method of testing, usually undertaken at the end of a unit of study, designed to ascertain how far a concept has been understood.

Teacher Learning Communities (TLCs)

A means of personal and professional development in which teachers work in partnership to support one another on self-selected development projects.

 FURTHER READING

Bartlett, J. (2015) *Outstanding Assessment for Learning in the Classroom*. Oxon: Routledge.

Practical strategies to support practitioners in making meaningful assessments in the classroom. Specifically focusing on how assessment can be embedded from the outset in the planning process.

Clarke, S. (2001) *Unlocking Formative Assessment*. Oxon: Hodder Education.

Practical suggestions as to how formative assessment can be used in the classroom, unpacking some of the key terms proposed by Black and Wiliam.

Clarke, S. (2005) *Formative Assessment in Action: Weaving the elements together*. Oxon: Hodder Education.

Informed through action research this book brings together key aspects of formative assessments linked to lesson plans and exemplars showing how these can be successfully applied to practice.

Wiliam, D. (2016) *Leadership for Teacher Learning: Creating a culture where all teachers improve so that all pupils succeed*. West Palm Beach, FL: Learning Sciences International.

Research-informed guidance as to how student achievement can be increased through the creation of a structured and rigorous learning environment.

REFERENCES

The Assessment Reform Group (1999) *Assessment for Learning: Beyond the Black Box*. Cambridge: University of Cambridge School of Education.

BBC (2010) The classroom experiment. Available at: www.bbc.co.uk/programmes/b00txzwp [accessed 12/03/18].

Black, P. and Wiliam, D. (1998) *Inside the Black Box*. Brentford: Department of Education and Professional Studies: GL Assessment.

Black, P., Harrison, C., Lee, C., Marshall, B. and Wiliam, D. (2003) *Assessment for Learning: Putting it into practice*. Maidenhead: Oxford University Press.

Bloom, B.S. (1969) Some Theoretical Issues relating to Educational Evaluation. In: Tyler, R.W. (ed.) *Educational Evaluation: New roles, new means: The 68th yearbook of the National Society for the Study of Education (part II)* (Vol. 68(2), 26–50). Chicago, IL: University of Chicago Press.

Butler, R. (1988) Enhancing and undermining intrinsic motivation: the effects of task-involving and ego-involving evaluation on interest and performance. *British Journal of Educational Psychology, 58*, 1–14.

Cambridge International Examinations Teaching and Learning Team (undated) *Getting started with assessment for learning*. Available at: www.cambridge-community.org.uk/professional-development/gswafl/index.html [accessed 12/03/18].

Christodoulou, D, (2016) *Making Good Progress? The future of Assessment for Learning*. Oxford: OUP.

Department for Children, Schools and Families (DCSF) (2009) *Getting to Grips with Pupil Progress*. Crown Copyright.

Didau, D. (2014) *Why AfL might be wrong and what to do about it*. Available at: www.learning-spy.co.uk/myths/afl-might-wrong/ [accessed 12/03/18].

Goodwin, G. (2008) *Dylan Wiliam: Profile interview with Gail Goodwin*. Slough: NFER. Available at: www.dylanwiliam.org/Dylan_Wiliams_website/Bios_files/Gail%20Goodwin%20%28NFER%29.doc [accessed 12/03/18].

Kirby, J. (2013) What can we learn from Dylan Wiliam and AfL? *Pragmatic Education*. Available at: https://pragmaticreform.wordpress.com/2013/03/30/afl/ [accessed 12/03/18].

Marshall, B. (2002) Thinking through assessment: an interview with Dylan Wiliam. *English in Education. 36*(3), 47–60.

McInerney, L. (2015) Profiles: Dylan Wiliam, emeritus professor of educational assessment, *Institute of Education*. Available at: https://schoolsweek.co.uk/dylan-wiliam/ [accessed 12/03/18].

Menzies, L. (2010) *Policy Diffraction*. Available at: www.lkmco.org/policy-diffraction/ [accessed 12/03/18].

Rowe, M.B. (1974) Wait time and rewards as instructional variables, their influence on language, logic and fate control. *Journal of Research in Science Teaching, 11*, 81–94.

Sadler, D.R. (1989) Formative assessment and the design of instructional systems, *Instructional Science, 18*, 119–44.

Scriven, M. (1967) The methodology of evaluation. In R.W. Tyler, R.M. Gagné and M. Scriven (eds), *Perspectives of curriculum evaluation 1* : 39–83. Chicago, IL: Rand McNally.

Wilby, P. (2011) Teaching guru is optimistic about education. Available at: www.theguardian.com/education/2011/jan/18/teaching-methods-government-reforms [accessed 12/03/18].

Wiliam, D. (2011) *Embedded Formative Assessment*. Bloomington, IN: Solution Tree Press.

Wiliam, D, (2014) '*Formative assessment and contingency in the regulation of learning processed*'. Paper presented in a symposium entitled Toward a Theory of Classroom Assessment as the Regulation of Learning at the annual meeting of the American Educational Research Association, Philadelphia, PA, April.

Wiliam, D. (2016) The secret of effective feedback. *Educational Leadership, 73*(7). (Association for Supervision and Curriculum Development.)

17

CAROL DWECK

MINDSETS AND MOTIVATION

LEARNING OUTCOMES

Having read this chapter you should be able to:

- Appreciate Dweck's notions of mindsets and their relationship with motivation for learning
- Identify and understand the differences between fixed and growth mindsets, and the connections with their respective entity and incremental theories
- Apply the principles of building a growth mindset with students, which involves creating a culture of accepting challenges and the use of appropriate praise
- Critically appraise Dweck's concepts.

KEY WORDS

fixed mindsets; growth mindsets; learned helplessness; entity theory; incremental theory; contingent self-worth

INTRODUCTION

Carol Dweck is generally considered as a renowned researcher in areas which span the studies of social psychology, developmental psychology, and personality. Her work encompasses the psychological tradition that emphasises the power of people's self-beliefs. She posits that whether people are aware of these beliefs, or not, they have a profound influence on what people aspire to and whether they succeed in their aspirations. Her work also demonstrates that shifting people's beliefs, even uncomplicated beliefs, can result in deep and meaningful consequences for their personal development (Dweck, 2012). Dweck's research and writing has mainly focused on the role of motivation, self-beliefs and self-theories in people's learning. Broadly speaking, she argues that learners can be classified into two separate groups. Firstly, those who she calls entity theorists who think that their intelligence is static and regardless of effort and resolve cannot be changed; these are learners who have **fixed mindsets**. Secondly, those who she calls incremental theorists who think that their intelligence can, by effort and perseverance, be developed; these are learners who have **growth mindsets**. It should be noted at this early stage that Dweck felt that 'learners may not have fixed mindsets in every context of their lives; they may believe that they can grow in one area of learning but not another' (Robins, 2012: 54).

Dweck contends that the way learners perceive intelligence, as either a static characteristic (fixed mindset), or as a flexible and developmental characteristic (growth mindset), can have a profound effect on their motivation and achievement (Dweck, 2009a). Those who possess a fixed mindset tend to be excessively anxious about how clever they are perceived to be. As such they are inclined to steer clear of challenges and fail to recognise the significance of effort, when confronted by adversity they fail to reach their potential. Conversely, learners who possess a growth mindset are more interested in the process of learning itself instead of trying to give the impression of looking clever. Growth mindset learners openly look for challenges, realise the importance of effort and tend to excel when confronted with complexity (Dweck, 2009a). In an article which explores who will be the successful learners in the future, she states that 'The twenty-first century will belong to the passionate and resilient learners' and urges teachers to 'foster the growth mindset in our students so that they can be among them' (Dweck, 2009b: 9).

Overall then, an important focus of Dweck's interests and subsequent research concerns the concept of self-theories or mindsets. These self-theories are the beliefs that children create for themselves about their personal qualities, including what they feel about their own intelligence. The impact of these self-beliefs on education as a whole is crucial because it can have an influence on how we motivate, teach and assess students as well as how we manage transition periods with learners. According to Dweck, by fostering growth mindsets educators can help learners overcome challenges, avoid the fear of failure and celebrate effort over outcome; this in turn will benefit children across all the stages of their educational development.

Moreover, she argues, perhaps somewhat optimistically, that people who have a growth mindset 'in a particular area of their lives are happier, healthier, more fulfilled and successful in … school, work, sports, business, love, friendships or family relationships' (Dweck, 2006: 20). Before this chapter considers the details of Dweck's theories of motivation and mindsets and application of her work, it is necessary to explore her academic background and writings to appreciate the context of her research findings and theories.

CAROL DWECK, THE PERSON

Carol Dweck is an American psychology professor who has been intrigued by 'outstanding achievement, especially in the face of adversity, and saddened by wasted potential' (Dweck, 2000: ix). For over forty years Dweck has dedicated her research towards a better understanding of motivation and achievement. Her research has been a collegiate endeavour and has included working alongside graduate students and post-doctoral fellows. She was, from an early stage in her research career, 'obsessed with understanding how people cope with failures, and … decided to study it by watching how students grapple with hard problems' (Dweck, 2012: 3). For Dweck, understanding how people coped with failure was of particular importance in a society which was preoccupied with the notion of inherent intelligence and effortless genius (Dweck, 2000). The research undertaken by Dweck and her associates drew on thousands of participants from a range of mainly educational settings, from early years to those attending colleges; her research also encompasses fields such as sport and business. Participants come from a variety of ethnic groups and span both urban and rural areas of the USA (Dweck, 2000).

She graduated with a Bachelor's degree in psychology from Columbia University in 1967, and a PhD, also in psychology, from Yale University in 1972. She is currently the Virginia and Eaton Professor of Psychology at Stanford University. Before this she was the William B. Ransford Professor of Psychology at Columbia University. Among her many other accolades she has been the elected member of the America Academy of Arts and Sciences, a position she has held since 2002. She portrays herself chiefly as a researcher in social psychology (Pound, 2009; Dweck, 2012; Dweck, 2017). Her research has been innovative and has transformed the study of motivation, specifically in such areas as how self-beliefs and goals impact on learning and achievement (Dweck, 2009a). The findings from her research have been documented in her numerous writings in the form of journal articles and books, all of which reflect her long-held enthusiasm for understanding matters of social psychology and in particular topics which come under the umbrella theme of motivation. Her writing, especially the books, offers some helpful advice on how her theories can be applied in classrooms.

Much of her well-regarded early writing was published in peer-reviewed journal articles in the early 1970s and focused around her concept of **learned helplessness**;

these included 'Learned helplessness and reinforcement responsibility in children' (1973) with N. Dickon Reppucci, and 'Role of expectations and attributions in alleviation of learned helplessness' (1975). There are two works which are of particular importance in both explaining her concepts and offering ideas for putting those concepts into practice. The first of these is *Self-theories: Their role in motivation, personality and development* (2000), a book which is especially useful for those working with young children. It is clearly written and offers numerous examples for practice, in which her main advice is that practitioners can help develop children's learning by nurturing their persistence and positivity (Pound, 2009). This book was also named 'book of the year' by the World Education Fellowship (Dweck, 2012). The second is *Mindset: The new psychology of success* (2006) and this text challenges the conventional way in which praise is used with learners. She contends that praising intelligence and ability could harm self-esteem and achievement; furthermore, it could also endanger success. Dweck also promotes the idea that knowing about how the brain works can foster a love of learning and enhance resilience (Pound, 2009). Her writings have also appeared in the broader media such as *Time Magazine*, *The Washington Post*, *The New York Times*, and *The Boston Globe* amongst others (Dweck, 2012). All of these writings were a result of the outcomes from her research, where she explains her concepts.

DWECK'S CONCEPTS

Dweck's concepts have developed from her quest to have a better insight regarding meaningful motivation and how this relates to learner achievement. As we have mentioned, her earlier research concerned learned helplessness which drew a great deal of interest from educators mainly because of the gender perspective she identified in her work. It is likely that the findings from this early work on learned helplessness acted as a guiding light for her future research. As such the notion of learned helplessness is briefly explored here as a way of understanding how Dweck's concepts have evolved. She discovered that girls would probably display learned helplessness more than boys. Interestingly though, teachers were apt to blame boys' failure on disinterest or poor behaviour. Conversely girls' failures were ascribed to an absence of ability. Moreover, girls' successes were thought to be merely a matter of hard work (Pound, 2009). Dweck found that children with learned helplessness (which she considered to be about half of all children) believe that when they fail it is irreversible. Also, when children with learned helplessness encounter failure they usually attribute such failure to being unintelligent and typically become pessimistic and lose their tenacity (Dweck, 2000; Pound, 2009). This early work set in motion Dweck's future research into motivation and achievement and involved a number of interrelated themes, including self-concept, self-esteem, intelligence, contingent worth, self-theories, mastery orientated learning, praise and the notion of gifted children. Her main concepts of **entity theory** and incremental theories, and the respective fixed and growth mindsets, are interwoven throughout this section.

Dweck discovered that there was a strong link between learners' self-concept and self-esteem and their accomplishment, and this was influenced by how they perceived their abilities and intelligence; either their abilities were a fixed factor, or they could be changed through effort and the use of learning strategies. She argued that learners who saw intelligence as a fixed factor came within the entity theory of intelligence as corroborated by IQ and summative assessment results; these learners felt that their results were finite and there was nothing they could do to improve. On the other hand, those learners who saw their abilities being flexible and a process of ongoing development came within the **incremental theory** of intelligence; these learners typically welcomed challenge, worked hard and had little fear of failure. Those learners who hold the entity theory see failure in their learning as a personal failure which is irretrievable, which in turn affects their self-concept. Thus they tend to shy away from challenges as they are seen as a threat to their self-esteem. To retain their self-esteem they require easy, risk-free tasks that will allow them to succeed. However, learners who hold the incremental notion of their abilities have little anxiety about failing from a personal point of view. Their self-concept and self-esteem are not affected by challenging themselves in a persistent manner with difficult tasks, regardless of outcome, as they see tasks and assessments as a process of development (Dweck, 2000; Race, 2007).

The findings from Dweck's research with young children indicated that those children who subscribed to the entity theory, or fixed mindset, of intelligence were aligned closely with what she termed **contingent self-worth**. For Dweck contingent self-worth is 'the idea that you are worthy when you are succeeding and unworthy when you are not' (Dweck, 2009a: 312). Although it is understandable for children to be disappointed when they do not achieve as well as they thought they should, some children who hold a fixed mindset, she argued, lose their self-respect and the feeling of being a person in their own right. When this happens children become unable to operate in a meaningful way, and thus 'these children conclude they are bad people when they fail or are criticised, and become too paralysed to fix the problem' (2009a: 312). These findings, particularly with such young learners, are disquieting for the long-term effects on their self-esteem. Dweck offers a more optimistic and progressive viewpoint concerning self-esteem. She considers that the notion of self-esteem should be about what learners experience because they are fully involved in trying to master something new. However, she also warns that this is not something we can just give to learners as a gift, but it is something we can as educators make possible, and when we do 'we can help ensure that challenge and effort are things that enhance self-esteem, not threats to the ego' (Dweck, 2000: 119). What teachers and parents can do is motivate children to develop an incremental or growth mindset position to their learning.

For Dweck 'motivation is the motor for intelligence' as it helps learners make the most of their intellectual capabilities over a period of time to reach their full potential (Dweck, 2009a: 311). She further argues against the common idea that intelligence is all that is needed to succeed, and cites examples of 'clever' children who achieve very little contrasting this with other people who did not appear too 'bright' when they were younger who have made massive contributions to their particular field of study, because they were passionate about their subject. She further questions the importance of spotting and celebrating ability and talent in young children:

> I do sometimes wonder whether what children come with is not talent or ability – but fascination with something. Prodigies, for example are not just little fonts of knowledge and skills, but are riveted by numbers, words, or music. Wouldn't it be interesting if the fascination comes first and the ability comes second? (2009a: 311)

She contends that what educators and parents should be doing when motivating learners is not building up their intellectual self-confidence, but creating a learning culture and a position of confidence which weathers obstacles and celebrates effort and persistence. This she states is best done by encouraging students to concentrate on the overall aim of learning, and teaching them the value of hard work and offering suggestions for strategies which the children can use to overcome setbacks (Dweck, 2009a).

According to Dweck such motivation should be driven by the concept of learners developing an incremental and growth mindset through a mastery-orientated approach to learning. She has contrasted this mastery-orientated approach with learned helplessness (entity and fixed mindset) in the way educators set two different and corresponding goals for their learners. Firstly, she identified a 'performance goal' relating to learners gaining positive feedback about their ability and side-stepping negative judgements; a measurement of their ability from their performance. Hence learners who seek performance goals are anxious about their level of intelligence, they aim to be perceived as being clever and not stupid, and therefore they try not to make mistakes and tackle tasks which they think they can accomplish. The second goal is a 'learning goal' and unlike the performance goal relates to mastering new tasks and learning new skills. The focus here is on discovering strategies that develop the learning process. With the learning goal it does not matter too much if things go awry in trying to achieve a task, learners do not blame their intelligence they merely consider that they have not yet found the correct strategy so they keep on looking (Dweck, 2000).

Dweck questions the idea of the use of certain forms of praise to boost learners' confidence and to motivate them to succeed. It might seem reasonable that praise is beneficial for learners if it helps them believe in their capabilities. However, she argues that praising children's intelligence can lead them to fear failure, evade challenges, become uncertain about themselves, and manage setbacks badly. As such they remain subscribed to the entity theory and fixed mindset, and fall short of embracing mastery-orientated learning. As she explains:

> Children love praise. And they especially love to be praised for their intelligence and talent. It really does give them a boost, a special glow – but only for a moment. The minute they hit a snag, their confidence goes out of the window and their motivation hits rock bottom. If success means they are smart, then failure means they're dumb. That's the fixed mindset. (Dweck, 2012: 175)

She does not suggest that educators or parents refrain from praising children altogether, only that they refrain from praise that judges their intelligence, or suggests pride in their intelligence and ability. Dweck promotes praise that enhances the growth mindset. This is praise that celebrates perseverance, effort, study, hard work and the use of learning strategies (Dweck, 2012). She advocates teaching children how the brain functions and how to make it work better to aid their study practices and form their own learning strategies. To help learners find out about the workings of the brain Dweck and her colleagues developed the 'Brainology' interactive computer program which she suggests schools use as part of a study skills curriculum (Dweck, 2007).

One final aspect of her vast work which merits inclusion, particularly as it appears to be a common phenomenon in many schools, is her unease with the term 'gifted children'. She feels that by using the classification 'gifted' that there is a likelihood of encouraging a fixed mindset for those children given this label. She justifies this:

> We are, in essence, telling them that they have been given a 'gift', a fixed ability that sets them apart from the others and makes them more special than others. I worry that some children will become so focused on showing they deserve the label that they will stop challenging themselves, avoiding any situation that might reveal an inadequacy and show that they do not have the gift. (Dweck, 2009a: 311)

Furthermore, there is a perception that a gauge of giftedness is the ability to think and learn quickly, if however a learner has to work hard, take time to think and learn slowly they are not gifted. Yet with a growth mindset learning and accomplishment come from a high degree of perseverance and effort over time: 'Instead of being markers for giftedness, speed and perfection are enemies of high-level learning. Real learning comes from a lot of hard work' (Matthews and Folsom, 2009: 22). Dweck does not condemn giftedness as such, but argues that 'such programmes should convey loudly and clearly that students' current ability is just a starting point and that challenge, effort, and learning are the only way to fulfil their potential' (Dweck, 2009a: 312).

Dweck's ideas are closely linked with other educational thinkers who have made connections between learning and personal growth, motivation, and those who have argued that intelligence is not a fixed and single entity.

LINKS WITH OTHER THEORISTS

Dweck's concepts have clear connections to the ideas of eminent past and present educational thinkers. Her fixed mindset in particular is closely linked with classical Freudian theory where people strive for pleasure and try and steer clear of pain. They acquire defence mechanisms 'that help them ward off anxiety and channel their impulses into socially approved activities' (Dweck, 2000: 136). However other theorists such as Abraham Maslow proposed that children strove for growth and personal development as part of their human nature, akin to Dweck's growth mindset. Similarly, Carl Rogers felt people who were fully functional were receptive to change and had faith in their own reasoning without recourse to external consent; 'for Rogers, learning and personal growth were interdependent' (Robins, 2012: 38). Nevertheless, Rogers also contested that such personal growth could be spoiled by unkind, cruel or rejecting behaviour from parents. Such treatment might lead to children feeling embarrassment and guilt, which in turn might prompt them to try and please their parents rather than being concerned with their own personal growth (Dweck, 2000). A.S. Neill also raised his concern at how guilt hindered children's personal development because, similar to Dweck's entity theory, failing to reach what they perceive as the required standards of society would bring censure from adults. Moreover, Neill argued that guilt restricted children's ability to be creative for fear of failure (Neill, 1960).

Dweck's notion of fostering an incremental theory and a growth mindset is also compatible with those of a number of social constructivist thinkers. Foremost among these is Piaget who thought that children should explore and discover during learning and not be anxious about making mistakes, and that the role of the educator is to facilitate the learning process and encourage further study. Piaget thought children were intrinsically motivated to learn and therefore did not need rewards. For him 'praise and reward is at best an irrelevance and at worst an interference in a child's self-determined learning journey' (Robins, 2012: 36). Similarly, Vygotsky believed that learning should be a progressive process and teaching should start with what the learner already knows through challenge and by giving precedence to how children learn rather than the product of the learning. Dweck's notion of encouraging children to adopt learning strategies which challenged their learning process, is aligned with Bruner's 'scaffolding' concept where educators help children reach their full potential rather than being fixed to their current level of ability. Bruner argued that it was the interest in the subject being taught that was the main motivator for children's learning and not the external motivation of test results. Furthermore, he suggested that educators refrain from extrinsic motivation such as giving rewards and praise. Praise and possible punishment were liable to impede children's intuitive and creative thought, which would probably deter them from taking risks because they might make mistakes (Robins, 2012).

Her concept of self-theories is similar to Albert Bandura's concept of self-efficacy. Bandura contends that people with a positive self-efficacy trust that they themselves can achieve any task that is required with confidence and persistence (growth mind-set). Those with negative self-efficacy are unsure of themselves and doubt their ability to achieve, they may avoid tasks altogether or concede defeat when they meet obstacles (fixed mindset) (Wentzel and Brophy, 2014). Like Dweck, Bandura advocates the fostering of 'intrinsic motivation and the resilience needed to buffer the negative effects of academic anxiety' (Mitchell, 2008: 78). Guy Claxton also promotes resilience in the learning process. He posits that the idea of intelligence being a fixed entity is harmful, as children will infer that difficulty is 'a sign of stupidity, [to] feel ashamed, and therefore switch to self-protection by hiding, creating diversions or not trying' (Claxton, 2002: 121). Several recent educational thinkers have, like Dweck, questioned the notion of intelligence being fixed by IQ scores and test results. Two of these theories have been well received by educators; firstly, Howard Gardner's multiple intelligences, and secondly, Daniel Goleman's emotional intelligence. Although Dweck's ideas have many connections with those of other educational thinkers, some of her notions have drawn a degree of criticism.

CRITIQUING DWECK

Reading about Dweck's concepts it seems difficult to be critical of her work mainly because of the empirical research that has been undertaken. Her ideas also appear to be quite straightforward and she is very optimistic about their practical application. Yet it is the very uncomplicated and optimistic nature of her work, particularly in an education system which increasingly demands and values test and exam scores, which attracts the most censure. Dweck herself has acknowledged a number of criticisms along these lines and has attempted to answer them, perhaps unconvincingly in some instances. Her concept of failure preceding and guiding the start of a more creative learning process is a worthy idea and certainly within her notion of incremental theory and growth mindset. However, sadly it is probably unrealistic for most schools, who have set time-limited curricula to work through, league tables to compete in and financial constraints, to give children the time to explore and learn inquisitively (Wilson, 2009). Her emphasis on hard work, effort and persistence could for some children, particularly the very young, be quite harmful as it could deny them their childhood (Dweck, 2000). This is especially the case if work overshadows play. Furthermore, an overemphasis on persistence could also cause children to be anxious and unable to cope with the stress that this effort brings, particularly if it is outside the reach of some children's ability level. Moreover, Dweck's claim that everyone has the potential to change from a fixed to a growth mindset is unrealistic.

Pound (2009) suggests there are two other aspects of her work that could also attract criticism. The first of these is related to the marketing of her interactive computer program Brainology which is designed to teach children the functions of the brain as part of a study skills course. Dweck's explicit promotion of the Brainology program as a product could perceivably diminish her impartiality as a researcher, and as such her work underpinning Brainology has the potential to lose its standing as a piece of research. The second possible criticism from Pound relates to her view that intelligence is flexible and her opposition to the value placed on IQ scores by education and society as a whole. This, Pound suggests, could draw censure from those who disagree with her views, such as those whose businesses make financial gains from the production and distribution of standard intelligence assessment material (Pound, 2009). The final and more generic points of criticism are associated with her writings. Dweck is somewhat repetitious in reporting the findings of her research and there is at times some duplication between terms such as 'entity theory' and 'fixed mindsets', as well as 'incremental theory' and 'growth mindsets'. Although a minor observation Dweck uses terminology which is relevant to the USA, which is perhaps not apt for countries which use the English language such as her use of 'smart' and 'dumb' when describing children's abilities. Nevertheless, these observations do not lessen the merit that Dweck's work thoroughly deserves. Her research and writings have a profound effect on how educators can endeavour to create a more progressive learning experience for children.

⚙ APPLYING DWECK IN THE CLASSROOM

What is evident in Dweck's ideas is that they make sense to educators who can relate to her concepts of mastery orientated learning and helplessness. Many educators know children who react differently to challenging situations, and the strategies she offers are straightforward to apply in a classroom situation, which has added to the impact her concepts have had for practitioners (Pound, 2009). This section will consider the different aspects of application in fostering children's growth mindsets. Dweck is confident that teachers can facilitate learners to cultivate a 'growth mindset which leads to not just a short-term achievement but also long-term success' (Dweck, 2010: 16). She argues that this can be done by educators encouraging learners to adopt the incremental theory of ability and a mastery orientation toward their learning endeavours. Broadly speaking this is achieved by educators depicting learning activities 'as opportunities to acquire (not just display) knowledge or skill and give feedback that reinforces this idea. Where relevant, help students to see how an activity fits into a larger strand' (Robins, 2012: 149).

To begin with Dweck recommends that educators try not to assume that those learners who are 'slow' to understand concepts will never be able to learn competently, or even excel, in the future. Rather educators should try and discover what these slower learners do not understand and which strategies they do not possess. From that point on educators should help learners formulate learning goals to enable them to achieve by portraying subjects and themes in a growth context and giving learners process feedback (Dweck, 2012). Such process feedback should not mention anything which relates to the learners' abilities. She also advocates keeping away from giving feedback which is general in its nature, instead recommending that educators give specific commentary in response to learners' work. Most importantly she warns against praising learners' abilities or intelligence. She proposes that feedback concentrates on effort, care, a focused approach to the learning process, and developing effective learning strategies (Robins, 2012). Petty offers some ideas and consequences regarding the application of praise for learners' developing growth mind sets.

Avoid giving 'personal orientated praise': e.g. 'I'm proud of you'; 'you're good at this'. Because it:

- assumes that success is due to personal attributes
- teaches students to interpret in terms of their personal weakness.

Instead, give 'process orientated praise' this is focused on the process required for success. For example, praise the student's effort and strategy.

E.g. 'You really tried hard', 'That was a good way to do it'. Because it:

- sells the idea that esteem comes from the use of striving and from the use of strategies
- teaches students to interpret setbacks in terms of a lack of effort, or inappropriate strategies
- allows every student to earn praise.

Use also 'task orientated praise'.

For example: 'All the labels are correct.'; 'There are hardly any spelling mistakes this time.'

(Petty, 2011)

Another way to develop growth mindsets, Dweck suggests, is to tell children stories about the accomplishments that have resulted from effort and hard work: for example, accounts of eminent scientists who were not born to be brilliant but through hard work and a love for their subject developed astonishing talents in their chosen field (Dweck, 2007). Stories about people such as Albert Einstein who did poorly during his early education, and Thomas Edison who was expelled from school because of his perceived lack of intelligence. Indeed, research evidence has demonstrated that some of the most innovative and high-achieving people have mediocre IQs. This could be enhanced by introducing children to past students who have flourished through hard work and a passion for their subject. Other methods to foster growth mindsets include using peer tutoring where older students teach younger children, coupling growth-mindset and fixed-mindset learners, developing growth-related induction programmes, and the introduction of computer games where learners are encouraged to work towards progressing from one level to the next through persistent effort (Petty, 2011). Educators should also stress that quick learning is not really the most meaningful learning, and that those learners who sometimes take longer to comprehend ideas learn at a deeper level. By adopting these ideas for advancing growth mindsets, educators are:

> ... transmitting crucial information - telling students that they view them all as having intelligence that they can choose to develop. The teachers are also communicating that their role is not to judge who is smart and who is not, but to collaborate with students to make everyone smarter. (Dweck, 2010: 18)

Dweck also recommends that educators should model taking pleasure in facing challenges and by being fascinated and enlightened by mistakes. She suggests using feedback to students who make mistakes such as 'Well that didn't work. How interesting! What did that tell us? What should we try next?!' (Dweck, 2009a: 311). Furthermore, educators should show their delight when children are progressing and indicate to the children how they challenged themselves in order to progress. Challenges for Dweck are opportunities for children to develop a growth mindset. She suggests that educators should present:

> ... challenges as fun and exciting, while portraying easy tasks as boring and less useful ... when students initially struggle or make mistakes, the teacher should view this as an opportunity to teach students how to try different strategies if the first ones don't work – how to step back and think about what to try next, like a detective solving a mystery. (Dweck, 2010: 18)

In a similar way Gilbert (2002) posits that educators should teach learners to aim high and use coping strategies when things do not work out as intended, but he argues this should not include disengagement in learning because of the prospect of failure: 'What chance do any of us have if we spend our lives avoiding possible defeat?' (Gilbert, 2002: 25). He also uses the analogy of children as small seedlings when he explains that children need nurturing as well as the ability to face challenges and difficulties in order to succeed in learning and in life. Seedlings need to endure 'being "hardened", ready for life beyond the mollycoddling glass walls of the nursery. Without this, when they are finally faced with the ravages of wind, weather and incompetent gardeners, they would not survive' (Gilbert, 2002: 25). Similar to Dweck, Gilbert argues that children also need 'hardening', particularly those who are used to high achievement, as they have not necessarily experienced failure. Although it may appear harsh the more educators do for children, the less children will try to do themselves, in turn generating an ongoing sequence of learned helplessness (Dweck, 2000; Gilbert, 2002).

An explicit aspect of fostering a growth mindset with children is teaching them that the brain works 'as a learning machine' (Dweck, 2007: 42). She contends that by explaining to children that the brain forms new networks each time they learn, children discover that their abilities can be extended and used to enhance their schoolwork. This contention comes from her research which revealed that students who had been taught about the workings of the brain showed substantial improvement in their motivation to learn. Furthermore, those students had also increased their grades. From this research she developed her Brainology interactive computer program which teaches children how the brain works, how it changes when learning takes place, and more importantly what learners can do to make the brain work better (Dweck, 2009a). However, it is argued that educators without access to the Brainology program can include the functions of the brain as part of their teaching, particularly during study skills lessons. This can be done by asking children to think about their brains as a muscle which is fortified by use during learning, and also by asking them to picture the brain making new connections as they learn (Pound, 2009).

Feedback from assessed tasks, Dweck argues, needs to give learners a sense of their progress towards mastery. Following assessment outcomes students should be motivated to tackle tasks they would not have attempted before, thereby enabling them to understand new ideas. In doing this, educators should indicate to learners that it was their efforts in completing the tasks set which led to their progress. She cites the practice, which might appear somewhat unconventional and even questionable, of some educators she has observed during her research, who make progress explicit by giving learners pre-tests at the start of a module of study. These pre-tests intentionally include matter which learners have not yet encountered. Then, when the learners contrast their unsurprisingly sub-standard grades on the pre-tests with their much enhanced grades on module post-tests, they get accustomed to the idea that learning improves with application (Dweck, 2010). Another assessment approach educators can use to help children adopt a growth mindset is not to recognise a grade which indicates failure. Again Dweck refers to the practice she has observed during her research, where educators use the grade 'Not Yet', because learners are not embarrassed or humiliated by this grade as they appreciate that mastery will come in time and with application. Dweck explains the significance of this for practice:

> The word 'yet' is valuable and should be used in every classroom. Whenever students say they can't do something or are not good at something, the teacher should add, 'yet'. This simple habit coveys the idea that ability and motivation are fluid. (Dweck, 2010: 19)

A further option, she suggests, to employ in assessment is to include additional growth mindset criteria into the grades awarded to learners. This could include grades for effort, resilience, tackling challenges, and improvement over time (Dweck, 2010).

Finally, Dweck contests that educators also need to consider what type of mindset they have themselves. They should also endeavour to motivate all learners with their enthusiasm and allow time for learners who are labouring to understand concepts (Pound, 2009). Furthermore, she advocates that all educators should be taught the growth mindset and how to employ it with their learners. This Dweck suggests can be embedded in teacher education curricula and reinforced during continuous professional development programmes for educators. Such training should include:

a. the latest findings in brain plasticity and the implications for all children's potential to learn
b. the findings that dedication and self-improvement – and not existing talent – bring students long-term success
c. the findings that process praise promotes more lasting confidence and motivation than intelligence praise or outcome praise, and
d. information on the need for students at all levels to be challenged appropriately.

(Dweck, 2008: 14)

Although Dweck's concepts have evolved from her extensive research in US schools, it is suggested that her ideas from practice can be adapted for educators outside the United States.

REFLECTIVE TASK

Dweck advocates that educators help children create an incremental theory for themselves and foster a growth mindset so that they can develop meaningful, long-term learning. Reflecting on experiences from your own schooling, to what extent and in what ways, do you consider that you were encouraged to adopt a growth mindset? List the strategies you could use to cultivate Dweck's notion of a growth mindset with learners as part of your future classroom practice.

SUMMARY

Dweck is an American psychology professor and researcher. She has published numerous works on motivation and self-theories in learning which are capable of being applied in educational settings. Her main concept advances that people can be placed into one of two different groups. Firstly, the entity theorists who think their intelligence is fixed and unchangeable – these people have what Dweck calls fixed mindsets. The second group of people are incremental theorists who conversely think that their intelligence can be changed and developed through application – these she argues have growth mindsets. She holds that educators should endeavour to help children to adopt growth mindsets which in turn would help them become learners who would welcome challenge and hard work. Some of the ideas she advocates to cultivate a growth mindset include the appropriate use of praise and feedback, the setting of challenging tasks, and negotiating with learners' personal process goals and strategies for learning. Her early research and writings concerned her concept of learned helplessness; this subsequently evolved into her future interest in mindsets and motivation.

Dweck's ideas, particularly the entity theory and fixed mindsets, can be associated with classical Freudian theory where people seek praise and avoid negative feedback. Her incremental theory and growth mindsets is closely associated with the ideas of social constructivists such as Piaget, Vygotsky and Bruner. Furthermore, her notions regarding self-theories are similar to Bandura's concept of self-efficacy, with positive self-efficacy being aligned with growth mindsets and negative self-efficacy with fixed mindsets. Her idea that intelligence is a fluid concept has parallels with recent thoughts on intelligence such as Gardner's multiple intelligences and Goleman's emotional intelligence. There are also comparable links between Dweck's thoughts on the importance of hard work and effort with Guy Claxton's emphasis of resilience in the learning process. Criticism of Dweck's work has included the simplistic and over-optimistic nature of her work, especially in an increasingly product-driven educational system. The prominence she gives to hard work and effort could, if inappropriately delivered, harm rather than help children. Her sponsorship of the Brainology program has also drawn censure because of her possible impartiality. Another criticism is that her writings are, at times, repetitious in nature. Regardless of these criticisms her work in promoting children developing a growth mindset has positive, and long-term, implications for learners being motivated to enjoy the challenges of meaningful learning.

GLOSSARY OF TERMS

Contingent self-worth

A notion that children feel that they are worthy when they succeed but unworthy when they fail. Although it is understandable that all children may be disappointed when they fail, some children also leave behind their self-respect and their belief of being a deserving individual. Having a fixed mindset can be a factor to contingent self-worth.

Entity theory

This is the self-theory which people hold which believes that intelligence is fixed and cannot be transformed through hard work or application. Entity theorists possess a fixed mindset.

Fixed mindset

People with fixed mindsets stay clear of difficult tasks, tend to give up and blame others when faced with challenge and obstacles. They also consider that effort and hard work are futile undertakings and tend to take no notice of negative comments from educators.

Growth mindset

Those people with growth mindsets welcome challenges, enjoy the process of learning, react positively and developmentally to their mistakes, and learn from negative comments from educators.

Incremental theory

The self-theory in which people think that intelligence is fluid in nature and that it can be developed by working hard and by resilience. Incremental theorists have a growth mindset.

Learned helplessness

A belief by children that if they fail it is their fault because they are not clever, and that failure is irreversible. They lose their persistence and tenacity as a result.

 ## FURTHER READING

Boaler, J. and Dweck, C. (2016) *Mathematical Mindsets: Unleashing students' potential through creative Math, inspiring messages and innovative teaching*. San Francisco, CA: Jossey-Bass.

Practical examples of teaching and learning methods in mathematics which help children develop creative mathematical mindsets.

Elliot, A., Dweck, C. and Yeager, D. (eds) (2017) *Handbook of Competence and Motivation: Theory and application* (Second Edition). New York, NY: Guilford Press.

A comprehensive text which explores the theory and associated classroom practice related to motivation and achievement.

Gershon, M. (2016) *How to Develop Growth Mindsets in the Classroom: The complete guide*. Scotts Valley, CA: Createspace.

A guide which offers innovative suggestions to enhance children's growth mindsets; in particular how to promote resilience and help children enjoy tackling challenges.

REFERENCES

Claxton, G. (2002) Learning and the Development of 'Resilience'. In: Pollard, A. (ed.) *Readings for Reflective Teaching*. London: Continuum.

Dweck, C. (1975) Role of expectations and attributions in alleviation of learned helplessness. *Journal of Personality and Social Psychology*, *31*(4), 674–85.

Dweck, C. (2000) *Self-theories: Their role in motivation, personality and development*. Hove: Psychology Press.

Dweck, C. (2006) *Mindset: The new psychology of success.* New York, NY: Random House.

Dweck, C. (2007) The secret to raising smart kids. *Scientific American Mind.* December 2007–January 2008, 36–43.

Dweck, C. (2008) *Mindsets and Math/Science Achievement.* Available from: http://opportunity equation.org [accessed 12/09/18].

Dweck, C. (2009a) Self-Theories and Lessons in Giftedness: A reflective conversation. In: Balchin, T., Hymer, B. and Matthews, D. (eds) *The Routledge Companion to Gifted Education.* Abingdon: Routledge.

Dweck, C. (2009b) Who will the 21st-Century learners be? *Knowledge Quest: Professional Practice, 38,* 8–9.

Dweck, C. (2010) Even geniuses work hard. *Educational Leadership, 68*(1), 16–20.

Dweck, C. (2012) *Mindset: How you can fulfil your potential.* London: Robinson.

Dweck, C. (2017) Biography. Available from: http://cap.stanford.edu/profiles/Carol_Dweck/ [accessed 12/03/18].

Dweck, C. and Reppucci, N. (1973) Learned helplessness and reinforcement responsibility in children. *Journal of Personality and Social Psychology, 1,* 109–66.

Gilbert, I. (2002) *Essential Motivation in the Classroom.* London: RoutledgeFalmer.

Matthews, D. and Folsom, C. (2009) Making Connections: Cognition, emotion and a shifting paradigm. In: Balchin, T., Hymer, B. and Matthews, D. (eds) *The Routledge Companion to Gifted Education.* Abingdon: Routledge.

Mitchell, G. (2008) Psychology in education. In: *An Introduction to the Study of Education* (Third Edition). London: Routledge.

Neill, A.S. (1960) *Summerhill: A Radical Approach to Child Rearing.* New York, NY: Hart.

Petty, G. (2011) *Dweck's Theory of Motivation.* Available from: http://teacherstoolbox.co.uk/T_ Dweck.html [accessed 12/03/18].

Pound, L. (2009) *How Children Learn. 3, Contemporary Thinking and Theorists.* London: Practical Pre-School Books.

Race, P. (2007) *The Lecturer's Toolkit: A practical guide to assessment, learning and teaching* (Third Edition). London: Routledge.

Robins, G. (2012) *Praise, Motivation and the Child.* London: Routledge.

Wentzel, K. and Brophy, J. (2014) *Motivating Students to Learn* (Fourth Edition). London: Routledge.

Wilson, H. (2009) Challenge and Creativity: Making the links. In: Balchin, T., Hymer, B. and Matthews, D. (eds) *The Routledge Companion to Gifted Education.* Abingdon: Routledge.

CONCLUSION

A NOTE FROM THE AUTHORS

While this book, to a large extent, reflects our own particular interest and enthusiasm for the theories underpinning education today, we were also keen to provide a text which would assist our students in unpacking some of the complexities seen in the work of theorists through the ages.

Our individual roles on education-based courses led us to the observation that there were a number of areas which undergraduate students found challenging when developing their understanding of the work of these key theorists. It was also observed that such challenges appeared to be consistent across a diverse student body, including those combining their study with work in early years settings, school-based settings and youth centres, and others who were embarking on higher education straight from school or college. Such challenges were loosely based around the application of theory to practice (particularly in the current educational climate), the relationship between the different theories and theorists and, perhaps most challenging, the ability to critique the work of those theorists in an objective manner.

In attempting to support our students in developing their understanding in some of these key areas we were able to direct them to some excellent generic texts, but there did not appear to be any one book which covered all of the areas as described above. The information required by the students could be found across a range of sources, but we observed that students starting out in higher education frequently found it overwhelming to search across a number of texts and wondered if it would be possible to provide a book which made some of these links for the students. It was our aim to provide them with a secure foundation on which they could build their own explorations of the key areas described above. However, this text is designed as a starting point only and we anticipate that the reader will explore further those areas which they find to be the most stimulating.

Our research provided us with a fascinating insight into the lives and works of our chosen theorists and the more we researched, the more common elements we found between their works. This ultimately led to our decision to present work chronologically rather than according to category. We also realised that a degree of selectivity would need to be applied if we were to avoid substantially exceeding the word count we had set ourselves, since many of the theories presented here are both complex and multi-layered. It was our intention, then, to capture the essence of the theories, which would then inspire readers to delve further into the work of the theorists – hence the inclusion of lists of further reading.

Our original intention was that this text could be used as a point of reference for both students and tutors, hence we selected those theorists who we believed were fundamental to education-related courses across the sectors of further and higher education. While we were careful in our selection to include a range of ideals, we recognise that there may be omissions. We have attempted to resolve this through making links to other theorists in order to ensure that other works have at least been acknowledged, but certainly recognise that the theorists represented here are a mere snapshot of the wider picture of the field of educational theory.

We hope that you enjoy reading this book as much as we have enjoyed writing it, but – more importantly – that it has served the purpose of our original intention to provide a simple and accessible introduction to the work of key theorists from a range of different perspectives.

INDEX